COMPLETE BOOKS OF ENOCH: ALL THREE: NEW TRANSLATION WITH EXTENSIVE COMMENTARY

1 Enoch (First Book of Enoch), 2 Enoch (Secrets of Enoch), 3 Enoch (Hebrew Book of Enoch)

DR. A. NYLAND

Complete Books of Enoch: ALL THREE: New Translation with Extensive Commentary

Dr. A. Nyland

Translations are by Dr. A. Nyland unless otherwise stated.

CHAPTER 2: FIRST BOOK OF ENOCH: INTRODUCTION

The *First Book of Enoch* contains accounts of a class of angel known as the Watchers, who, against God's orders, came to earth to teach humankind all about weapons, spell potions, root cuttings, astrology, and astronomy, and alchemy. The Watchers had sex with human women, the result of which was the mysterious Nephilim. The *First Book of Enoch* states that God punished them being ordering that they be bound in Tartarus. This is also mentioned in the New Testament.

Scholars cannot agree about the author of The *First Book of Enoch*, although it is generally accepted that several authors were responsible for The *First Book of Enoch*.

The *First Book of Enoch* was excluded from the Christian Bible Canon, despite the fact that Jude quotes a passage from *First Book of Enoch*. Early Christians objected upon Jude's inclusion in the New Testament canon on this basis. (Jerome, *Letter* 181.4.) The Church Father Tertullian stated that the *First Book of Enoch* should be included in the canon. Jerome, the third century Bible translator Jerome agreed, stating, "Jude, James' brother, left a short letter which is considered among the seven broad letters, and because in it he quotes from the apocryphal book of Enoch it is rejected by many. Nonetheless by age and use it has gained authority and is considered among the Holy Scriptures." (Jerome, *Letter* 181.4.)

Angels and Nephilim in the First Book of Enoch.

The following will likely make more sense after you have read the First Book of Enoch, but I am placing it here for easy reference so you can refer to it. I have included passages from where the angels and Nephilim mentioned in the First Book of Enoch appear in other ancient sources.

Angels were actually "messengers." "Angel" is the transliteration of the Greek word, and not a translation. To "transliterate" (noun, "transliteration") means to put the Greek letters into English letters. "Angels" is the transliteration but the meaning is "messengers." The Hebrew word for "angel" actually means one dispatched as a deputy. The word occurs for an ordinary messenger as well as a supernatural messenger.

Notes

For the pagan supernatural messenger (pagan "angel") context see inscriptions *ZPE* 30 (1978) 257 n. 7, and *EG* IV.210 (2nd c AD), as well as dedication to pagan *TAM* V, 1.185. The word also occurs in *TAM* V, 1.159 but it is not clear whether the messenger was a human or supernatural messenger. There is evidence for the term occurring in contexts where a derivation from Judaism has been ruled out. There is as yet no conclusive evidence as to whether the famous "Thera angels" were in fact Christian, cf. *IG* XII, 3 (1898) 455, 933-74, *IG* XII, *Suppl.* (1904) 1636, 1637 (2nd – 3rd c. AD)

The Archangel Gabriel

Parallel Accounts in the New Testament.

Luke 1

5-7 In the time of Herod, the king of Judea, there was a certain priest named Zacharias. He was a member of the priestly order of Abijah. His wife was one of the descendants of Aaron, and her name was Elizabeth. 6 They were both right before God, and they acted blamelessly as to all the commandments and regulations of the Lord. 7 But they didn't have any children, as Elizabeth was barren and they were both getting on in years.

8-11 Now it turned out that while Zacharias was serving God with his priestly duties when his priestly division was on duty, he was chosen by lot – 9 this was in line with the priestly custom - to burn incense when

he went into the temple of the Lord. 10 At the time of
the incense offering, the whole crowd of people was
praying outside. 11 A Messenger of the Lord appeared in
front of him, standing on the right side of the incense
altar.

12-17 When Zacharias saw him, he got all mixed up
and he became quite scared. 13 But the Messenger reas-
sured him, "Zacharias, don't be afraid! Your earnest
request has been heard. Your wife Elizabeth will bear
you a son, and you must give him the name 'John'. 14 He
will be a joy and a delight to you, and lots of people will
shout joyfully because of him. 15 He will be important
in the Lord's sight! He'll never take wine or sweet
fermented liquor and he will be filled with the Holy
Spirit even from birth. 16 He will bring back many
Israelites to the Lord their God. 17 He will go on ahead
of the Lord to prepare people for the Lord. He will be
equipped with the same spirit and power that Elijah
had, to correct the attitudes of parents to their children. He will correct disobedient people so that they
will have the common sense of the people who are right
with God, and make ready for the Lord people who are
well prepared for him."

18-20 "What's going to make me believe that this is
the case! Zacharias asked the Messenger. "Me - I'm an
old man, that's for sure, and my wife's well and truly
getting on years!"

19 The Messenger answered, "I am Gabriel, who
stands in the presence of God, and who was sent to

announce this Good News to you! 20 Well then! You will be silent! As you didn't believe my words, which will in fact turn out just as I said, you won't be able to speak a word until the very day it actually happens!"

21-23 The people waited for Zacharias. They were surprised that he was spending such a long time in the temple. 22 When he came out, he couldn't speak to them. They realized that he had seen a vision, because he kept on making signs and stayed firmly speechless the whole time. 23 And it turned out that as soon as his time of priestly ministry was completed, he went back home.

24-25 After these events his wife Elizabeth became pregnant and lived in seclusion for five months. 25 "The Lord has done this for me!" she exclaimed. "He was watching over me to take away my inability to have children which the people considered to be a disgrace."

26-29 When Elizabeth was six months pregnant, God sent the Messenger Gabriel to Nazareth, a city in Galilee, 27 to an unmarried girl who was engaged to a man named Joseph, a descendant of David. The unmarried girl's name was Mary. 28 The Messenger greeted her, "Hello there, you highly favored person! The Lord is with you!" 29 But she was deeply disturbed and wondered what sort of greeting this was!

30-38 The Messenger continued, "Don't be afraid, Mary! You've found favor with God! 31 You will become pregnant and give birth to a son, and you are to name him Jesus. 32 He will be very important, and will be

called the Son of the Most High, and the Lord God will
give him the throne of his ancestor David. 33 He will
reign over the house of Jacob forever, and his Realm will
never end."

34 "How can this be?" Mary asked the Messenger.
"I'm a virgin: I haven't been with a man!"

35 The Messenger answered, "The Holy Spirit will
come upon you and the power of the Most High will
spread his shadow over you. The one to be born will be
sacred and will be called the Son of God. 36 Your rela-
tive Elizabeth has also become pregnant with a son in
her old age. They said she was unable to have children
but now she is six months pregnant! 37 Every spoken
word from God has power!"

38 "Fantastic!" Mary exclaimed. "I am the Lord's
slave servant! May everything you've said come true!"
And then the Messenger left her.

Notes.

Verse 11: The place of honor (the south side). The Messenger was standing between the altar and the golden candlestick. At the left side (north side) of the altar was the table with the sacred bread.

Gabriel in the Old Testament / Hebrew Bible

Daniel 8:15-27

Then it came about that when I, Daniel, had seen the vision and was looking for its meaning, that suddenly someone who looked like a human stood in front of me. I heard a human voice calling out from the

Ulai river banks, "Gabriel, tell this man the meaning of the vision."

So he approached the place where I was standing and then I became terrified and I fell on my face. He said to me, "Human, understand that the events you have seen in your vision relate to the future."

Now, as he was speaking with me, I was in a deep sleep with my face to the ground, but he touched me, and stood me upright. He said, "I'm here to reveal to you what will happen later in angry times. What you have seen pertains to the very end of time. The two-horned ram you saw represents the kings of Media and Persia. The hairy goat demon you saw is the king of Ionia, and the large horn between its eyes is the first king. As for the horn that was broken, and the four others that took its place, four kingdoms will rise from that nation, but not by his power. And at the end time of their kingdom, when the wrongdoers have reached their limit, a king of bold appearance, one who understands enigmas, will arise. He will be very powerful but not by his own power. He will cause a huge amount of destruction and everything he does will succeed. He will destroy powerful leaders and devastate the sacred people. He will cunningly make deceitfulness prosper by his power, and he will praise himself. He will carelessly destroy many. He will rise up against the Leader of leaders, but in the end his power will be broken. The vision of the evening and morning that has been told to you is true, but hide the vision, as it's about the distant future."

And I, Daniel, was weak for several days. Afterward I got up and attended to the king's business, but I was appalled by the vision and no one understood it.

Daniel 9:21-27

While I was praying, the one Gabriel, whom I had seen in the vision at the beginning, ran swiftly, and approached me about the time of the evening offering.

He explained to me, "Daniel, I've come here to give you insight and understanding. At the beginning of your prayers the word went out, and I've come to report it to you, for you are loved. So discern the utterance and understand the vision. Seventy weeks are marked out for your people and your sacred city, to stop rebellion, to put wrongdoing to an end, to make atonement for crime, to bring in continual justice, and to hide the vision and prophecy, and to anoint the most sacred.

"So perceive and understand that from the going out of the word to restore and build Jerusalem to the coming of the anointed one, a prince, there will be seven weeks. Then for sixty-two weeks it will be built again with streets and moat, but in a time of distress. After the sixty-two weeks, the anointed one will be cut off and will have nothing. The people of the leader who is to come will destroy the city and the sanctuary. Its end will come with a flood, and devastations are decreed up to the end of the war. And he will cut a covenant with many for one week, and for half the week he will make the sacrifice and offering cease. He will devastate the edges of the detestable, until that which is decided is poured out on the devastator."

The Archangel Michael

Accounts in the New Testament

Jude 9 (quoting from the pseudegraphical *The Assumption of Moses.*)

But Michael the Chief Messenger, when he was deciding the dispute, discoursing with Slanderer-Liar about Moses' body, did not dare to impose an abusive sentence on him, but said, "May the Lord impose the penalty on you!"

Revelation 12

7-9 War broke out in heaven. Michael and his
Messengers waged war against the dragon, and the
dragon and his Messengers fought back. 8 But the
dragon wasn't strong enough, and thus they no longer
had a place in heaven. 9 The mighty dragon was thrown
down - that ancient snake called "Slanderer-Liar", and
also called "Adversary," who leads the whole earth astray.
He and his Messengers were hurled to the earth.

Accounts in the Old Testament / Hebrew Bible

Daniel 10:2-21

In those days I, Daniel, was mourning for three weeks. I did not eat any tasty food, no meat or wine touched my lips, and I did not use any lotions at all until the three weeks were over. On the twenty-fourth day of the first month, as I was standing on the bank of the great river, the Tigris, I looked up and there in front of me was a man dressed in linen, and wearing a belt of fine gold from Uphaz around his waist.

His body was like a precious yellow gemstone, his face shone like lightning, his eyes were like fiery torches, his arms and legs gleamed like burnished bronze, and his voice sounded like a crowd of people speaking.

I, Daniel, was the only one who saw the vision. The people with me did not see it, but such fear came on them that they fled and hid themselves. So I was left alone and saw this great vision. No strength was left in me. My vigor was completely destroyed and I had no strength at all. Then I heard the sound of his words, and when I heard the sound of his words, I was on my face in a deep sleep with my face to the ground. A hand touched me which shook me to my knees and on the palms of my hands!

He said to me, "Daniel, you greatly loved person, discern the words I'm about to tell you, and stand up! I have now been sent to you."

When he said this to me, I stood up shuddering. Then he said to me, "Don't be afraid, Daniel. Since the first day you began to pray for understanding and to be occupied with Elohim's presence, your words were heard, and I've come because of your words. But the spirit leader of the kingdom of Persia withstood me for twenty-one days, but Michael, one of the foremost spirit leaders, came to help me, as I was left there with the spirit kings of Persia. Now I've come to explain to you what will happen to your people in the future, for the vision concerns a time yet to come. Now I've come so you will discern what will happen to your people in the future, as the vision is about the future."

When he said this to me, I bowed with my face toward the ground and I was unable to speak. Then the one who looked like a human (Note: The *Septuagint* says, "The one touched me with what looked like a human hand.") touched my lips, and I opened my mouth and spoke. I said to the one standing in front of me, "I'm utterly distressed by the vision, and my strength has left me! How can someone like me, your master's servant, talk to you, my master? I have no strength left, and I can hardly breathe."

Then the one who looked like a human touched me again and gave me strength. He said, "Don't be afraid, you loved person. Be at peace, be strong, be strong!"

As he spoke these words, I suddenly grew stronger and said to him, "Now please speak, my master, you've strengthened me."

He replied, "Do you know why I've come? Soon I have to return to fight against the spirit prince of the kingdom of Persia, and then when I have left, the spirit leader of the kingdom of Ionia will come! But I will tell you what is written in the truthful writings, and there is no one who supports me against these except Michael, your spirit leader."

Daniel 12:1

"At that time Michael, the great spirit leader who takes a stand for your people, will take a stand. There will be a time of trouble such as has not happened from the beginning of nations until then. But at that time your people - those whose names are found written in the book - will escape."

The angels Raphael and Uriel

Raphael and Uriel are not mentioned in the Old Testament / Hebrew Bible or the New Testament. Raphael features strongly in the *Book of Tobit*, a book of scripture that is part of the Catholic and Orthodox Biblical canon (and used by the Amish). The *Book of Tobit* is also found in the Septuagint, the ancient Greek Old Testament/Hebrew Bible text from the 3rd to 2nd centuries BC, which was translated from the Hebrew texts of the times. The Septuagint is quoted in the New Testament. It was widely used by the Hellenistic Jews of the era.

Hebrew and Aramaic fragments of the *Book of Tobit* were discovered in Cave IV at Qumran in 1952. The *Book of Tobit* was put forward by the Council of Carthage of 397 and confirmed for Roman Catholics in 1546 by the Council of Trent. The *Book of Tobit* is considered apocryphal by

Protestants, and was not included as canon by ancient Judaism.

In The *Book of Tobit* 3:8., Raphael tells Tobit that God sent him to cure his blindness and to help his daughter-in-law Sara as the evil spirit Asmodeus had killed her 7 husbands. The *Book of Tobit* 3:17 states, "Raphael was sent to heal them both, that is, to scale away the whiteness of Tobit's eyes, and to give Sara the daughter of Raguel as a wife to Tobias, Tobit's son, and to bind the evil spirit Asmodeus."

The *Book of Tobit* 12:15 states, "I am Raphael, one of the seven sacred angels who present the prayers of the people devoted to God, and I go in and out in the presence of the splendor of the Sacred One."

Raphael is not mentioned in the Qur'an.

Raphael, Gabriel, Uriel and Michael are all mentioned in *The Testament of Solomon. The Testament of Solomon* is an Old Testament pseudepigraphical work, said to be, as the name suggests, written by King Solomon. It describes how Solomon was able to build the Temple by commanding demons, thanks to a ring given to him by the archangel Michael.

When a demon named Ornias harasses a servant, who happens to be a favorite of Solomon's, by stealing half his pay and sucking out his life-force through the servant's thumb, Solomon prays for help. As a result, the archangel Michael gives him a ring with the seal of God on it. The ring gives him the power to command demons. Solomon gives the ring to the servant and tells him to throw it at the demon Ornias's chest while ordering Ornias to go to Solomon.

Ornias tells Solomon he is the offspring of the archangel Uriel. Solomon had trouble with Ornias, so prayed that the archangel Uriel would come and help him. Uriel came from heaven and made the sea monsters come out of the deep. Uriel told the demon Ornias to cut the stones for the Temple. Solomon ordered the demon Ornias to take the ring and do the same thing to Beelzebub, the prince of demons. Beelzebub says he used to be the highest ranking angel in Heaven.

Solomon questions all the demons as to which angel can frustrate them.

The demon Error is frustrated by Uriel, as is the demon Artosael.

The demon Ruaz is frustrated by Michael.

The demon Barsafael is frustrated by Gabriel.

The demon Asmodeus is frustrated by Raphael, as is the demon Obizuth.

Solomon eventually has control over all the demons and gets them to build the Temple.

The Nephilim

Here is the parallel account in Genesis 6:1-4: "When humankind began to increase on the face of the earth, and daughters were born to them, those associated with God saw that the human women were beautiful and so they took wives for themselves from any they chose. ... The Nephilim were on the earth in those times, and also afterward, when those associated with God were having sex with the human women, who gave birth to their children. They were the Gibborim of ancient times, the famous ones."

The Septuagint, Philo of Alexandria, Josephus, Justin Martyr, Irenaeus, Athenagoras, Clement of Alexandria, Tertullian, Lactantius, Eusebius, Ambrose of Milan, Jerome, Sulpicius Severus, and Augustine of Hippo all identified the "Sons of God" (correctly, "the associates of God") of Genesis 6:1-4 with the angels who came to earth and had sex with human women.

Note

The words "those associated with God are often mi)translated as "sons of God" (but the word sons/children with a noun indicates an association with the noun and should be translated thus). This occurs only elsewhere in Job 1:6, 2:1, 38:7, where it is clear these are angels.

Nephilim in Numbers 13:33

The word "Nephilim" occurs only twice in the Old Testament /Hebrew Bible, in Genesis 6:4 (see above) and Numbers 13:33. Here is the mention in Numbers 13:33: "And there we saw the Nephilim (the Anakims, who come from the Nephilim), and we seemed to ourselves to be like grasshoppers, and we seemed the same to them."

Nephilim is the Aramaic word for Giants. It is translated by the English word "giants" in several Bible versions, which can be misleading, as the Giants of ancient times were not like the fairy tale giants we think of today. The word "Rephaim" is also translated by the English word "giants" or as "the dead" in several Bible versions.

Deuteronomy 2:11

Like the Anakims, they too were considered Rephaim, but the Moabites called them *Emims*.

Deuteronomy 2:20

That area, too, was once considered to be the land of the Rephaim, and the Ammonites referred to them as Zamzummims.

2 Samuel 21:20

In still another battle, which took place at Gath, there was a man of stature with six fingers on each hand and six toes on each foot, twenty-four in all. He also was descended from the Rephaim.

Deuteronomy 3:11

King Og of Bashan was the last of the Rephaim. His iron bed was more than 9 cubits (13 feet = 4.1 meters) long and 4 cubits (6 feet = 1.8 meters) wide. It remains today in the Ammonite city of Rabbah.

Deuteronomy 3:13

I gave the rest of Gilead and also all of Bashan, the kingdom of Og, to the half tribe of Manasseh. The whole region of Argob in Bashan used to be known as a land of the Rephaim.

Note: Goliath is often said to be one of the Nephilim, but there is no evidence for this and the Bible itself does not say this. As we have seen, the two passages in Old Testament / Hebrew Bible which mention Nephilim have nothing to do with Goliath.

1 Samuel 17:4.

"And a champion went out from the camp of the Philistines. His name was Goliath, and he was from Gath, and his height was six cubits and a span."

Note: The Septuagint, the Dead Sea Scrolls, and Josephus have his height as 4 cubits and a span, which is 6 ¾ feet tall (2 meters). Six cubits and span is 9 feet tall. However, Goliath was not called a Nephilim.

Which angel was the Leader of the Watchers?

Account in 2 Enoch

"These are the Grigori, who with their chief Satanail rejected the Lord of light, and after them are those who are held in the great darkness on the second heaven, and three of them went down on earth to the place Hermon, and broke their vows on the shoulder of the Mount Hermon and saw the human women, and slept with them, and contaminated the earth with their deeds. In their times they caused lawless mixing, and Nephilim were born, amazing big people, and great hostility. So God judged them strongly, and they weep for their associates. They will be punished on the Lord's great day." (2 Enoch 18:3-4.)

Account in Psalms.

Psalm 82

A psalm of Asaph.

1 Elohim presides over the assembly of El,
he gives judgment in the midst of the elohim: (Elohim)
2 How long will you defend the unjust
and show favoritism to the wicked? Selah
3 Defend the cause of the poor and the fatherless,
defend the rights of the oppressed and suffering.
4 Rescue the poor and needy,
rescue them from the power of the wicked.
5 They know nothing, they understand nothing,
they walk around in the dark,
all the foundations of the earth are shaken.
6 I said, 'You are elohim,
all of you are associates of Elyon.'
7 Yet you will die like mortals,
you will fall like the other rulers."
8 Rise up, Elohim, and judge the earth,
for you own all the nations.

Note

Verse 1: Equally possible from the text, "the assembly of El," or "the mighty assembly."

. . .

Account in Isaiah 14:12-21

"How you are fallen from heaven, Lucifer, ("Light bearer") associate of dawn! How you are cut down to the ground, you who weakened the nations!"

"For you said to yourself, 'I will ascend to heaven and set my throne above El's stars. I will preside on the appointed mountain in the sides of the north. I will climb to above the height of the clouds, I will be like Elyon.'

"But instead, you will be brought down to Sheol, to the sides of the pit. Everyone there will stare at you and ask, 'Is this the one who shook the earth and the kingdoms of the world, that made the world a wilderness and demolished its cities and did not free the prisoners from Sheol?'

"The kings of the nations lie in splendid tombs, but you will be thrown out of your grave like a ritually abominable branch. You will be dumped like the remainder of those slain by the sword with those killed in battle like a corpse trampled underfoot, you will go down to the dungeon. You will not be given a proper burial, because you have destroyed your land and killed your people. The offspring of evildoers will never be proclaimed. Kill the children of this wrongdoer so they do not rise and conquer the land or rebuild the cities of the world."

Account in Ezekiel 28:11-19

"The word of Yahweh came to me, 'Human, weep for the king of Tyre and say to him, "Adonai Yahweh says, 'You were full of wisdom and beauty. You were in Eden, Elohim's garden. Your clothing had every precious stone: sardius, chrysolite, diamond, beryl, onyx, jasper, sapphire, and emerald, carbuncle, gold, and the making of the settings was crafted for you on the day you were created.

'You are the anointed cherub that defends. You had access to Elohim's sacred mountain and walked among the fiery stones. You were complete in everything you did from the day you were created until the day injustice was found in you.

'Your great wealth filled you with violence, and you sinned. So I banished you from Elohim's mountain. Mighty guardian, I expelled you from your place among the fiery stones. Your heart was filled with pride because of your beauty. You corrupted your wisdom because of your splendor. So I threw you to the earth and exposed you to the gaze of kings.

'You defiled your sanctuaries with your many wrongdoings and your dishonest trade. So I brought fire from within you, and it consumed you. I will burn you to ashes on the ground in the sight of all who are watching. All who knew you are appalled at your destruction. You have come to a terrible end, and you are no more."

Account in Luke 10:17-20

The seventy came back and were very happy. They said, "Lord, even the demons yield to us in your name!"

"Yes, I know," Jesus replied. "I was watching Adversary fall like a flash of lightning from the sky. I have given you the authority to trample on snakes and scorpions, and authority over all the enemy's power, and nothing will harm you. But all that aside, don't be happy just because the spirits yield to you, but instead be happy that your names have been written down in the heavenly places."

Account in Revelation

Ch.12:1-2 And a mighty sign appeared in heaven. It
was a woman clothed with the sun, with the moon
under her feet and a crown of twelve stars on her head.
2 She was pregnant, and cried out in torture as she was
in labor and about to give birth.

3-6 And I saw another sign in heaven. It was a huge
red dragon with seven heads, ten horns, and seven
diadems on the heads! 4 Its tail dragged a third of the
stars out of the sky and hurled them to the earth. The
dragon stood in front of the woman who was about to
give birth, so that he could eat her child the moment it
was born. 5 She gave birth to a son, who is destined to
rule all the nations with an iron rod. Her child was
snatched away and carried up to God and to his throne.
6 The woman escaped into the desert to a place that
God had prepared for her, so that she would be taken
care of for 1,260 days.

7-9 War broke out in heaven. Michael and his
Messengers waged war against the dragon, and the
dragon and his messengers fought back. 8 But the
dragon wasn't strong enough, and thus they no longer
had a place in heaven. 9 The mighty dragon was thrown

down - that ancient snake called "Slanderer-Liar", and
also called "Adversary", who leads the whole earth astray.
He and his Messengers were hurled to the earth.

10-12 Then I heard a loud voice in heaven saying:
"Just now have come salvation and power and the
kingdom realm of our God, and the authority of his
Anointed One. Because the accuser of our fellow believers, who accuses them in front of our God day and
night has been hurled down. 11 And they conquered him
by the Blood of the Lamb and by the Message of their
testimony. They were willing to give up their lives. 12
For this reason rejoice, you heavenly places and those
who encamp in them. But alas for the earth and the sea,
because Slanderer-Liar has gone down to you! He is in a
major rage, because he knows the time is short!"

13-18 And when the dragon realized that it had been hurled to the earth, it chased the woman who had given birth to the male child.

14 The woman was given the two wings of a huge
eagle, so that she could fly to the place prepared for
her in the desert. In that place she would be taken care
of for a time, times, and half a time. 15 And the snake
spat out water like a river from its mouth, in order to
overtake the woman and sweep her away in the
current. 16 The earth helped the woman by swallowing
the river that the dragon had spat out of its mouth. 17
The dragon was furious with the woman and went off
to make war against the rest of her offspring - those
who obey God's commandments and hold onto to

Jesus' testimony. 18 And the dragon stood on the seashore.

Who was the angel Azazel?

Azazel figures strongly in the *First Book of Enoch*. The word *Azazel* was mistranslated "scapegoat" by several Bible versions, a mistranslation started by Tyndale's 16th century English translation and followed by such versions as the King James Version, and the New International Version. It is translated correctly as "Azazel" in the Revised Standard Version and the English Standard Version. Tyndale misread the Hebrew word to mean "escaped goat" and coined the word "scapegoat."

The name Azazel occurs 3 times in the Old Testament /Hebrew Bible, in Leviticus 16: 8, 10, 26. The context is that on Yom Kippur, the Day of Atonement, the high priest performed the set sacrifices for himself and his family then presented the victims for the sins of the people. These were a ram for the burnt offering, and two young goats for the sin-offering. The high priest brought the goats before Yahweh at the door of the tabernacle, and cast lots for them, one lot "for Yahweh" and the other lot "for Azazel." The goat that fell by lot to Yahweh was killed as a sin-offering for the people. The high priest laid his hands on the head of the goat that fell by lot to Azazel and confessed the sins of the people over it. The goat was then handed over to a man who led it to an isolated region and let it go in the wilderness.

Leviticus 16:6: "Aaron will offer the bull as a sin offering for himself and shall make atonement for himself and for his family.

7 Then he will take the two goats and set them before the Lord at the entrance of the tent of meeting.
8 And Aaron will cast lots over the two goats, one lot
for the Lord and the other lot for Azazel. 9 And Aaron
will present the goat on which the lot fell for the Lord
and use it as a sin offering, 10 but the goat on which the
lot fell for Azazel will be presented alive before the Lord to make atonement over it, and it will be sent away into the wilderness to Azazel.

26 And he who lets the goat go to Azazel will wash his clothes and bathe his body in water, and then afterward he may come back into the camp."

The 13th century Nahmanides' (Rabbi Moses ben Nachman's) commentary on Leviticus 26:8 states that Azazel belongs to the class of se'irim, hairy goat like demons. This follows Rabbi Abraham ibn Ezra's commentary although Ibn Ezra did not state this explicitly. Isaiah 34:15 states, "The wild animals of the desert will meet with the howlers, and the hairy goat demon (se'irim) will cry to its fellow. Lilith will settle there and find for herself a resting place." Isaiah 13:21 states, "But the desert dwellers will recline there, and their dwellings will be full of howling creatures, and female unclean birds (*meaning unclear*) will live there, and hairy goat demons (se'irim) will dance there."

2 Chronicles 11:15 states, "And he appointed his own priests for the high places, and for the hairy goat demons (se'irim), and for the calf idols which he had made."

The Septuagint (ancient Greek translation of the Hebrew scriptures), translates se'irim by an ancient Greek word meaning "profane" or "useless."

In the 1st to 2nd century Jewish text (originally Jewish, but preserved today only in Slavonic) the *Apocalypse of Abraham*, Azazel is portrayed as an unclean bird which came down upon the sacrifice prepared by Abraham. (See also *Genesis 15:11*: "Birds of prey came down on the carcasses, and Abram drove them away.")

It describes Azazel as an evil spirit, a liar, and as an entity that brings troubles to humans who live wickedly. (13:4-9) The *Apocalypse of Abraham* 31:5 states that the wicked will decay in the belly of the cunning worm Azazel, and be burned by the fire of Azazel's tongue." Azazel's appearance is described as a dragon with hands and feet like a human's, and having six wings on the right and six wings on the left of his back." (23.7) God is said to share the earth with Azazel. (20.5)

Islam tradition holds Azazel as one of the Jinn. Jinn (or Djinn) are Arabian spiritual beings who are shape shifters, evil spirits, and treacherous spirits who can create illusions. They are creatures of flame and were created from smokeless fire and the searing wind. There are many different kinds of Jinn. Jinn are considered to be the cause of shooting stars, whirlwinds, and sandstorms. They prefer to live in desolate places.

In Islamic tradition, Azazel is identified with Iblis (Eblis). (cf. J. Knappert, *Islamic Legends: Histories of the Heroes, Saints and Prophets of Islam* (Leiden: E.J. Brill, 1985), 31-3.) The Qur'an states that when the angels were told to submit to Adam they did, but Iblis refused and was arrogant. (Surah 2:35.) It also states that Iblis said Allah created him out of fire while humans were created out of clay, and that Allah banished him. (Qur'an, Surah 7:13-19. See also Surah 15:31-48, 17:61-65, 18:50, 20:116-123, 38:71-85.)

This is an excerpt from the Islamic *Twenty-first Discourse On Addressing Iblis the Accursed*: "The Shaikh (may Allah be well pleased with him, and may He grant him contentment) said: I saw Iblis in a dream, where I was in the midst of a big crowd. I was on the point of killing him, when he said to me (may Allah curse him): 'Why are you going to kill me? What is my offense? If evil is entailed by destiny, I am powerless to change it and transform it into good, and if good is so entailed I cannot change it and transform it into evil. So what do I control?'

"Hermaphroditic in appearance, he was soft-spoken, with distorted features, wisps of hair on his chin, misshapen and deformed. When he smiled at me, the smile was bashful and apprehensive.

"This happened on the night of Sunday, 12th of

Dhu'l-Hijja in the year 516 [of the Hijra].

"Allah is the Guide to all that is good!"

Note

Abd al-Qadir al-Jilani, *Revelations of the unseen : Futuh al-Ghaib. A collection of seventy-eight discourses*, Abd al-Qadir al-Jilani, translated from the Arabic by Muhtar Holland, Houston, Texas, Al-Baz Publishing, 1992.

The Watchers

THIS IS THE ACCOUNT IN THE BOOK OF JUBILEES: "And in the second week of the tenth jubilee Mahalalel took Dinah as a wife. She was the daughter of Barakiel, the daughter of his father's brother, and she bore him a son in the third week of the sixth year. He named him Jared, and in his days the Lord's angels named the Watchers came down to the earth, in order to instruct the humans, and so that they could carry out judgment and justice on the earth." (Jubilees 4:15)

God was exceedingly angry with the angels he had sent upon the earth. (Jubilees 5:6)

The Punishment of the Watchers

THE PASSAGE IN 2 PETER 2:4-8 IS ABOUT THE Watchers who came down to earth and rebelled against God's ordinances by whoring after human women (including those of Sodom and Gomorrah as can be seen in the *Testament of Naphtali* 3.3.4-5).

"God didn't spare the Messengers who sinned but handed them over to Tartarus in ropes in the underworld's gloom where they are firmly held for judgment."

The Book of Jude in the New Testament mentions the three elements that are linked in accounts of the Watchers, sorcery, going after a different flesh, and punishment of angels (messengers). Jude quotes 1 Enoch in verses 14-15:

"And as for the Messengers who did not uphold their own office but deserted their own places, he has held them firmly in eternal ropes down in the gloom, waiting for the Judgment of the Great Day. Just like these, Sodom and Gomorrah as well as the surrounding cities, which in a similar way committed *porneia* and went after different flesh, serve as an example of those who undergo punishment in the eternal fire."

Note

Porneia. There is no equivalent English term of this word. It is a term referring to acts condemned in the Law of Moses, acts encompassing idolatry and/or pornography, vice, certain sexual acts. Leviticus 18 lists idolatry and ritually unclean sexual acts against the laws of Moses, and in 18:3 states, "You must not do the deeds of the land of Canaan into which I am about to bring you." These included incest, sex with in-laws, sex with a woman as a rival to her sister, women or men having sex with animals, child offerings to Molech, sex with a woman during menstruation. Note also that the polytheistic Canaanites were particularly despised in the Old Testament, and male temple prostitution was part of their worship of their goddess Asherah. Cult prostitution and eunuchs castrating themselves (and thereafter dressing in women's clothing, cf. Deuteronomy 22:5) both figured in the worship of the Canaanite goddess Astarte.

"Went after different flesh." Angels having sex with human women.

Book of Jubilees

The Book of Jubilees 5 sets out the punishment by God upon the Watchers and says that the flood was due to the Watchers taking human wives but that God saved Noah from it.

The Book of Jubilees 7:20-2 states, "Noah... encouraged his sons...to avoid porneia, uncleanness, and injustice. For it was on account of these three things that the flood came on the earth, since it was due to sexual misconduct in which the Watchers, against the regulations of their authority, had illicit sex and went a whoring after human women. When they married whomever they liked, they committed the first acts of uncleanness. They fathered as children the Nephilim."

"And he testified about the Watchers, who had sinned with the female humans, for they had begun to sleep with the female humans causing defilement, and Enoch testified against them all." (Jubilees 4:22)

"It happened when the humans began to increase

on the face of the earth and daughters were born to them, that the angels of God saw them on a certain year of this jubilee, and saw that they were beautiful to look at, and they chose wives, anyone they wanted, and the wives bore them children and they were Nephilim. Lawlessness increased on the earth and everything of the earthly realm became corrupt, humans, cattle, wild animals, birds, and everything that walked on the earth - all of them corrupted their ways and their orders, and they began to eat each other.

Lawlessness increased on the earth and every imagination of all human thought was continually evil. And God looked at the earth, and saw it was corrupt, and everything of the earthly realm had corrupted its order, and all that were on the earth had done all kinds of evil in front of his eyes. He said: "I will destroy humans and all living things on the face of the earth that I created." (Jubilees 5:1-4)

Testament of Naphtali 3.3.4-5

The Testament of Naphtali 3.3.4-5 states that the women of Sodom had sex with the Watchers. It states, "In the same way also the Watchers changed the order of their nature. The Lord cursed the Watchers at the flood, and made the earth desolate because of them, so that it would be uninhabited and fruitless." Note the term "changed the order of their nature" which is similar to Jude's term, "went after different flesh" and to Paul's statement, "for the females exchanged natural sex for what is other than nature. And the same goes for males too," in Romans 1:26.

The Church Father Irenaeus

The Church Father Irenaeus stated, "And wickedness very long-continued and widespread pervaded all the races of men, until very little seed of justice was in them. For unlawful unions came about on earth, as angels linked themselves with offspring of the daughters of men, who bore to them sons, who on account of their exceeding great were called Giants. The angels, then, brought to their wives as gifts teachings of evil, for they taught them the virtues of roots and herbs, and dyeing and cosmetics and discoveries of precious materials, love-philtes, hatreds, amours, passions, constraints of love, the bonds of witchcraft, every sorcery and idolatry, hateful to God, and when this was come into the world, the affairs of wickedness were propagated to overflowing, and those of justice dwindled to very little." (Irenaeus, Demonstration, 18. Joseph P. Smith, St. Irenaeus: Proof of the Apostolic Preaching, London, 1952, p. 58.)

The 2nd century theologian Tatian

The 2nd century theologian Tatian, 2 Apology 5, stated, "God committed the care of humans and everything under heaven to angels whom he appointed over them. But the angels disobeyed this appointment, and were captivated by the love of women. They produced children who are called demons, and not only that, they later subjugated the human race for themselves, partly by magical writings, partly by fears and the punishments they brought about, and partly by teaching them to offer sacrifices, incense, and libations, as they needed these things after they were enslaved by lust. Among humankind they sowed murders, wars, adulteries, awful actions, and all kinds of wickedness."

Clement of Alexandria

Clement of Alexandria, Miscellanies 5.1.10 stated, "To this we will also add, that the angels who had obtained the superior rank, after sinking into pleasures, told the women the secrets which had come to their knowledge."

The Second Book of Enoch

Second Book of Enoch 10: "1 Those two men led me up on to the north side, and showed me there an awful place. There were all kinds of tortures in that place, brutal darkness and the gloom of darkness. There is no light there, but a gloomy fire constantly burning high, and a fiery river coming out. The whole place is on fire, and everywhere there is frost, ice, thirst, and cold. The bonds are very cruel, and the angels frightening and without compassion. They carry fierce weapons and harsh torture. I said, 2 "Woe, woe, this place is so awful!" 3 And those men replied, "Enoch, this place is prepared for those who dishonor God, who on earth practice crime against nature, child-corruption, magic-making, enchantments, and devilish witchcrafts, and who boast of their wicked deeds, stealing, lies, slander, envy, resentment, porneia, murder. They are accursed and steal people's lives, and take away the possessions of the poor in order to make themselves rich, harming them, and although they are able to feed the hungry, make them starve to death, and although they can clothe people, they strip them naked. They did not acknowledge their creator, and bowed down to the soulless and lifeless gods who cannot see nor hear, useless gods, and they also built carved images and bowed down to unclean work. This whole place is prepared for their eternal inheritance."

CHAPTER 3: FIRST BOOK OF ENOCH: TRANSLATION

The Book of the Watchers

1:1-9.

The word of the blessing of Enoch, how he blessed the chosen ones and the just, who were to live in the time of trouble, rejecting all the wicked who would be removed.

Enoch was a just person, whose eyes were opened by God, and saw a sacred vision in the heavens and told about it. The angels showed me this. I heard everything from them, and understood what I saw. It will not take place in this generation, but in a generation which will come at a future point.

I spoke, and conversed with him about the chosen ones. The sacred mighty one will leave his dwelling. The eternal God will tread on the earth, on Mount Sinai. He will appear with his hosts, and appear with his powerful strength from heaven. Everyone will be afraid, and the

Watchers will be terrified. Great fear and trembling will grip them, as far as to the ends of the earth. The high mountains will be shaken, and the high hills brought low, melting like wax in the flame. The earth will be ripped open, and everything in it will perish, and there will be judgment on all. But he will give peace to the just. He will safeguard the chosen and show them compassion. Then they will all belong to God and they will be prosperous and blessed. His light will appear to them. The Lord comes with tens of thousands of his devoted people, to carry out judgments on everyone, to cross-examine every soul among them who has committed sacrilege, about their sacrilegious acts, and about all the harsh things that sacrilegious wrongdoers have said about him.

Commentary

This was quoted by Jude in the New Testament, verses 14-15: "14 Now Enoch, the seventh from Adam, prophesied to these people too. He said, 'The Lord comes with tens of thousands of his devoted people, 15 to carry out judgments on everyone, to cross-examine every soul among them who has committed sacrilege, about their sacrilegious acts, and about all the harsh things that sacrilegious wrongdoers have said about him.' 16 These people are complaining grumblers going the way of their own wants and wishes.

They boast excessively about themselves, and flatter other people for their own benefit." "The Watchers" - also known as "Grigori" after the Greek.

2:1-3

All who are in the heavens know what happens there. They know that the heavenly luminaries do not change their paths, that each rises and sets regularly at the proper time, without wandering off from their appointed order. Observe the earth, and take notice of what happens there, from the beginning to the end, how nothing changes, but God's work is apparent. Observe the summer and winter, how the whole earth is full of water, and that the cloud, the dew, and the rain lie on it.

3:1.

Observe how every tree appears to wither and shed its leaves, except for fourteen trees, which are not deciduous but retain their old leaves for two or three winters until the new leaves appear.

4:1.

And again, observe the days of summer, how the sun is on it at the very beginning, while you look for a covered and shady spot due to the burning sun. The earth burns with scorching heat, and because of that heat you cannot walk on the ground or the rocks.

5:6-9.

Observe how the trees cover themselves with green

leaves and produce fruit. Observe that he who lives forever has made all these things, and that his works continue from year to year, and that all the tasks they do for him do not change, but things are brought to pass as God has appointed them to do so.

Observe how the seas and the rivers together do what they are meant to do. But you have not been unwavering, nor have you carried out the Lord's instructions, but you have misbehaved and spoken nasty, spiteful words with your polluted mouths against his magnificence You hard hearted, no peace will come to you! Therefore you will curse your days, and your lives will come to an end, you will be the object of increasing and perpetual cursing, and you will not find compassion.

In those times, all the just will consider your names to be an abhorrent curse, and all who curse, will curse by you. All the wrongdoers and the unjust will invoke evil by you, and for you, the godless, there will be a curse. Then they will celebrate, and there will be forgiveness for wrongdoings, and compassion, peace and tolerance. There will be rescue for them, a good light. But on you all there will be a curse. But for the chosen ones there will be light, favor, and peace, and they will inherit the earth.

Wisdom will be given to the chosen ones. They will live and not do wrong whether through godlessness or pride, but the wise ones will be humble. They will not do wrong again for the rest of their lives. They will not die as a result of anger or torment, but will live out the full term of their lives. They will grow old in peace, while their lives will increase with happiness, and with peace, for all the days of their lives.

6:1-8.

It happened after the humans had multiplied, that in those times daughters were born to them, and they were attractive and beautiful.

Commentary
"The Humans"

The phrase often mistranslated "sons of men," "children of men," actually meant "people," "humans." The word children/sons with a noun refers to a member of a class of people, and should not be translated as "son/child of." The phrase "sons of (place name)" /"children of (place name)" again refers to inhabitants of that place. The Benai Israel, translated in the King James Version as "children/sons of Israel" actually means "members of the class of people called Israel" and should be translated as "Israelites." The expression is also Greek, and found as early as Homer. The same is the case in the New Testament, where the Greek word *huios* is placed with the word "Israel," referring to "members of the class of people called Israel" and should be translated as "Israelites." Prop-

erly, it is not to be translated "children of Israel" or "sons of Israel." Likewise, Autenrieth's Homeric Dictionary notes that *huios* with the word Achaeon means "Achaeans." This is typical Greek usage.

The word *huios* is often used with a noun to express a similarity with the noun. For example, an ancient Greek would put the word *huios* (son, child) with a word meaning "perfume" to mean "the perfumed one" or to refer to a person who smells nice. In word-for-word Greek, the same expression would appear as "child/son of Perfume," but such a (mis)translation is not the correct meaning. Sometimes Greek simply used the genitive case instead of inserting the word huios. For example, in Aristophanes' (the famous comic playwright of the 5th century B.C.) play Acharnians, 1150, *Antimachon ton Psakados* appears to be word-for-word "Antimachos child/son of showers" but proper translation method demands we translate as "Antimachos the spitter" or similar. The scholiast states that he was so-named because he spat when speaking and "showered spray on those who were talking to him."

The standard ancient Greek language lexicon (dictionary) Liddell-Scott(-Jones) lists the meanings for *huios* as 1. son, 2. with a place name simply to mean inhabitants of the place name, 3.

children, 4. used with numbers of years to indicate age, as well as several other meanings. Thus "sons of God" is a mistranslation for "associates of God", and "daughters of men" is a mistranslation for "human women."
See lengthy discussion in J. Massingberd Ford, "'Son of Man – A Euphemism?" JBL 87 (1968), 257-67: Albright, W.F. and Mann, C.S. Matthew: A New Translation with Introduction and Commentary, (New York: Doubleday, 1982), pp. CLVI-CLVII, 95, G. Dalman, The Works of Jesus, Eng. trans. by D.M. Kay, (Edinburgh, 1902), V. Taylor, *The Gospel According to St. Mark: The Greek text with Introduction, Notes and Indexes*, London, Macmillan, 195, p. 197.

WHEN THE ANGELS, THE INHABITANTS OF HEAVEN, saw them, they lusted after them and said to each other, "Come on, let's choose consorts for ourselves from the humans, and let's produce children!"

Commentary
Watcher/s

An Aramaic text reads "Watchers," Cf. J.T. Milik, *Aramaic Fragments of Qumran Cave 4*, Oxford, Clarendon Press, 1976, p. 167. Daniel 4:17 mentions a "Watcher." Nebuchadnezzar tells Daniel that he saw in a vision or dream a "sacred

Watcher" who appeared to him and made an announcement. In the vision the Watcher concluded, "This announcement is by the decree of the Watchers, this command is by the word of the sacred ones, so that those who are alive may understand that the Supreme has authority over the human kingdoms, and he gives it to whomever he wishes. He sets up even the lowest ranked human beings over them." (From *The Source Bible*.) The *Septuagint* (Greek Old Testament) translates the word for "Watcher" as "angel." However, Theodotion (c. 200 A.D.), the Jewish scholar who made a translation of the Hebrew Bible into Greek, transliterates the word. That is, he simply put it into Greek letters without attempting to translate it, as one does with names.

The angels in this verse is: *bene ha 'elohim*.

***Bene ha 'elohim* is often (mis)translated "Sons of God" but in fact refers to the inhabitants of heaven or associates of God (Elohim). Both the ancient Rabbis and the Church fathers did not acknowledge *bene ha 'elohim* as "associates of God," (properly, "associates of Elohim"). The Rabbis saw them as righteous men and the Church Fathers saw them as Seth's descendants.**

Job 2:1
Again there was a day when the associates of God came to present themselves before Yahweh, and Satan also came with them to present himself before Yahweh.

Job 38:7
When the morning stars sang together, and all the associates of God shouted for joy?

Psalm 29:1
A psalm of David.
Assign to Yahweh, you mighty ones (bene 'elim), assign to him splendor and strength!

Psalm 89:7
El is respected in the great assembly of the sacred ones,
he is more awe-inspiring than all who surround him.

Then their leader Semjaza said to them, "I'm concerned as I fear that perhaps you won't agree to carry out this venture, and that I alone will have to pay the penalty for such a serious crime."

But they answered, "Let's all swear an oath, and bind ourselves by mutual curses, that we will not change our minds but carry through this venture."

So they swore all together and bound themselves by

mutual curses. They were two hundred in number, they descended in the time of Jared, on the top of Mount Hermon. They called it Mount Hermon because they had sworn an oath on it and bound themselves by mutual curses.

These are the names of their leaders: Semjaza, who was their leader, Arakiba, Rameel, Kokaqbiel, Ramuel, Tamiel, Ramiel, Danel, Ezeqeel, Baraqijal, Asael, Armaros, Batarerl, Ananel, Zaqiel, Samsapeel, Satareil, Turel, Jomjael, Sariel. These were the leaders of the groups of ten.

Commentary

Semjaza

Other spellings of the name include Samyaza, Semiaza, Samjaza, Shemhazai, Shemyazaz, Semihazah.

On the top of Mount Hermon

Or "On Ardis."

Mutual curses

"Herem" was the practice of sanctification by total obliteration carried out against certain peoples, such as Jericho, by God's command, around the time of Joshua. See Joshua 6:17-19.

Sariel

The Aramaic texts have an earlier catalog of the Watchers' names: Semihazah, Artqoph, Ramtel, Kokabel, Ramel, Danieal, Zeqiel, Baraqel, Asael, Hermoni, Matarel, Ananel, Stawel, Samsiel, Sahriel, Tummiel, Turiel, Yomiel, and Yhaddiel, cf. Milik, *opt .cit.*, p. 151.

7:1-6.

They and the rest took consorts. Each one chose their own. They had sex with them and defiled themselves with them. They taught them charms and sorceries, the cutting of roots, and the uses of plants.

The women got pregnant and gave birth to Nephilim whose height was three hundred cubits. They consumed everything humans produced. When humans could no longer sustain them, they turned against them, in order to consume them. They began to do wrong against birds, beasts, reptiles, and fish, and to eat each other's flesh, and to drink their blood. Then the earth laid accusation against the lawless ones.

Commentary

Here the Greek texts differ from the Ethiopic. One Greek manuscript adds to this section, "And the women bore to the Watchers three races:

first, the great giants who brought forth the Nephilim, and the Nephilim brought forth the Elioud. And they existed and their power and greatness increased."
"To to eat each other's flesh" or, "and to eat their flesh one after another."

8:1-4.

Azazel taught humans to make swords, knives, shields, breastplates, and showed them metals of the earth and the art of alchemy, and bracelets and ornaments, the use of antimony and paint, the beautifying of the eyelids, the use of all types of precious stones, and all sorts of dyes. Then wickedness and immorality increased, and they disobeyed, and everything they did was corrupt.

Semjaza taught spell potions, and root cuttings,
Armaros taught the resolving of spell potions,
Baraqijal taught astrology,
Kokabel taught the constellations,
Ezeqeel taught the knowledge of the clouds,
Araqiel the signs of the earth,
Shamseil the signs of the sun,
and Sareil the course of the moon.

And as humans perished, they cried out, and their voice reached heaven.

9:1-11.

Then Michael, Uriel, Raphael, and Gabriel looked down from heaven and saw much bloodshed on earth, and all the lawlessness that was happening on the earth. They said one to another, "It's the voice of their cries! The earth deprived of her children has cried as far as the portal of heaven. And now people's souls complain to you, you sacred ones of heaven! They say, "Bring our case to the Most High!" Then they said to their Lord, "You are Lord of lords, God of gods, King of kings. Your splendid throne lasts forever and ever, and is your name is sacred, magnificent, and blessed forever and ever. You have made everything and you have power over everything, everything is open and clear before you. You see everything, and nothing can be hidden from you.

"You have seen what Azazel has done, how he has taught every lawless act on earth, and has disclosed to the world all the secret things which are done in the heavens which humans were keen to know - also Semjaza, to whom you have given authority over his associates. They have gone together to the human women, have had sex with them, and have defiled themselves, and have revealed these crimes to them. And the women likewise have given birth to Nephilim, and so the whole earth has been filled with blood and lawlessness. And now the souls of those who are dead cry out and complain, even at heaven's portals! Their groaning ascends!

It cannot stop due to the lawlessness which is committed on earth.

"You know everything before it happens. You know

these things, and what has been done by them, yet you do not tell us what we are supposed to do about it?"

10:1-22.

Then the Most High, the sacred great one spoke. He sent Uriel to Lamech's son, and said to him, "Tell him in my name, 'Hide yourself!', then explain to him the event that is about to happen, that the whole earth will be destroyed, that a flooding deluge will cover the whole earth, and everything in it will be destroyed. And now tell him how he may escape, and how his descendants may remain for all generations on the earth."

Commentary

"Tell him" - i.e. tell Noah.

Again the Lord said to Raphael, "Bind Azazel hand and foot, cast him into the darkness! Make an opening in the desert which is in Dudael, and throw him in there! Put him on rough and pointed stones, and cover him with darkness. Let him stay there forever, and cover his face so he can't see the light. And in the day of the great judgment he will be thrown into the fire. Restore the earth, which the angels have corrupted, and proclaim life to it, that they may restore it. And all the humans will not perish as a result of all the secrets of the Watchers, and which they have taught to their offspring. All the earth has been corrupted by the works that were taught by Azazel. The blame for the whole crime rests on him!"

The Lord said to Gabriel, "Go to the bastards, to the reprobates, to the offspring of immorality, and destroy them, the offspring of the Watchers, from among the humans, and send them against one another so that they will perish by killing one another, for they will not live long lives. No request their fathers make of you will be granted on their behalf. They wish to live eternally but each one of them will live for five hundred years."

The Lord said to Michael, "Go and bind Semjaza and his associates who have had sex with women and so have completely polluted and contaminated themselves! And when their sons have slain one another, and they have seen the destruction of their beloved ones, bind them for seventy generations under the earth, until the day of their judgment and of their end, until the judgment that lasts forever is completed. In those times they will be taken away to the lowest depths of the fire and tormented and they will be shut up in prison forever. Immediately after this he will, together with them, be condemned and destroyed, and they will be bound together for generation after generations."

Destroy all the lustful spirits, and the offspring of the Watchers, for they have committed crimes against humankind. Let all oppressors perish from the face of the earth and let every evil work be destroyed. Let the plant of justice and truth appear and become a blessing. Justice and truth will be forever planted with enjoyment.

And then all the devoted people will be thankful, and live until they have produced a thousand children, while the whole time of their youth, and their old age, will come to an end peacefully.

In those times the whole earth will be cultivated with justice, and will be planted with trees and be filled with blessings. And all desirable trees will be planted on it. They will plant vines on it. The vines which they plant will yield abundant wine. Every seed which is sown on it will produce a thousand measures for one measure, and produce ten presses of oil for one measure of olives.

Cleanse the earth from all oppression, from all injustice, from all crimes, from all godlessness, and from all the pollution which is committed on it. Eliminate them from the earth. Then all the humans will be just, and all nations will highly respect me and bless me, and all will esteem me. The earth will be cleansed from all defilement, from every crime, from all punishment, and from all torment, and I will never again send torment on it for generation after generation, forever.

11:1-2.

In those days I will open the storehouses of blessing which are in heaven, so as to make them descend on earth over all the work and labor of humankind. Peace and fair play will associate with humankind for all the days of the world, in every generation.

12:1-6.

Before all these things, Enoch was hidden, and none

of the humans knew where he was hidden, where he had been, and what had happened. His days were with the sacred ones, and his actions were with the Watchers.

I, Enoch, was blessing the great Lord and King of ages, when the Watchers called me - Enoch the scribe - and said to me, "Enoch, you just scribe of justice, go and tell the Watchers of heaven, who have deserted the high heaven, the sacred everlasting place, who have been defiled with women and have done as the humans do, by taking wives for themselves, 'You have greatly caused corruption on the earth. You will never have peace or forgiveness for your crimes. You will have no delight in your offspring, for you will see the slaughter of their loved ones, and you will lament for the destruction of your children. You can make petition forever, but you will not obtain compassion or peace!"

13:1-10.

Then Enoch went on and said to Azazel, "You will not find peace. A severe sentence has gone out against you, that you are to be bound. You will find no relief, compassion, or granting of requests, because of the injustice you have taught, because of every act of blasphemy, lawlessness, and wrongdoing, which you have shown to humankind."

Then I left him and spoke to them all together, and they were terrified, seized with fear and trembling. They asked me to write a petition for them so that they might find forgiveness, and for me to read their petition in the presence of the Lord of heaven, because from then on they could not address him, or lift up their eyes to heaven on account of the appalling offence for which they were judged.

Then I wrote out their petition and the prayer for their spirits, for everything which they had done, and in regard to their requests, that they should have forgiveness and rest. Then I continued on and sat down at the waters of Dan, in the land of Dan, to the right of the west of Hermon. I read their petition until I fell asleep.

And a dream came to me, and visions fell on me. I saw visions of punishment, so that I might relate it to the heavenly ones, and reprimand them. When I awoke I went to them. They were all sitting gathered together in Abelsjail, which is situated between Lebanon and Seneser, crying, with their faces covered. I related in their presence all the visions which I had seen, and my dream. And I began to utter the just words of justice, reprimanding the heavenly Watchers.

Commentary

Abelsjail was near Damascus.

14:1-25.

This is the book of the just words, and of the reprimand of the Watchers, who are from eternity, according to what the sacred and great one commanded in the vision. I saw in my dream, what I will now speak with a tongue of flesh, and my breath, which the Mighty One has given to the human mouth to converse with and to understand with the heart. As he has created and given to humans the power of comprehending the word of understanding, so has he created and given to me the power of reprimanding the Watchers, the heavenly ones.

"I have written your petition, and in my vision it appeared to me, that what you request will not be granted to you as long as the world lasts. Judgment has been passed on you: your request will not be granted to you. From this time forward, you will not ascend into heaven for all eternity, and he has said that you will be bound on the earth as long as the world lasts. And before these things, you will see the destruction of your loved offspring. You will not have them, but they will fall in front of you by the sword. Your petition on their behalf will not be granted, nor for yourselves, despite your crying and praying and speaking all the words in the writing which I have written."

A vision appeared to me. In that vision clouds and a mist invited me. The pathway of the stars and flashes of lightning summoned me and pressed me forwards, while the winds in the vision caused me to fly, speeding up my progress, and lifted me to heaven. I continued until I arrived at a wall built with crystals and surrounded by tongues of fire which began to terrify me.

I went into the tongues of fire and drew close to a large dwelling also built with crystals. Its walls and pavement were made with crystals, and the ground was also crystal. Its roof was like the path of the stars and flashes of lightning, and among them were fiery cherubs in a watery sky. A flaming fire surrounded the walls, and its doorway blazed with fire. When I entered the dwelling, it was as hot as fire and cold as ice. There was no trace of delight or life there. Terror seized me, and a dread shaking seized me.

Commentary
Cherubs

The plural of "cherub" is often written as "cherubim." Cherubs are described as winged beings. Numbers 7:89 states that Yahweh's voice spoke to Moses from between the two cherubs on top of the Ark of the Covenant. Ezekiel describes cherubs in 1 and 10.

Violently disconcerted and trembling, I fell on my face. In the vision I saw another dwelling bigger than the former. Every entrance to it stood open in front of me. It was built of fiery flames. In every way it so excelled in splendor and magnificence and size that it is impossible to describe to you either the splendor or the extent of it. Its floor was on fire and above it were flashes of lightning and the path of the stars. Its roof was flaming fire. I looked and saw that it contained a high throne, the appearance of which was like a crystal, while its circumference resembled the brilliant sun, and there was the voice of the cherubs.

From underneath the throne came rivers of flaming fire. To look on it was impossible. The splendid one sat on it. His robe was brighter than the sun, and whiter than snow. No angel could enter and look at his face because of the splendor and grandeur, nor could any mortal look at him. The flaming fire was around him. A huge fire also continued to rise up in front of him and no one who surrounded him was able to approach him, among the myriads of myriads who were in front of him. He needed no counselor. The most sacred ones who were near him did not leave him by night or by day, nor did they go far from him. Until then I had been on my face, and trembling. Then the Lord called me with his own mouth and said, "Come here, Enoch, and hear my word."

He made me rise up and approach the entrance. My face was directed to the ground.

15:1-12.

Then he answered me, and I heard his voice. He said, "Don't be afraid, Enoch, you are a just scribe of justice. Approach, and hear my voice. Go, and say to the heavenly Watchers, who have sent you to pray for them, 'You ought to pray for humans, and not humans for you. You have left the high and sacred heaven, which lasts forever, and have slept with women. You have defiled yourselves with the human women and have taken wives, you have acted like the humans, and you have produced Nephilim as your offspring!

"And although you were sacred, spiritual, and possessing eternal life, you have defiled yourselves with the blood of women, have produced with the blood of the natural realm, have lusted like humans and have done as those who are flesh and blood do. These however die and perish. Therefore have I given them wives, that they might get them pregnant and produce children with them, and that this might be conducted on the earth. But you from the beginning were made spiritual, having eternal life, immortal for all generations. Therefore I did not make wives for you, because, being spiritual, your dwelling is in heaven.

"Now the Nephilim, who are produced from spirit and flesh, will be called on earth evil spirits, and they will live on earth. Evil spirits have proceeded from their bodies, because they were created from humans: from the sacred Watchers was their beginning and primary origin. Evil spirits they will be on earth, and the spirits of the wicked they will be called.

"As for the spirits of heaven, they will live in heaven, but as for the spirits of the earth which were born on the earth, they will live on the earth. The spirits of the Nephilim will oppress, afflict, destroy, do battle, and bruise on the earth. They will cause grief. They will not eat food, and they will be thirsty, they will cause trouble. They will rise up against the humans, and against women, because they have proceeded from them."

Commentary

Most manuscripts here read "they will not rise up against the humans," but scholars such as Charles and Knibbs attribute the "not" to scribal error.

16:1-4.

"During the days of slaughter and destruction of the Nephilim, whenever their spirits depart from their bodies, their flesh will be destroyed before the judgment. Thus they will perish, until the day of the great end of the great world. A destruction will take place of the Watchers and the wicked. And now as for the Watchers, who have sent you to pray for them, who previously were in heaven, say to them, 'You have been in heaven, but all the mysteries had not been revealed to you. You knew worthless ones, and because of your stubbornness you have related these to the women, and through these mysteries women and humankind have done much evil on the earth. Say to them, 'You will never obtain peace!'"

Enoch's travels through the Earth and through Sheol

17:1-8.

They took me to a certain place, and those who were there were like flaming fire, and when they wished to, they assumed the appearance of humans. They carried me to the place of darkness, to a mountain, the top of which reached heaven. And I saw the receptacles of the luminaries and of thunder at the uttermost extremities, where it was deepest. There was a fiery bow, and arrows in their quiver, a fiery sword, and every type of lightning.

Then they took me to living water, and to a fire in the west, which received every setting of the sun. I came to a river of fire, which flowed like water, and emptied itself into the great sea toward the west. I saw every large river, until I arrived at the great darkness. I went to the place where no flesh walks. I saw the mountains of the gloom of winter, and the place from which the water of every abyss flows. I saw the mouths of all the rivers in the world, and the mouth of the deep.

18:1-16.

I then saw the holders of all the winds. I saw how they contributed to the whole creation and the foundations of the earth. I saw the cornerstone of the earth. I also saw the four winds, which bear up the earth, and the structure of the sky. And I saw the winds occupying the high sky, being in the midst of heaven and of earth, and constituting the pillars of heaven.

I saw the winds of the sky, which turn and cause the orb of the sun and of all the stars to set, and over the earth I saw the winds carrying the clouds. I saw the paths of the angels. I saw the structure of the sky above at the extremity of the earth. Then I headed south, and saw a place which burns day and night, where there are seven mountains formed of superb stones, three toward the east, and three toward the south. Of those which were toward the east, one was a colored stone, one was of pearl, and another of healing stone. Those toward the south were of a red stone.

The middle one reached to heaven like God's throne. It was of alabaster, and the top was of sapphire. I also saw blazing fire. Over all the mountains is a place on the other side of a large territory, where waters were collected. I also saw a deep abyss, with columns of heavenly fire. And in the heavenly columns I saw fires, which were beyond measure both as regards their height and depth. Over this abyss I also saw a place which did not have the structure of the sky above it, nor the solid ground underneath it. There was no water above it, nor any birds, but it was a desolate place. And there I saw seven stars, like great blazing mountains, and like spirits entreating me.

There I saw seven stars like great burning mountains, and when I inquired about them, the angel said, "This place is the end of heaven and earth: this has become a prison for the stars and the host of heaven. The stars which roll over the fire are those which disobeyed the Lord's instruction in the beginning of their time, because they did not come at their appointed times. Therefore he was angry with them, and bound them until the time when their sentence would be completed, in ten thousand years."

19:1-3.

Then Uriel said to me, "The angels who were promiscuous with women will stand here. Their spirits will assume many different forms. They will defile humankind and lead them astray into sacrificing to demons as gods. They will stand here until the great day of judgment, in which they will be judged, until they are made an end of. But their wives who led astray the angels of heaven will find peace."

And I, Enoch, alone saw the vision of the end of all things. No other human saw what I saw.

The Watchers who did not fall

20:1-8.

These are the names of the sacred angels who watch. Uriel, one of the sacred angels, who presides over the world and Tartarus.

Commentary
Tartarus

The Greeks considered Hades to be the underworld, full of ghosts or wraiths of people who had died. Homer's Odyssey speaks of Odysseus raising spirits from Hades and notes that these spirits could be strengthened when they drank blood. It also speaks of people continuing their earthly ways – for example, one person was professionally hunting. It was spoken of as a terrifying, eerie place, but not specifically a place of punishment like Tartarus. Hades is commonly translated as "Hell" in most Bible versions, as are "Gehenna" and "Tartarus," yet to the Greeks,

they were separate places. Tartarus was the lowest region of the underworld, said to be as far below Hades as the earth is under the sky. Tartarus was the place where the very wicked were punished. The Greeks believed Hades to be midway between heaven and Tartarus. See Aeschylus, Prom. 152-6: "Would that he had hurled me underneath the earth and underneath the House of Hades, host to the dead – yes, down to limitless Tartarus, yes, though he bound me cruelly in chains breakable." (Trans. David Grene.)
The Septuagint translated Sheol as "Hades."

Raphael, one of the sacred angels, who is over human spirits. Raguel, one of the sacred angels, who inflicts punishment on the world and the luminaries. Michael, one of the sacred angels who is over the most part of humankind, in charge of the nations. Saraqael, one of the sacred angels, who presides over the spirits of the humans that do wrong. Gabriel, one of the sacred angels, who presides over the seraphim, over paradise, and over the cherubim.

Remiel, one of the sacred angels, whom God set over those who rise.

Commentary
Seraphim

The Ethiopic word is *Ikisat* which means "serpents" and was translated by the Greeks as *drakon*, which means a huge serpent, a python, a dragon. The Hebrew word "Seraphim" can also mean "serpents."

Paradise

In the Greek, *paradeisis*, commonly transliterated as "paradise," is a Persian loan word meaning a garden of fruit trees (or orchard) which first occurs in Greek in Xenophon's *Anabasis*, 1.2.7. It appears commonly in the papyri and inscriptions in the same meaning. See *I.Tyre* 1.108 (pl.47.1) (late Roman), "I solemnly request those who are going to acquire this orchard...", *P.Petr*. i.16.2.7 (230 B.C.), "the produce of my orchards", *P.Tebt* 1.5.53 (118 B.C.), "the tithes which they used to receive from the holdings and the orchards". *P.Lond* 933.12 (A.D. 211) notes a payment on account of an "olive orchard". See also the Rosetta Stone (*OGIS* 90.15, 196 B.C.).

The word occurs frequently in the *Septuagint* as a garden, sometimes as the abode of the blessed, see *Cant*. 5.13, *Eccl*. 2.5, and *Neh*. 2.8. The *Midrash Haggadah* (*Midrash* means a verse-by-verse interpretation of Scripture, and *Haggadah* is an interpretation and expansion of the non-legal

portions of Scripture) describes Paradise in detail, as far as giving specific dimensions and furnishings of the chambers. The details are said to have been supplied by individuals who visited Paradise while alive. It states that 9 mortals visited heaven while alive, and that one of these is Enoch. Ezekiel's description of Paradise is similar to that of Enoch's: a great mountain in the middle of the earth which has streams of water flowing from under it. A palm tree grows in the middle of the center of the sacred enclosure. Similar descriptions are to be found in other apocalypses (e.g. *Apoc. Baruch*, 5, 2 *Esd.* 8.52). In Rabbinical literature the conception of paradise stands in contradistinction to hell. Paradise is occasionally referred to as "the world to come". The word occurs 3 times in the New Testament: Luke 23:43, 2 Cor. 12:4 and Rev. 2:7.

Enoch's second journey

21:1-10.

Then I went to a place where things were dreadful. There I saw neither a high heaven nor an established earth, but a desolate appalling spot. There I saw seven stars of heaven bound together in it, like great mountains of blazing fire. I said, "For what type of crime have they been bound, and why have they been thrown into this place?"

Then Uriel, one of the sacred angels who was with

me, and who guided me, answered, "Enoch, why do you ask, why do you earnestly inquire? These are those of the stars which have disobeyed the Lord's commandment, and are bound here until ten thousand years, the time of their crimes, have come to pass."

Afterward I went on from there to another dreadful place, more ghastly than the former, where I saw a huge blazing and glittering fire, in the middle of which there was a split as far as the abyss. It was full of huge columns of fire, and their descent was deep. I could not discover its measurement or magnitude, nor could I perceive its source. Then I exclaimed, "How horrifying this place is, and how difficult to explore!"

Then Uriel, one of the sacred angels who was with me, answered me, "Enoch, why are you alarmed and amazed at this appalling place, at the sight of this place of pain?" He told me, "This is the prison of the angels, and they are kept here forever."

22:1-14.

From there I went to another spot, and he showed me an immense high mountain of hard rock in the west. There were four hollow places in it which were deep and very smooth. Three of them were dark and one was bright, and there was a fountain of water in the middle of it. I said, "These beautiful places are so smooth, and so and deep and dark to look at!"

Then Raphael, one of the sacred angels who was with me, answered, "The beautiful places have been created for this very purpose, for the spirits of the souls of the dead to assemble in them, so that all the souls of humans should assemble here. They will stay in these places until the day of their judgment, until their appointed time. Their appointed time will be long, until the great judgment."

And I saw the spirits of humans who were dead, and their voices reached heaven in complaint. Then I asked Raphael, the angel who was with me, "Whose spirit is that, the voice of which reaches to heaven in complaint?"

He answered me, "This is the spirit of Abel who was slain by his brother Cain, and who will accuse that brother, until his descendants are wiped off the face of the earth, until his descendants are annihilated from the descendants of the human race."

At that time I asked about him, and about the general judgment, "Why is one separated from another?"

He answered, "These three have been made so that the spirits of the dead might be separated. This division has been made for the spirits of the just, in which there is the bright spring of water. And this has been made for wrongdoers when they die and are buried in the earth when judgment has not been executed on them in their lifetime. Here their spirits will be separated in this great pain, until the time of the great judgment, the scoldings, and the torments of the accursed, whose souls are punished and bound there forever. Thus has it been from the beginning of the world.

"And this division has been made for the spirits of those who make complaints, who give information about their destruction, when they were killed in the days of the wrongdoers. This has been made for the spirits of unjust humans who are wrongdoers, those who have committed crimes, and are godless associates of the lawless. But their spirits will not be annihilated in the day of judgment, nor will they arise from this place."

Then I blessed the splendid Lord, "Blessed are you, just Lord, who reigns over everything forever and ever!"

23:1-4.

From there I went to another place, toward the west, to the extremities of the earth. There I saw a blazing fire which ran without ceasing, and did not change its course day or night, but always continued the same.

I asked, "What is this, which doesn't cease?"

Then Raguel, one of the sacred angels who was with me, answered, "This blazing fire, which you see running toward the west, is the fire of all the heavenly luminaries."

The Fragrant Trees

24:1-7.

I went from there to another place, and saw a mountain of fire which burned day and night. I went past it, and saw seven impressive mountains, which were all different from each other.

Their stones were dazzling and beautiful, all were brilliant and splendid to look at, and their surface was attractive. Three mountains were toward the east, and one placed on the other, and three were toward the south, one placed on the other. There were deep ravines, which did not join each other. The seventh mountain was in the middle of them and was taller, resembling the seat of a throne, and fragrant trees surrounded it.

Among these there was a tree such as I have never smelled. None of the others there were like it. It had a fragrance beyond all other fragrances. Its leaf, its flower, and its bark never withered, and its fruit was beautiful. Its fruit resembled the cluster of the palm. I exclaimed, "This tree is beautiful! Its leaves are gorgeous, and its fruit is a delight to the eye!"

Then Michael, one of the sacred splendid angels who was with me, and was their leader,

25:1-7.

responded, "Enoch, why do you inquire about the fragrance of this tree? Why are you inquisitive to know about it?"

Then I answered him, "I would like to know everything, but particularly about this tree."

He answered me, "That mountain which you saw, whose summit resembles God's throne, will be the seat on which the sacred and great splendid Lord, the everlasting king, will sit when he comes down to visit the earth for the good. And as for that perfumed tree of an agreeable smell, no mortal is permitted to touch it, until the time of the great judgment, when he will punish all and bring everything to an end forever. It will be then be given to the just and sacred. Its fruit will be food for the chosen. It will be transplanted to the sacred place, by the house of the Lord, the everlasting king. Then will they celebrate greatly and be happy. They will enter the sacred place and its fragrance will enter their bones. They will live a long life on the earth as your ancestors lived. No sorrow, plague, trouble, or tragedy will touch them."

Then I blessed the splendid Lord, the everlasting king, because he has prepared this tree for the just ones, and declared that he would give it to them.

26:1-6.

From there I went to the middle of the earth, and saw a blessed fertile spot, which contained branches continually sprouting from the trees which were planted in it. There I saw a sacred mountain, and underneath the mountain to the east there was a stream which flowed toward the south. I also saw to the east another mountain higher than it, and between them was a deep, narrow ravine. A stream ran under the mountain. To the west was another mountain, lower and smaller, and a deep and dry ravine ran between them. In the middle of them was another deep and dry ravine at the extremities of the three mountains. All these ravines, which were deep and narrow, and formed of hard rock, had no trees planted on them. And I was in awe of the rock and of the ravine; I was very much in awe.

27:1-4.

Then I said, "What is the purpose of this blessed land, which is full of trees, and the accursed valley between them?"

Then Uriel, one of the sacred angels with me, replied, "This valley is for those who are accursed forever. Here all those who speak inappropriate language against the Lord, and speak harsh things about his splendor will be collected. Here will they be collected, here will be their territory. In the last times, in the time of judgment in the presence of the just ones, those who have received compassion will bless the splendid Lord, the everlasting king, for all their days, forever. In the time of judgment they will bless him for his compassion, as he has assigned it to them." Then I blessed the splendid Lord, addressing him, and making mention of his greatness.

28:1-2.

From there I headed east to the middle of the mountain range in the desert, and saw a wilderness, full of trees and plants, and water gushed down on it. A cascade of water appeared there. It was composed of many cascades of water both to the west and the east. On one side were trees, and on the other side were water and dew. The watercourse rushed to the north-west causing clouds and spray to go up on all sides.

29:1-2.

Then I went to another place in the desert, and approached the east of that mountain range. There I saw first rate trees, those which produce frankincense and myrrh, and the trees were not alike.

30:1-3.

And beyond them, I went to the east and saw another place with valleys full of water. In there was a tree, the color of the fragrant trees such as the mastic. And on the sides of these valleys I saw sweetly smelling cinnamon. Past these I advanced toward the east.

31:1-3.

Then I saw other mountains containing trees, from which water flowed like nectar called sarara and galbanum. And beyond these mountains I saw another mountain, and the trees were full of fruit like a hard almond. This fruit smelt sweeter than any fragrance.

32:1-6.

After these things I saw the entrances of the north east and saw seven mountains full of first-rate nard, mastic, cinnamon, and pepper. From there I passed on above the summits of those mountains to some distance eastwards, and went over the Erythraean Sea. When I had gone far beyond it, I passed along above the angel Zotiel, and arrived at the garden of justice. There I saw from afar off, trees more numerous and greater than these trees. They were sweet smelling, large, fine-looking and elegant. The tree of knowledge was there. If any one eats from it, they gain great wisdom.

It was like the carob tree, bearing fruit which resembled very fine grapes, and its perfume extended a great distance. I exclaimed, “How beautiful is this tree, and how delightful is its appearance!”

Then the sacred angel Raphael who was with me, responded, “This is the tree of wisdom, of which your ancient father and your ancient mother ate, who came before you, and they obtained wisdom and their eyes were opened, and then they knew that they were naked, and were expelled from the garden.”

33:1-4.

From there I went on toward the extremities of the earth, where I saw large beasts different from each other, and birds also differing in appearance, beauty and voice, different from each other. To the east of these beasts I saw the extremities of the earth, where heaven rests, and the portals of heaven stood open. I saw the celestial stars come out. I counted them as they proceeded out of the portal, and wrote them all down, as they came out one by one according to their number and their names, their times and their seasons, as the angel Uriel, who was with me, pointed them out to me. He showed them all to me, and wrote them down for me. He also wrote down for me their names, their regulations, and their operations.

34:1-3.

From there I went toward the north, to the extremities of the earth. There I saw a great and glorious wonder at the extremities of the whole earth. There I saw three heavenly portals open, and the north winds proceed from them, blowing cold, hail, frost, snow, dew, and rain. From one of the portals they blew mildly, but when they blew from the two other portals, it was with violence and force. They blew over the earth strongly.

35:1.

From there I went to the west to the extremities of the earth and there I saw three heavenly portals such as I had seen in the east, the same number of portals, and the same number of passages.

36:1-4.

From there I went south to the extremities of the earth, where I saw three heavenly open portals, from which issued dew, rain, and wind. From there I went east to the extremities of heaven, where I saw three eastern heavenly portals open, and these had smaller portals within them. Through each of these small portals the stars of heaven pass west by a path which is shown to them.

Every time they appeared, I blessed the splendid Lord, who had made those great splendid signs, in order to display the magnificence of his works to angels and to spirits and to humans, so that these would praise all his works and operations, would see his powerful works, and would praise his amazing labor, and bless him forever.

The Parables

37:1-5.

The second vision he saw, the vision of wisdom, which Enoch, the son of Jared, the son of Mahalalel, the son of Cainan, the son of Enos, the son of Seth, the son of Adam, saw. This is the start of the word of wisdom, which I received to declare and tell to those who live on earth. Listen, you people of old, see, and you who come after, from the beginning, and understand to the end, the words of the sacred one which I will speak in the presence of the Lord of spirits. It would have been better to declare them only to the people of old, but we will not withhold the beginning of wisdom from those who come after. Until the present time there never has been such wisdom given by the Lord of spirits as that which I have received, wisdom according to my insight, according to the wish of the Lord of spirits, by whom the portion of eternal life has been given to me. And I obtained three parables, and I lifted up my voice and told them to the inhabitants of the earth.

The First Parable

38:1-6.

The first parable.

When the congregation of the just appears, and wrongdoers are judged for their crimes, and are driven from the face of the earth.

When the just one appears in the presence of the just themselves, who will be elected for their good works duly weighed by the Lord of spirits, and when the light appears to the just and the chosen ones, who live on earth, where will the dwelling of wrongdoers be? And where will be the place of rest for those who have rejected the Lord of spirits? It would have been better for them if had they never been born.

When the secrets of the just will be revealed and the wrongdoers judged, and the impious driven from the presence of the just and the chosen, from that time those who possess the earth will cease to be powerful and exalted. They will not be able to look at the faces of the sacred, for the Lord of spirits has made his light appear on the faces of the sacred, the just, and the chosen. The mighty kings of that time will be destroyed and delivered to the hands of the just and sacred. From then on no one will attain compassion from the Lord of spirits, because their lives will be at an end.

Commentary
"When the just one appears," or, "When justice appears."

39:1-13.

In those days the chosen and sacred race will descend from the upper heavens, and their offspring will become one with the humans. In those days Enoch received books of indignation and anger, and books of agitation and confusion.

"They will never obtain compassion," says the Lord of spirits.

In those days a whirlwind snatched me up, and raised me above the earth's surface, setting me down at the extremity of the heavens.

There I saw another vision. I saw the dwellings and resting places of the sacred ones and the resting places of the just. There my eyes saw their dwellings with the sacred ones. They were entreating, interceding, and praying for the humans. Justice flowed in front of them like water, and compassion was scattered over the earth like dew. And so it will be with them forever and ever.

At that time my eyes saw the dwelling of the chosen ones of truth, faith, and justice. There will be justice in their days, and the just and chosen ones will be without number, in his presence, forever and ever. I saw his dwelling under the wings of the Lord of spirits. All the sacred and the chosen ones sang in his presence looking like a blazing fire. Their mouths were full of blessings, and their lips were praising the name of the Lord of spirits. And justice was always before him.

I wished to stay there, and my inner self longed for that dwelling. There my allotment had been previously assigned to me in the presence of the Lord of Spirits.

In those times I praised and extolled the name of the Lord of spirits with blessings and praises, for he has destined me with blessing and favor, according to his own good pleasure. My eyes contemplated that place for a long time. I blessed him and said, "May he be blessed, blessed from the beginning and forever!"

In his presence there is no end. He knew before the world was created what the world would become, for generation after generation. Those who do not sleep bless you. They stand in the presence of your splendor and bless, praise, and exalt you, saying, "The sacred, sacred, sacred Lord of spirits fills the earth with spirits."

There my eyes saw all who do not sleep and stand in his presence and bless him, saying, "May you be blessed, may the name of God be blessed forever and ever!"

Then my face became changed until I was incapable of seeing.

40:1-9.

After this I saw thousands of thousands, and ten thousand times ten thousand, and an infinite number of people, standing in front of the Lord of spirits. On the four sides of the Lord of spirits, I saw four figures, different from those who were standing before him and I learnt their names, because the angel, who went with me, told them to me, and showed me every secret thing.

Then I heard the voices of the four figures praising the splendid Lord. The first voice blessed the Lord of spirits forever and ever. I heard the second voice blessing the chosen one, and the chosen ones who rely on the Lord of spirits. I heard the third voice interceding and praying for those who live on earth, and requesting in the name of the Lord of spirits.

I heard the fourth voice expelling the satans, and prohibiting them from entering the presence of the Lord of spirits to accuse the inhabitants of the earth.

After that I asked the angel of peace who went with me, to explain everything that is hidden. I asked, "Who are the four figures I have seen, whose words have I heard and written down?"

He replied, "The first is the merciful, patient, and sacred Michael.

The second is the sacred Raphael, who is set over all diseases and afflictions of humans. The third is Gabriel, who is set over all the powers. And the fourth is Phanuel, who is set over repentance, and the hope of those who will inherit eternal life." These are the four angels of the Lord of spirits, and their four voices, which I heard in those times.

41:1-9.

After this I saw the secrets of the heavens and how the kingdom is divided, and how human action is weighed there in the balances. I saw the dwellings of the chosen ones, and the dwellings of the sacred ones. And there my eyes saw all the wrongdoers who denied the Lord of spirits, being dragged away, as they could not stay because of the punishment proceeding against them from the Lord of spirits.

There, too, my eyes saw the secrets of the lightning and the thunder, and the secrets of the winds, how they are distributed as they blow over the earth, and the secrets of the clouds and dew. There I saw the place from which they issued, and from where they saturate the earth's dust. There I saw the closed containers, out of which the winds are distributed, the container of hail, the container of snow, the container of the clouds, and the cloud itself, which remained over the earth before the creation of the world.

I also saw the containers of the sun and moon, where they come from, and where they go to, their glorious return, and how one became more splendid than the other. I marked their majestic course, their unchangeable course, how they do not add or subtract anything to their course, and how they keep faith in each other by their stable oath. The sun goes out first and completes its course in accordance with the commandment of the Lord of spirits; his name is powerful forever and ever!

After this I saw the path, both concealed and apparent, of the moon, and how the moon's path progresses by day and by night. One stands opposite the other in front of the Lord of spirits, honoring and praising without ceasing, since praising is like a rest to them.

For the splendid sun makes many revolutions both for a blessing and a curse. The course of the moon's path is light for the just, but darkness for the wrongdoers. In the name of the Lord, who made a division between light and darkness, and divided the spirits of humans, and strengthened the spirits of the righteous in the name of his justice. No angel hinders this, and no power is able to hinder it, because the judge sees them all, and judges them all in his own presence.

42:1-3.

Wisdom found no place on earth where she could live, and her dwelling was in heaven. Wisdom went out to live among the humans, but did not find a place to live. Wisdom returned to her place, and took her seat in the midst of the angels. But wickedness went out of her chambers. She found those she did not seek, and lived among them, like rain in the desert and on a thirsty land.

43:1-4.

I saw flashes of lightning and the stars of heaven. I saw that he called them all by their names, and that they heard. I saw that he weighed them with a just balance, according to their light, according to the width of their areas and the day of their appearance and how their revolution produces lightning. I saw their revolutions, according to the number of the angels, and how they keep faith with each other.

I asked the angel who went with me, and explained secret things to me, "What are their names?"

He answered, "The Lord of spirits has shown you their parable. They are the names of the sacred ones who live on earth, and who believe the name of the Lord of spirits forever and ever."

44:1.

I saw other things with regard to the lightning - how some of the stars rise and become lightning but cannot lose their form.

The Second Parable

45:1-6.

This is the second parable, about those who deny the name and the dwelling of the sacred ones, and of the Lord of spirits. They will not ascend to heaven, nor will they come to the earth. This will be the fate of wrongdoers, who deny the name of the Lord of spirits, and who are reserved for the day of punishment and affliction.

On that day the chosen one will sit on a splendid throne, and will consider their actions, and they will have countless resting places. Their inner selves will be strengthened, when they see my chosen one, and those who have called on my sacred, splendid name. At that time I will cause my chosen one to live amongst them, and I will change the face of heaven and make it a blessing and a light forever. I will also change the face of the earth and make it a blessing, and cause my chosen ones to live on it. But those who have committed wrongdoing and wickedness will not live on it. I have taken note and satisfied my just ones with peace, and placed them in my presence, but as for the wrongdoers, their judgment will draw near so that I may destroy them from the face of the earth.

46:1-8.

There I saw the Ancient of Days, whose head was like white wool, and with him another, whose appearance looked like a human's. His appearance was very elegant, like one of the sacred angels. And I asked the angel who went with me, and explained secret things to me, about that human, who he was, and where did he come from, and why did he go with the Ancient of Days.

He answered me, "This is the human, to whom justice belongs, and with whom justice lives. He will reveal all the treasures of that which is hidden, for the

Lord of spirits has chosen him, and because of his justice, his share has surpassed all others in the presence of the Lord of spirits forever.

"This human, who you have seen, will stir up kings and the powerful from their dwellings, and the strong from their thrones, will loosen the reins of the strong, and break the teeth of the wrongdoers. He will throw kings from their thrones and their kingdoms, because they do not exalt and praise him, and do not respectfully acknowledge the source by which their kingdoms were granted to them. He will throw down the appearance of the strong and fill them with shame. Darkness will be their dwelling, and worms will be their bed. They will have no hope of being raised from their bed, because they have not praised the name of the Lord of spirits.

"They will judge the stars of heaven, and will lift up their hands against the Most High. They will tread on and inhabit the earth, exhibiting all their wicked actions. Their power rests on their wealth, and their faith is in the gods whom they have formed with their own hands. They deny the name of the Lord of spirits, and will expel him from his assembly places, and with him the faithful, who depend on the name of the Lord of spirits."

47:1-4.

In those days the prayer of the sacred and the blood of the just will ascend from the earth into the presence of the Lord of spirits. In those days the sacred ones, who live above the heavens, will unite with one voice, and petition, pray, praise, extol, and bless the name of the Lord of spirits, because of the blood of the just which has been shed, and so that the prayer of the just will not be in vain in the presence of the Lord of spirits, and so that justice may be done for them, and so that they don't have to wait patiently forever.

In those days, I saw the Ancient of Days while he sat on his splendid throne, and the books of the living were opened in his presence, while his entire host in the heavens above and his council stood around in his presence. The hearts of the sacred ones were very happy that the number of the just had been reached, and that the prayer of the just had been heard, and that the blood of the just had not been required in the presence of the Lord of spirits.

48:1-10.

In that place I saw a spring of justice which never ceased, surrounded by many springs of wisdom. All the thirsty drank from them, and were filled with wisdom, and their dwelling was with the honest, the chosen, and the sacred. At that hour that human was called in the presence of the Lord of spirits, and his name brought into the presence of the Ancient of Days.

Before the sun and the signs were created, before the stars of heaven were formed, his name was called in the presence of the Lord of spirits. He will be a support for the just and the sacred to lean on and not fall, and he will be a light to the nations. He will be the hope of those whose hearts are troubled. All who live on earth will fall down and worship him and will bless and praise him, and sing praise songs celebrating the name of the Lord of spirits.

Therefore he has been chosen and hidden in his presence, before the world was created, and forever. But the wisdom of the Lord of spirits has revealed him to the sacred and the honest, for he has kept the share belonging to the just ones safe, because they have hated and rejected this world of wickedness, and have detested all its works and ways, in the name of the Lord of spirits. For they are saved by his name, and his wishes will be their life.

In those days the kings of the earth and the strong, who possess the land by their achievements, will have downcast faces. For in the day of their anguish and trouble they will not be able to save themselves, and I will hand them over to my chosen ones. Like hay in the fire, they will burn in the presence of the honest, and like lead in the water, they will sink in the presence of the sacred. No trace of them will ever be found.

But in the day of their trouble, there will be rest on the earth. And they will fall down in his presence and not get up. There will be no one to lift them back up, as they have denied the Lord of spirits and his anointed. May the name of the Lord of spirits be blessed!

49:1-4.

Wisdom is poured out like water, and magnificence does not fail in his presence for evermore, for all his just secrets are powerful. But wickedness disappears like a shadow, and does not continue, for the chosen one stands in the presence of the Lord of spirits, and his splendor lasts forever and ever, and his power lasts for all generations.

The spirit of wisdom lives in him, as does the spirit which gives understanding and power, and the spirit of those who have fallen asleep justly. He will judge secret things. No one will be able to tell a lie in his presence, for the chosen one is in the presence of the Lord of Spirits, in accordance with his wish.

50:1-5.

In those days the sacred and the chosen ones will change. The light of days will rest on them, and the splendor and glory of the sacred will be changed. In the day of trouble disaster will be heaped upon wrongdoers, but the honest will triumph in the name of the Lord of spirits.

He will show this to others so that they will change their minds and stop what they are doing. They will have no honor in the presence of the Lord of spirits, but by his name they may be rescued. The Lord of spirits will have compassion on them, as he has much compassion. His judgment is just, and wickedness will not be able to stand against his judgment. The one who does not change their mind will perish. "From then on I will not have compassion on them," says the Lord of spirits.

51:1-5.

In those days the earth will give back that which has been entrusted to it, and Sheol will return that which has been entrusted to it, that which it has received. Destruction will return what it owes. He will select the honest and sacred from among them, for the day when they will be rescued has approached.

In those days the chosen one will sit on his throne, and all the secrets of wisdom will pour from his mouth, for the Lord of spirits has given them to him and exalted him.

In those days the mountains will skip like rams, and the hills will leap like lambs full of milk, and the faces of all the angels in heaven will be lit up with happiness, for in those days the chosen one will be praised. The earth will celebrate. The honest will live on it, and the chosen ones will walk on it.

52:1-9.

After those days in the place where I had seen all the visions of that which is hidden, I was carried away by a whirlwind, and it took me off to the west. There my eyes saw the secrets of heaven, and everything which existed on earth, a mountain of iron, a mountain of copper, a mountain of silver, a mountain of gold, a mountain of soft metal, and a mountain of lead.

I asked the angel who went with me, "What are these things which I have seen in secret?"

He answered me, "All these things which you have seen will be for the anointed one's dominion, so that he may be strong and powerful on the earth."

The angel of peace answered me, "Wait just a short time, and you will see that every secret thing which the Lord of spirits has decreed will be revealed to you. Those mountains which you have seen, the mountain of iron, the mountain of copper, the mountain of silver, the mountain of gold, the mountain of soft metal, and the mountain of lead, all these will melt like wax in a fire in the presence of the chosen one. Like the water that descends from above on these mountains, they will become powerless before his feet. It will come to pass in those days, that people will not be able to save themselves by silver or gold, nor will they be able to flee.

"There will be no iron for war, no material for a breastplate. Bronze will be of no use, tin will be of no use and will count for nothing, and lead will not be wanted. All these things will be rejected, and destroyed off the face of the earth, when the chosen one appears in the presence of the Lord of spirits."

53:1-7.

There my eyes saw a deep valley, and its entrance was open.

Everyone who lives on the earth, on the sea, and on islands, will bring him gifts, presents, and offerings, yet that deep valley will not become full. Their hands will commit wrongdoing. Whatever they produce by working, the wrongdoers will devour with crime. But they will be destroyed in front of the Lord of spirits, and from the face of his earth, incessantly, forever and ever.

I saw the angels of punishment, who were living there, and preparing every instrument of the adversary.

Then I asked the angel of peace, who went with me, "For whom are they preparing these instruments?"

He said, "They are preparing them for the kings and powerful ones of the earth, so that they will perish. After this the honest and chosen one will cause the house of his worshippers to appear, and from then on they will not be hindered anymore, by the name of the Lord of spirits. In his presence these mountains will not be solid like the earth, and the hills will be like fountains of water. And the honest will have rest from oppression by wrongdoers."

54:1-10.

Then I looked and turned to another part of the earth, where I saw a deep valley burning with fire. They brought monarchs and the powerful and threw them in this valley. There my eyes saw how they made instruments for them, iron chains of immeasurable weight. Then I asked the angel of peace, who went with me, "For whom are these chain instruments being prepared?"

He replied, "These are being prepared for the hosts of Azazel, so that they may take them and throw them into the lowest part of the abyss, and cover their jaws with rough stones, as the Lord of spirits commanded. Michael, Gabriel, Raphael, and Phanuel will take hold of them on that great day and will throw them into a furnace of blazing fire, so that the Lord of spirits may take vengeance on them for their crimes, because they became servants of the adversary, and led astray those who live on earth.

"In those days the punishment of the Lord of spirits will go out, and the containers of water which are above the heavens, and the fountains which are under the earth, will be opened. All the waters will be mixed with the waters that are above the skies. The water which is above heaven will be the male, and the water which is under the earth will be the female. All the inhabitants of earth will be wiped out and all who live under the ends of heaven will be wiped out. Because of this they will understand the wickedness they have done on earth, and they will be destroyed by these means."

55:1-4.

Afterward the Ancient of Days changed his mind, and said, "I have destroyed all the inhabitants of the earth for no purpose!"

And he swore by his great name, "From now on I will not act like this to all the inhabitants of the earth. But I will place a sign in the heavens, and it will be a guarantee of good faith between me and them forever, as long as the days of heaven and earth last on the earth. This will be in agreement with my command. When I wish to seize them, by the hands of angels, in the day of trouble and pain, I will certainly cause my anger and my rebuke to stay on them," says the Lord, the Lord of spirits. "You powerful kings who live on the earth, you will see my chosen one sitting on my splendid throne. And he will judge Azazel, all his associates, and all his hosts, in the name of the Lord of spirits."

56:1-8.

There I saw hosts of the angels of punishment, as they went, and they were holding chains of iron and bronze. Then I asked the angel of peace, who went with me, "To whom are those angels who are holding the chains going?"

He answered, "To their chosen and loved ones, so that they may be thrown into the chasm of the valley's abyss, and then that valley will be filled with their chosen and their loved ones, and the days of their life will be at an end, but the days of their leading astray will be innumerable.

"In those days, the angels will assemble, and will throw themselves toward the east, on the Parthians and Medes. They will stir kings, so that a spirit of unrest comes on them. They will fling them from their thrones, and will spring out like lions from their dens, like hungry wolves in the middle of the flock. They will go up and trample underfoot the land of his chosen ones, and the land of my chosen ones will become a threshing floor and beaten path in front of them. The land of their chosen ones will be in front of them. But the city of my just ones will hinder their horses. They will begin to fight amongst themselves, and their own right hand will be strong against them. A person will not acknowledge their friend or sibling, or a child their father or mother, until the number of the corpses is fulfilled, and their punishment will be not in vain. In those days Sheol will open its mouth, and they will be swallowed up in it and destroyed. Sheol will swallow up wrongdoers in the presence of the chosen."

57:1-3.

After this I saw another army of chariots with men riding in them.

They came on winds from the east, from the west, and from the south. The sound of the noise of their chariots was heard and when that uproar happened, the sacred ones observed it from heaven and the pillars of the earth shook from their foundations. The sound of it was heard from the ends of the earth and to the ends of heaven at the same time. And they will all fall down, and worship the Lord of spirits. This is the end of the second parable.

The Third Parable

58:1-6.

I now began to speak the third parable, about the honest and the chosen. Blessed are you, you honest and chosen, for your allotment will be magnificent! The honest will be in the light of the sun, and the chosen in the light of eternal life, the days of their life will never end, and the days of the sacred will be without number. They will seek the light and will find justice with the Lord of spirits.

There will be peace for the honest with the Lord of the world.

After this the sacred will be told to seek in heaven

the secrets of justice and the share of faith, for it has become as bright as the sun on the earth, while darkness has passed away. There will be light which never ends, and they will not come to the limit of time, for darkness will first have been destroyed, and light will last in the presence of the Lord of spirits. The light of justice will last in the presence of the Lord of spirits forever.

59:1-3.

In those days my eyes saw the secrets of the lightnings and the lights, and their judgment. They lighten for a blessing or for a curse, according to the desire of the Lord of spirits. There I saw the secrets of the thunder, when it booms above in heaven, how its sound is heard. The judgments of the earth were shown to me, whether for peace and for a blessing, or for a curse, according to the word of the Lord of spirits. Afterward all the secrets of the lights and of the lightnings were shown to me, and they cause light for blessing and for satisfaction.

The Book of Noah - a fragment

60:1-24.

In the five hundredth year, and in the seventh month, on the fourteenth day of the month, in the life of Enoch. In that vision, I saw that the heaven of heavens was shaken fiercely, and that the host of the Most High, and the angels, thousands and thousands, and ten thousand times ten thousand, were agitated and greatly disturbed. And when I looked, the Ancient of

Days was sitting on his splendid throne, while the angels and the honest were standing around him. A great trembling seized me, and terror took hold of me. My loins buckled and gave way, my strength dissolved, and I fell on my face.

Then sacred Michael sent another sacred angel, one of the sacred ones, and he raised me up, and when he raised me, my spirit returned, for I had been unable to endure the sight of the host, the disturbance, and the shaking of heaven.

Then sacred Michael said to me, "Why are you disturbed by this vision? The time of compassion lasted until now, and he has been compassionate and patient toward all the inhabitants of the earth. But the day will come when the power, the punishment, and the judgment will take place, which the Lord of spirits has prepared for those who do not worship the just judgment, those who deny that judgment, and for those who take his name in vain. That day has been prepared for the chosen as a day of covenant, and for wrongdoers as a day of inquisition."

On that day two monsters will be separated from one another, a female monster named Leviathan, to live in the depths of the sea, above the springs of waters, and a male monster named Behemoth, which moves on its chest, and occupies a large desert named Dendayen in the east of the garden, where the chosen and the just live, where my grandfather was received. My grandfather was human, the seventh from Adam, the first human whom the Lord of spirits made. Then I asked the other angel to show me the power of those monsters, how they became separated on the same day, one being thrown into the depths of the sea, and one onto the dry desert. He answered, "You, human, are here wishing to understand secret things."

Commentary

Job 41 describes Leviathan as huge, fierce, with scales on its back, states that it breathes fire and smoke, and that arrows and clubs have no effect on it, and that it stirs up the sea when it moves. Job 31 also states that there is no other creature like it on earth.
Psalm 71:14 says, "You crushed the heads of Leviathan." The Ugaritic texts have the dragon with 7 heads defeated by the god Baal and by the goddess Anat. *KTU2* 1.3 3 38-39 and *KTU2* 1.5 I 1-3. Psalm 71:13 says, "You broke the heads of the dragon in the water." The dragon is called "Rahab" (proud one) in Isaiah 51:9 and Job 26:12. Isaiah 27:1 and Job 26:13 describe the dragon as "squirming." Job 41:19-21 states that the dragon breathed fire and smoke.

And the angel of peace, who was with me, said, "These two monsters are prepared by God's power so that God's punishment won't be in vain. Then children will be slain with their mothers, and sons with their fathers. When the punishment of the Lord of spirits comes on them, it will continue, so that the punishment of the Lord of spirits won't take place in vain. After that, judgment will be with compassion and patience."

Then another angel, who went with me, spoke to me, and showed me the first and last secrets in heaven above, and in the depths of the earth, in the ends of heaven, and its foundations, and in the container of the winds. He showed me how the winds were divided, how they were balanced, and how both the springs and the winds were numbered according to their power. He showed me the power of the moon's light, that its power is a fitting one, as well as the divisions of the stars, according to their respective names, how every division is divided.

He showed me that the lightning flashes, that its host immediately obeys, and that it stops during the progression of the sound of thunder. Thunder and lightning are not separated. They do not occur together, yet they are not separate. For when the lightning flashes, the thunder sounds, and their essence pauses at a proper interval, making an equal division between them, as the container, on which their intervals depend, is as flexible as sand. Each of them at their proper time is bridled and turned by the power of their essence, which propels them as far as the whole extent of the earth.

The essence of the sea is also powerful and strong, and a strong power causes it to ebb, and drives it forwards, and it disperses amongst the mountains of the earth. The essence of the frost has its angel, in the essence of hail there is a good angel, the essence of snow leaves its own place due to its strength, and a special essence is in it, which ascends from it like vapor, and is called frost. The essence of mist does not live with them in their container, but it has a container to itself, for its progress is majestic in light, and in darkness, in winter and in summer. Its container is bright, and an angel is in it.

The spirit of dew lives in the extremities of heaven, and is connected with the containers of rain, and its progress is in winter and in summer. The cloud produced by it, and the cloud of the mist, are connected. One gives to the other, and when the spirit of rain is in motion from its container, angels come and open its container and bring it out. When it too is sprinkled over all the earth, it forms a union with every kind of water on the ground. The waters stay on the ground, because they give nourishment to the earth from the Most High, who is in heaven. For this reason there is a regulation in the quantity of rain, and the angels are in charge of it.

I saw all these things near the garden of justice.

61:1-13.

In those days I saw long cords given to those angels, who took to their wings, and flew, advancing toward the north. I asked the angel, "Where have they taken those long cords, and gone off?"

He said, "They have gone off to measure."

The angel, who went with me, said, "These are the measures of the just, and the just bring cords, so that they may depend on the name of the Lord of spirits forever and ever. The chosen will begin to live with the chosen. And these are the measures which will be given to faith, and which will strengthen justice. These measures will reveal all the secrets of the depths of the earth and those who have been destroyed in the desert, and those who have been devoured by the fish of the sea, and by wild beasts, will return, and rely on the day of the chosen one, for none will perish in the presence of the Lord of spirits, nor will any be capable of perishing.

"And all who live in the heavens above received a command, a power, one voice, and one light like fire. And they blessed him with their voice, they exalted him, and they praised him with wisdom. They were wise with their speech, and with the breath of life. Then the Lord of spirits seated the chosen one on his splendid throne. He will judge all the deeds of the sacred, in heaven above, and will weigh their actions in a balance. When he lifts up his face to judge their secret ways in accordance with the word of the name of the Lord of spirits, and their progress along the path in accordance with the just judgment of the Lord most high, then they will all speak with united voice, and bless, praise, exalt, and extol, the name of the Lord of spirits.

"He will call all the host of the heavens, and all the sacred ones above, and the host of God, the Cherubim, the Seraphim, and the Ophanin, all the powerful angels, and all the angels of the principalities, and the chosen one, and the other host that is on earth and over the water on that day.

"They will raise their united voice, and will bless, praise, and exalt with the spirit of faith, with the spirit of wisdom and patience, with the spirit of compassion, with the spirit of judgment and peace, and with the spirit of goodwill. All will say with united voice, 'Blessed is he, and may the name of the Lord of spirits be blessed forever and ever.'

"All who do not sleep in heaven above will bless him. All the sacred ones in heaven will bless him, all the chosen who live in the garden of life, and every spirit of light, who is capable of blessing, praising, exalting, and extolling your sacred name, and all of the natural realm will beyond measure praise and bless your name forever and ever. For the compassion of the Lord of spirits is vast. He is patient. All his works and all his power, all the great things he has done, he has revealed to the just and to the chosen, in the name of the Lord of spirits."

62:1-16.

Thus the Lord commanded the kings, the mighty, the exalted, and the inhabitants of the earth, "Open your eyes, and raise your horns, if you are able to recognize the chosen one."

The Lord of spirits seated him on his splendid throne. The spirit of justice was poured out over him. The word of his mouth will destroy all the wrongdoers and all the unjust, who will perish in his presence. In that day all the kings, the mighty, the exalted, and those who possess the earth, will stand up, see, and perceive that he is sitting on his splendid throne, and that the just are judged justly in his presence, and no useless word is spoken in his presence.

Then pain will come on them, as on a woman in childbirth whose labor is severe, when her child comes to the mouth of the womb, and she has difficulty birthing. One part of them will look at the other. They will be astounded, and have downcast faces. Pain will seize them, when they see this human sitting on his splendid throne.

Then the kings, the mighty, and all who possess the earth, will praise him who has dominion over all things, him who was hidden, for from the beginning the human existed in secret, and the Most High kept him in the presence of his power, and revealed him to the chosen. The assembly of the sacred and of the chosen will be sown, and all the chosen will stand in his presence on that day. All the kings, the mighty, the exalted, and those who rule over all the earth, will fall down on their faces in worship before him. They will set their hope on this human, will pray to him, and petition him to show compassion.

Then the Lord of spirits will hurry to expel them from his presence. Their faces will be full of confusion, and darkness will grow deeper on their faces. The angels of punishment will take them, so that they will be repaid for the wrong done to his children and his chosen. They will become an exhibition to the just and to his chosen. They will celebrate because of them, as the anger of the Lord of spirits will rest on them. Then the sword of the Lord of spirits will be drunk with their blood, but the just and the chosen will be safe on that day, and they will never again see the face of the wrong-doers and the unjust.

The Lord of spirits will remain over them, and they will live, eat, lie down, and get up, with this human, forever and ever. The just and the chosen have risen from the earth, have stopped having downcast faces, have stopped having depressed appearances, and have put on the clothing of life. The clothing of life is from the Lord of spirits, in whose presence your clothing will not get old, nor will your magnificence decrease.

63:1-12.

In those days the mighty kings who possess the earth will beg the angels of his punishment, to whom they have been handed over, to give them a little rest, so that they may fall down and worship in the presence of the Lord of spirits, and admit their wrongdoings to him. And they will bless and praise the Lord of spirits: "Blessed is the Lord of spirits, the Lord of kings, the Lord of the mighty, the Lord of the rich, the Lord of splendor, and the Lord of wisdom. Every secret thing is clear to you, and your power lasts for generation after generation, and your splendor lasts forever and ever. Your secrets are deep and numberless, and your justice is beyond measure. Now we realize that we should praise and bless the Lord of kings and him who is king over all kings." They will say, "If only we could have some rest so we could praise, thank, and bless him, and admit our wrongdoings in the presence of his splendor?"

And now we long for a little rest but do not find it, we are driven away and do not possess it. Light has passed away from in front of us, and darkness will be where we will live forever. For we have not believed him, we have not praised the name of the Lord of spirits, we have not praised the Lord for all his works, but we have trusted the scepter of our kingdom and of our magnificence.

On the day of our affliction and of our trouble he will not save us, neither will we find any rest to agree that our Lord is faithful in all his actions, in all his judgments, and in his justice. His judgments have no respect for persons, and we must leave his presence on account of our deeds as our wrongdoings are certainly without number. Then will they say to themselves, "Our inner beings are full of criminal gain, but that doesn't prevent us from going down into the fiery middle of Sheol!"

Afterward, their faces will be filled with darkness

and confusion before the human, and they will be driven from his presence, and the sword will remain in their midst, in his presence. The Lord of spirits says, "This is the decree and the judgment against the mighty, the kings, the exalted, and those who possess the earth, in the presence of the Lord of spirits."

Commentary
The following is a vision of Noah and not of Enoch.

64:1-2.

I also saw other figures hidden in that place. I heard the voice of an angel saying, "These are the angels who went down from heaven to earth, and have revealed what is hidden to the humans, and seduced the humans into doing wrong."

65:1-12.

In those days Noah saw that the earth had tilted, and that destruction approached. He set off from there and went to the ends of the earth, and called out to his grandfather Enoch. Noah said three times with a bitter voice, "Hear me, hear me, hear me!"

And I said to him, "Tell me, what is happening to the earth, as it is so badly affected and violently shaken, surely I will perish with it!"

Then immediately there was a great disturbance on the earth, and a voice was heard from heaven. I fell down on my face. Then my grandfather Enoch came and stood by me, and said, "Why have you cried out to me so bitterly and wept? A decree has gone out from the Lord against the inhabitants of the earth, that they must be destroyed. They know all the secrets of the angels, and all the oppressive and secret powers of the satans, and every power of those who commit sorcery, and the power of those who make molten images in the whole earth. They know how silver is produced from the dust of the earth, and how soft metal originates from the earth. For lead and tin are not produced from earth like the former, for there is a spring that produces them, and there is an angel standing on it, and that angel allocates them."

Afterward my grandfather Enoch seized me with his hand, and raised me up, and said to me, "Go! I have asked the Lord of spirits about this disturbance on the earth, and he replied, 'Because of their wickedness, their judgment has been completed, and I will not withhold it, forever. Because of the sorceries which they have searched out and learnt, the earth and its inhabitants shall be destroyed. There will be no place of refuge for them forever because they showed them what was hidden, and they are damned. But this is not the case with you, my son. The Lord of spirits knows that you are good, and innocent of the reproach concerning the secrets. He has established your name in the midst of the sacred ones, and will preserve you from amongst the inhabitants of the earth. He has destined your just offspring for dominion and great honor, and countless numbers of the just and the sacred will flow from your offspring forever."

66:1-3.

After this he showed me the angels of punishment, who were ready to come and release all the force of the waters under the earth in order to bring judgment and destruction of all the inhabitants of the earth. The Lord of spirits commanded the angels who were going out not to make the waters rise but to keep an eye on them, for those angels were in charge of the force of the waters. Then I left Enoch.

67:1-13.

In those days God's word came to me, and said, "Noah, your allotment has come up before me, an allotment void of blame, an allotment of love and justice. Now the angels are working with timber, but when they have finished this, I will place my hand on it, and preserve it. The seed of life will come out of it, and change will take place, so that the earth will not be left empty. I will establish your offspring before me forever and ever, and I will scatter those who live with you over the face of the earth. It will not happen again on the earth. They will be blessed and multiplied on the earth, in the name of the Lord."

They will lock up those angels who acted wickedly in that burning valley, which my grandfather Enoch had previously shown me in the west, where there were mountains of gold and silver, of iron, of soft metal, and of tin. I saw that valley in which there was a great disturbance, and where the waters heaved.

And when all this happened, a smell of sulfur was produced from the fiery molten metal and the disturbance which troubled them in that place, and the smell came from the waters. The valley of the angels who had been guilty of leading humans astray, burned underneath the ground. Rivers of fire flowed through that valley, where those angels who led the inhabitants of the earth astray will be condemned.

But in those days, those waters will be for healing the inner self and the body, and for judgment of the spirit, for kings, the mighty, the exalted, and the inhabitants of the earth. Their spirits will be full of lust and they will be judged in their bodies, because they have denied the Lord of spirits, and although they see their punishment daily, they do not believe his name.

The more they are burned, the more a change will take place in their spirits forever and ever, for no one can speak a useless word in the presence of the Lord of spirits. Judgment will come on them, because they trusted their bodily lust, but denied the spirit of the Lord. In those days the waters of that valley will be changed, for when the angels are judged, the temperature of those springs of water will change. When the angels come up, the water of the springs will change, and become cold. Then I heard the sacred Michael answering.

He said, "This judgment by which the angels are

judged, will bear witness against the kings and the mighty who possess the earth. For these waters of judgment will be for their healing, and for the lust of their bodies. But they will not recognize and believe that the waters will change and become a fire which burns forever."

68:1-5.

After this my grandfather Enoch gave me the signs of all the secrets in the book, and of the parables which had been given to him, and he inserted them for me in the words of the book of parables. At that that time the sacred Michael answered and said to Raphael, "Spiritual power seizes me, and urges me on because of the severity of the angels' judgment. Who can endure the severe judgment which has been executed, before which they melt away?"

Again the sacred Michael answered the sacred Raphael, "Who is there whose heart is not softened by it, and whose mind is not disturbed by this word? Judgment has gone out against them by those who have dragged them away!"

But it came to pass that when they stood in the presence of the Lord of spirits, the sacred Michael said to Raphael, "I will not take their part under the Lord's eye, because the Lord of spirits has been angry with them because they acted as if they were masters.

Because of this the secret judgment will come on them forever and ever, and neither angel nor human will receive any part of it, but they alone will receive their judgment forever and ever.

69:1-29.

"After this judgment they will be terrified and shaken, because they have shown this to the inhabitants of the earth."

Here are the names of those angels! The first of them is Semjaza, the second, Artiqifa, the third, Armen, the fourth, Kokabel, the fifth, Turael, the sixth, Rumjal, the seventh, Danjal, the eighth, Nuqael, the ninth, Baraqel, the tenth, Azazel, the eleventh, Armaros, the twelfth, Batarjal, the thirteenth, Busasajel, the fourteenth, Hananel, the fifteenth, Turel, the sixteenth, Simapesiel, the seventeenth, Yetarel, the eighteenth, Tumael, the nineteenth, Turel, the twentieth, Rumael, the twenty-first, Azazel. These are the chiefs of their angels, and the names of the leaders of their hundreds, and the leaders of their fifties, and the leaders of their tens.

The name of the first is Jeqon. He was the one who led all the sacred associates of God astray and brought them down to earth, and led them astray with humans. The name of the second is Asbeel. He suggested an evil plan to the sacred associates of God, so that they defiled their bodies with humans. The name of the third is Gadreel. He showed every deadly blow to the humans. He led Eve astray, and showed the humans the weapons of death, the coat of mail, the shield, and the sword for killing, every deadly weapon he showed to the humans. Because of him they have proceeded against the inhabitants of the earth forever and ever.

The name of the fourth is Penemue. He showed humans bitterness and sweetness, and showed them all the secrets of their wisdom. He taught humans writing with ink and paper, and through that, numerous have gone astray through every time of the world, even to this day. For humans were not born for this, to confirm their faith with pen and ink. For humans were created just like the angels, so that they would stay just and pure, and death, which destroys everything, would not have touched them. But they perish because of this knowledge, and death consumes them through this power.

The name of the fifth is Kasdeja. He showed the humans every wicked strike of spirits and of demons, the strike at the embryo in the womb, to miscarry it, the strike of the spirit by the bite of the serpent, and the strike which is given in the midday by the offspring of the serpent, the name of which is Tabaaet.

This is the task of Kasbeel, the chief of the oath which he showed to the sacred ones when he lived in splendor. His name is Biqa. He told sacred Michael to show him the secret name, so that they might say it in the oath, so that those who showed every secret thing to the humans would shake at that name and oath. This is the power of that oath, for it is powerful and strong.

He placed this oath Akae in the charge of the sacred Michael.

These are the secrets of this oath, and they are strong through this oath. Heaven was suspended by it before the world was created, and forever. By it the earth was founded on the water, and from the secret parts of the mountains the beautiful waters come, from the creation of the world to eternity. By that oath the sea was created, and its foundation. During the time of anger he placed the sand against it, and this continues unchanged forever. By this oath the depths were made firm, and they do not move from their place, forever and ever.

By that oath the sun and moon complete their course, never wandering from the regulation given to them forever and ever. By this oath the stars complete their course, and he calls their names, and they answer him, forever and ever.

In same goes for the spirits of the water, and of the winds, and of all the breezes, and their paths from all the groups of spirits. There the containers of thunder's voices are kept, and the light of the lightning. There the containers of hail and of frost, and the containers of snow, the containers of rain and of dew are kept. All these believe and praise in the presence of the Lord of spirits and praise him with all their power. He sustains them with every act of thanks, while they praise, extol, and exalt the name of the Lord of spirits forever and ever. This oath is strong over them. Through it, they are kept safe and their progress is preserved. They were very happy, and they blessed, praised, and exalted, because the name of the human was revealed to them. He sat on his splendid throne, and the whole judgment was assigned to him, the human. Wrongdoers will disappear and perish from the face of the earth, while those who led them astray will be bound with chains forever. They will be imprisoned in the assembly place of their destruction, and all their works will disappear from the face of the earth. From then on there will be nothing to corrupt, for the human has appeared, sitting on his splendid throne. Everything wicked will disappear and leave his presence, and the human's word will be powerful in the presence of the Lord of spirits. This is the third parable of Enoch.

The Storehouses

70:1-4.

It came to pass, that after this, during his lifetime, his name was lifted up by the inhabitants of the earth to the presence of the human, and to the presence of the Lord of spirits. He was lifted by the spiritual chariots, and his name vanished among them. From that time I was no longer counted among them, but he sat me between two winds, between the north and the west, where the angels took the ropes to measure for me the place for the chosen and the just. There I saw the ancestors of the first humans, and the sacred, who live in that place forever.

71:1-17.

And it came to pass after this that my spirit was carried away, and went up into the heavens. I saw the sacred associates of God treading on flaming fire. Their garments and clothes were white, and their faces were as light as snow. I saw two rivers of fire glittering like a hyacinth. Then I fell on my face in the presence of the Lord of spirits. The angel Michael, one of the archangels, took me by my right hand, lifted me up, and led me to where there were all the secrets of compassion and secrets of justice. He showed me all the secrets of the extremities of heaven, all the containers of the stars, and the luminaries, from where they come out in the presence of the sacred ones.

And he carried off Enoch to the heaven of heavens. There I saw, in the middle of that light, a structure made with ice crystals, and in the middle of these crystals were tongues of living fire. My spirit saw a circle of fire, and it surrounded the fiery structure. All around it were rivers full of living fire. The Seraphim, the Cherubim, and Ophanin surrounded it. These are those who never sleep, but guard his splendid throne. And I saw innumerable angels, thousands of thousands, and ten thousand times ten thousand, surrounding that structure. Michael, Raphael, Gabriel, Phanuel and the sacred angels who were in the heavens above, went in and out of it. Michael, Raphael, Gabriel, and innumerable sacred angels went out of that structure.

With them was the Ancient of Days. His face was white and pure as wool, and his clothing was indescribable. Then I fell on my face, my whole body melted, and my spirit became changed. I cried out loudly, with a powerful spirit, blessing, praising, and exalting. And those blessings which came out of my mouth were pleasing in the presence of the Ancient of Days. The Ancient of Days came with Michael, Gabriel, Raphael, and Phanuel, and with thousands of thousands, and thousands and ten thousands of angels without number.

Then that angel came to me, and greeted me with his voice, "You are a human who was born for justice, and justice has rested on you and the justice of the Ancient of Days will not leave you." He continued, "He proclaims peace to you in the name of the world which is to come, for from there peace has gone out since the world was created. And so it will be for you forever and ever. All who will exist, and who will walk in your pathway of justice, will never leave you. They will live with you. You will be their allotment, and they will not be separated from you forever and ever. So long life will be with that human, and the just will have peace, and the just will walk along the pathway of integrity, in the name of the Lord of spirits, forever and ever.

The book of the revolutions of the heavenly luminaries

72:1-37.

The book of the revolutions of the heavenly luminaries, according to their respective classes, their respective powers and seasons, their respective names and places of origin, and their respective months, which

Uriel, the sacred angel who was with me and is their guide, showed me. He showed me all their regulations, for each year of the world and forever, until a new creation is made, which will be eternal.

This is the first law of the luminaries. The luminary, the sun, rises in the portals of heaven, which are on the east, and sets in the west in the western portals of heaven. I saw six portals from where the sun rises, and six portals where the sun sets. The moon rises and sets in these portals. I saw the leaders of the stars, together with those whom they lead. There are six in the east and six in the west. All these, one after the other, are in the same place, and there are numerous windows on the right and on the left sides of those portals.

First that great luminary called the sun goes out. Its orb is like the heaven's orb, the whole of it being filled with splendid and flaming fire. The wind blows the chariot on which it ascends. The sun sets in heaven, and, returning by the north, goes to the east, and is led so as to enter by that portal, and illuminate the face of the sky. In the same manner it goes out by the large portal in the first month. It goes out through the fourth of those six portals, which are in the east. And in the fourth portal, through which the sun rises in the first month, are twelve window-openings, and a flame goes out of them whenever they are opened at their proper time.

When the sun rises in heaven, it goes out through this fourth portal for thirty days, and sets exactly in the fourth portal in the west of heaven. During that time the day grows longer daily, and the night grows shorter nightly until the thirtieth morning. On that day the day is longer by two parts than the night. The day amounts to precisely ten parts, and the night to eight parts. The sun rises through this fourth portal, and sets in it, and returns to the fifth portal in the east for thirty days, and rises from it, and sets in the fifth portal.

Then the day becomes longer by two parts, so the day amounts to eleven parts, while the night becomes shorter, amounting to seven parts. The sun now returns to the east, entering the sixth portal, and rising and setting in the sixth portal for thirty-one mornings, on account of its sign. On that day, the day is longer than the night, being twice as long as the night, and the day becomes twelve parts, and the night becomes shorter and amounts to six parts. Then the sun rises so that the day may be shortened, and the night lengthened. And the sun returns to the east and enters the sixth portal, where it rises and sets for thirty days.

When that has happened, the day becomes shortened by precisely one part, so that it is eleven parts, while the night is seven parts. Then the sun goes from that sixth portal in the west, and goes to the east, rising in the fifth portal for thirty days, and setting again in the fifth portal of the west. At that time the day becomes shortened by two parts, so that is ten parts, while the night is eight parts. Then the sun goes out from the fifth portal, and sets in the fifth portal of the west, and rises in the fourth portal for thirty-one days, on account of its signs, and sets in the west. At that time the day is made equal with the night and, being equal with it, the night amounts to nine parts, and the day to nine parts.

Then the sun goes out from that portal, and sets in the west, and returns to the east by the third portal for thirty days, and sets in the west at the third portal. At that time the night decreases in length, and the night amounts to ten parts and the day to eight. The sun then rises from the third portal, as it sets in the west and returns to the east. It rises in the third portal of the east for thirty one days and sets in the west.

In the same way too it sets in the second portal in the west of heaven. At that time the night is eleven parts, and the day is seven parts. Then at that time the sun goes from the second portal, as it sets in the second portal in the west, but returns to the east by the first portal for thirty-one days, and sets in the west in the first portal.

At that time that night is lengthened as much as the day. It is precisely twelve parts, while the day is six parts. The sun has thus completed its beginnings, and a second time goes around from these beginnings. In that first portal it enters for thirty days, and sets in the opposite part of heaven in the west. At that time the length of the night is shortened by a fourth part, that is, one portion, and becomes eleven parts. The day is seven parts.

Then the sun returns, and enters the second portal in the east. It returns on these divisions for thirty days, rising and setting. At that time the night decreases in length. It becomes ten parts, and the day eight parts. Then the sun goes from that second portal, and sets in the west, but returns to the east, and rises in the third portal in the east for thirty-one days, setting in the west of the sky. At that time the night becomes shortened. It is nine parts. The night is equal to the day. The year is precisely three hundred and sixty-four days. The length of the day and night and the shortness of the day and night, are different from each other by the progress of the sun. By means of this progress the day is lengthened daily, and the night is greatly shortened. This is the sun's regulation and progress, and its return, returning for sixty days, and going out. This is the great everlasting luminary, that which is named the sun, forever and ever.

That is a great luminary which goes forth, and which is named after its kind, as the Lord commanded. And thus it rises and sets, neither getting shorter nor resting, but running on by day and by night. It shines a seventh portion of light more than the moon, but the dimensions of both are equal.

73:1-8.

After this law I saw another law of a lesser luminary, named the moon, the shape of which is like the shape of the sun. The wind blows the chariot on which it rides, and light is given to it by the measure. Every month its rising and setting change and its days are like the days of the sun. When its light is full, its light is a seventh part of the sun's light.

And it rises like this, and its first phase is to the east: it rises on the thirtieth day. At that time it appears and becomes the first phase of the moon for you on the thirtieth day, together with the sun in the portal from which the sun goes out. One half of it goes out by a seventh part, and the whole of its orb is empty of light, except for a seventh part, the fourteenth part of its light. And in a day it receives a seventh part, or half that part, of its light. Its light is one seventh and a half. It sets with the sun, and when the sun rises, the moon rises with it, receiving half a part of light. On that night, at the beginning of its morning, at the beginning of the moon's day, the moon sets with the sun and on that night it is dark in its fourteen and half parts. But it rises on that day with precisely one seventh part, and it goes out and recedes from the rising of the sun. During the remainder of its time its light increases.

Commentary
Scholars do not agree on the number of portions here.

74:1-17.

Then I saw another course and regulation and how it makes its monthly journey according to that regulation. Uriel, the sacred angel who is the leader of them all, showed me all these and their positions, and I wrote down their positions as he showed them to me. I wrote down their months as they occur, and the appearance of their lights, until fifteen days have passed.

It completes its setting in the west in seven parts and completes its rising in the east in seven parts. But in certain months it changes its settings, and in certain months it makes its own way. In two months the moon sets with the sun, that is, in those two portals which are in the middle, in the third and fourth portal. It goes out for seven days, then returns to the portal from where the sun goes out, and in that completes its whole light. Then it recedes from the sun, and in eight days enters the sixth portal from which the sun rises. When the sun rises from the fourth portal, the moon goes out for seven days, until it rises from the fifth portal. Then it returns in seven days to the fourth portal, and completing all its light, recedes, and enters the first portal in eight days.

Thus I saw their position, according to the fixed order of the months the sun rises and sets At those times there is a surplus of thirty days of the sun in five years, and all the days add up to each year of the five years, and amount to 364 days. The surplus of the sun and stars amounts to 6 days, 6 days in each of the 5 years, thus 30 days. Thus the moon has 30 days less than the sun and stars.

The moon carries out all the years precisely, so that their positions may come neither too early nor too late even for a single day, but change the year in precisely in

364 days. In 3 years the days are 1092 days, in 5 years 1820 days, and in 8 years there are 2912 days.

For the moon alone, the days in 3 years amount to 1,062 days, and in 5 years amount to 50 days behind. In 5 years there are 1,770 days so that the days of the moon in eight years amount to 2,832 days. In 8 years the difference is 80 days, by which it falls short. The year then becomes completed according to the position of the moon and the position of the sun, as they rise from the portal in which the sun rises and sets for 30 days.

75:1-9.

These are the leaders of the chiefs of the thousands, those which preside over the whole creation and over all the stars, with the four days which are added and never separated from their allotted place, according to the calculation of the year. And these serve the four days which are not calculated in the calculation of the year. People go greatly wrong because of these, as these luminaries truly serve in the stations of the world, one in the first portal, one in the third portal, one in the fourth portal, and one in the sixth portal. And the harmony of the world is completed by the 364 stations.

The signs, the seasons, the years, and the days, were shown to me by Uriel, the angel whom the splendid Lord appointed over all the heavenly luminaries of the sky and the world, so that they would rule in the face of the sky, and appear over the earth, and become leaders of the days and nights: the sun, the moon, the stars, and all the serving creatures which make their circuit with all the heavenly chariots.

Likewise, Uriel showed me twelve portals open for the circle of the chariots of the sun in the sky, from which the rays of the sun shoot forth. From them heat comes out over the earth, when they are opened in their appointed seasons. They are for the winds, and the spirit of the dew, when in their seasons they are opened, being opened in the extremities of the heavens. I saw twelve portals in heaven at the extremities of the earth, through which the sun, moon, and stars, and all the works of heaven, rise and set. Many windows also are open on the right and on the left. One window at its appointed season grows hot corresponding to those portals from which the stars go out as they are commanded, and in which they set corresponding to their number. I also saw the heavenly chariots, running in the world, above those portals in which the stars turn, which never set. One of these is bigger than all the others, and it goes around the whole world.

76:1-14.

And at the extremities of the earth I saw twelve portals open for all the winds, from which they go out and blow over the earth. Three of them are open in the front of heaven, three in the back, three on the right side of heaven, and three on the left. The first three are those which are toward the east, three are toward the north, three behind those which are on the left, to the south, and three on the west. From four of them winds of blessing and health go out, and from eight of them winds of punishment go out in order to destroy the earth, all its inhabitants, and everything that is in the waters or on dry land.

The first of these winds goes from the portal called the eastern, through the first portal on the east. The one that goes from the south brings destruction, drought, heat, and devastation. From the second portal, the middle one, goes fairness. From it go rain, fruitfulness, prosperity, and dew. From the third portal which is northwards, go cold and drought. After these the south winds come out through three portals. A hot wind comes through the first portal, which is to the east. But from the middle portal come lovely fragrances, dew, rain, prosperity, and life. Dew, rain, locusts, and destruction go out from the third portal, which is to the west.

After these are the north winds. From the seventh portal on the east, come dew, rain, locusts, and destruction. From the portal exactly in the middle come rain, dew, life, and prosperity. From the third portal which is to the west, come mist, frost, snow, rain, dew, and locusts. After these are the west winds. Through the first portal, which is to the north, come dew, rain, frost, cold, snow, and ice. From the middle portal come dew, rain, prosperity, and blessing. Through the last portal, which is to the south, come drought, destruction, scorching, and devastation. The account of the twelve portals of the four quarters of heaven is complete. I have explained to you all their regulations, all their infliction of punishment, and the good produced by them, my son Methuselah.

77:1-8.

The first quarter is called the eastern, because it is the first. The second is called the south, because the Most High descends there, he who is blessed forever and descends there frequently. The western quarter is named "reduced", because there all the luminaries of heaven are diminished and go down. The fourth quarter, which is named the "north", is divided into three parts, one of which is for human habitation, another for seas of water, with the deeps, forests, rivers, shady places, and mist, and the third part contains the garden of justice.

I saw seven high mountains, higher than all the mountains of the earth, and snow comes from them, while days, seasons, and years depart and pass away. I saw seven rivers on the earth larger than all rivers, one of which comes from the west and flows into the Great Sea. Two come from the north to the sea, and their waters flow into the Red Sea in the east. And the remaining four flow out on the north side, to their seas, two to the Red Sea, and two into the Great Sea, where it is also said there is a desert. I saw seven large islands, in the sea and on the earth, and five in the Great Sea.

78:1-17.

The names of the sun are these: the first Orjares, and the second Tomas. The moon has four names. The first is Asonja, the second, Ebla, the third, Benase, and the fourth, Erae. These are the two great luminaries, whose orbs are like the orbs of heaven, and the dimensions of both appear equal. In the orb of the sun there are seven portions of light, which is added to it more than to the moon and light is transferred to the moon until a seventh portion of the light of the sun is depleted. Then they set and enter the western portal, and make their circuit by the north, and go out over the face of heaven through the eastern portal.

When the moon rises, it, one fourteenth portion of light is all that appears in heaven. In fourteen days the whole of its light is full. But fifteen parts of light are transferred to it until the fifteenth day when its light is full, according to the signs of the year, and it becomes fifteen parts, and the moon grows by the addition of fourteen parts.

During its waning on the first day the moon's light decreases to a fourteenth part, on the second day it decreases to a thirteenth part, on the third day to a twelfth part, on the fourth day to an eleventh part, on the fifth day to a tenth part, on the sixth day to a ninth part, on the seventh day it decreases to an eighth part, on the eighth day it decreases to a seventh part, on the ninth day it decreases to a sixth part, on the tenth day it decreases to a fifth part, on the eleventh day it decreases to a fourth part, on the twelfth day it decreases to a third part, on the thirteenth day it decreases to a second part, on the fourteenth day it decreases to a half of its seventh part, and on the fifteenth day the remainder of its light disappears fully.

On certain months the moon has twenty-nine days and once twenty-eight days. And Uriel showed me another regulation: when light is poured into the moon, and on which side it is poured into it by the sun.

All the time that the moon's light is increasing; it is transferring it to itself when opposite the sun, until in fourteen days its light is full in the sky. And when it is wholly lit up, its light is full in the sky.

On the first day it is called the new moon, for on that day light rises on it. It becomes a full moon on the day that the sun sets in the west, while the moon ascends at night from the east. The moon then shines all the night, until the sun rises opposite it, when the moon is seen opposite the sun. On the side on which the moon's light appears, it wanes there again until all its light disappears, and the days of the month are at an end. Then its orb remains empty of light.

For three months it achieves thirty days at its proper time, and for three more months it achieves twenty-nine days, during which it effects its waning in the first period of time, and in the first portal for 177 days. And at the time of its rising for three months it appears for thirty days each month, and for three more months it appears twenty-nine days each month. In the night for twenty days each time it looks like a human face, and by day like heaven, and there is nothing else in it except its light.

79:1-6.

And now, my son Methuselah, I have shown you everything, and the account of every regulation of the stars of heaven is finished. He showed me every regulation for these, and for every time, and for every rule, and for every year, and for its end, for the order prescribed to it for every month and every week. He showed me also the waning of the moon, which takes place in the sixth portal. Its light becomes full in the sixth portal and after that it is the beginning of the month. Its waning happens in the first portal, at its proper time, until 177 days are completed - according to the mode of calculation by weeks, twenty-five weeks and two days. It falls behind the sun, according to the regulation of the stars; by five days in one period of time when it has completed the pathway you have seen. Such is the appearance and likeness of every luminary, which Uriel, the great angel who is their leader, showed me.

80:1-8.

In those days Uriel answered me, "I have showed you everything, Enoch, and I have revealed everything to you. You see the sun, the moon, and the leaders of the stars of heaven, which cause all their operations, seasons, and departures. The years will be shortened in the times of wrongdoers. Their offspring will be backward in their prolific soil, and everything done on earth will be subverted, and will not appear in its season. The rain will be held back, and heaven will withhold it. In those days the fruits of the earth will be late, and will not flourish at their proper time, and in their season the fruits of the trees will be withheld at their proper time.

"The moon will change its laws, and not be seen at its proper time. But in those days it will be seen in heaven, on top of a great chariot in the west. It will shine more than light should shine. Many leaders of the stars will wander off, change their ways and actions. Those will not appear at their proper times which have been prescribed for them, and all the classes of the stars will be shut up against wrongdoers. The thoughts of the inhabitants of the earth will go astray concerning them, and they will go astray from their ways. They will do wrong, and think themselves gods, and evil will increase among them. Punishment will come on them and destroy them."

Enoch's Letter to Methuselah

81:1-10.

He said to me, "Enoch, look at the heavenly tablets and read what is written in it, and understand every individual fact."

Then I looked at everything that was written, and read everything that was written and understood it all, all the works of humankind, and of all the humans on earth for all generations of the world. Then I immediately blessed the Lord, the splendid king, because he made all the world's works. I praised the Lord because of his patience, and I blessed him because of the world's humans. At that time I said, "Blessed is the person who will die just and good, and against whom no record of crime has been recorded, and against whom no felony has been found."

Then those three sacred ones brought me and placed me on the earth, in front of the door of my house. They said to me, "Explain everything to Methuselah your son, and inform all your children, that no flesh will be acceptable in the Lord's presence, for he is their creator. We will leave you with your children for one year, until you recover your strength, so that you may instruct your family, write these things, and explain them to all your children. But in the second year they will take you from their midst and your heart will be strong. For the chosen will point out justice to the chosen, the just will celebrate with the just, congratulating each other, but the wrongdoers will die with wrongdoers and the traitor will be drowned with the traitor. Those who act justly will die on account of the works of humans, and will be collected because of the works of the wicked."

In those days they finished conversing with me, and I returned to my fellows, blessing the Lord of worlds.

The Regulations of the Stars

82:1-20.

Now, my son Methuselah, I am telling you all these things and writing them down for you. I have revealed everything to you, and have given you books about all these things. My son Methuselah, preserve the books written by your father, so that you may reveal them to future generations. I have given wisdom to you, to your children, and your descendants, so that they may reveal to their children, for generations, this wisdom that is beyond their thinking. Those who understand it will not sleep, but hear it with their ears in order to learn this wisdom, and it will be considered better than eating this good food.

Blessed are all the just, blessed are all who behave in a just manner, in whom no crime is found, as in wrong-doers. In the numbering of all the days in which the sun progresses through heaven, it goes in and out of each portal for thirty days, with the leaders of the thousands of classes of the stars, together with the four which are added, and which divide the four quarters of the year, which lead them, and accompany them for four days. Because of these, people very much get it wrong, and do not calculate them in the calculation of the whole year, for they very much get it wrong in respect of them, for they do not know this accurately. But indeed these do belong in the calculation of the whole year, and are recorded forever, one in the first portal, one in the third, one in the fourth, and one in the sixth, and the year is completed in 364 days.

It has been accurately calculated and recorded. Uriel has explained to me, and communicated to me, about the luminaries, the months, the fixed times, the years, and the days. The Lord of all creation, on my account, commanded, according to the might of heaven, and the power which it possesses by day and night, Uriel to explain to people the laws of light, of the sun, moon, and stars, and of all the heavenly powers, which revolve with their respective orbs. This is the regulation of the stars, which set in their places, in their seasons, in their times, in their days, and in their months. These are the names of those who lead them, who watch that they enter at their times, according to their regulation, in their months, in the times of their influence, and in their stations.

Their four leaders, who separate the four quarters of the year, enter first. After these, twelve leaders of their classes, who divide the months and the year into 364 days, with the leaders of a thousand, who divide the days, and for the four additional ones, there are leaders which divide the four quarters of the year.

These leaders of a thousand are in the midst of the leaders, and the leaders are added each behind a station, and their leaders make the division. These are the names of the leaders, who divide the four quarters of the year, which are appointed: Milkiel, Heeammelek, Melejal, and Narel. The names of those who lead them are Adnarel, Ijasusael, and Elomeel. These are the three who follow the leaders of the classes of stars, each following after the three leaders of the classes, which in turn follow after the leaders of the stations, who divide the four quarters of the year. In the first part of the year Melkejal rises and rules, this is named the southern sun. All the days of his influence, during which he rules, are 91 days.

And these are the signs of the days which are seen on earth in the days of his influence: sweat, heat, and calm. All the trees become fruitful, the leaf of every tree buds, the grain is harvested, the rose and every species of flower blossoms in the field, and the trees of winter wither. These are the names of the leaders who are under them: Berkael, Zelebsel, and another additional leader of a thousand is named Hilujaseph, the days of whose influence have come to an end. The next leader after them is Helemmelek, whose name they call the splendid sun, and all the days of his light are 91 days. These are the signs of the days on earth, heat and drought, while the trees bring forth their fruits, ripe and prepared, and produce their harvest.

The flocks breed and bear young. All the fruits of the earth are harvested, with everything in the fields, and the winepress. This takes place during the time of his influence.

These are their names and orders, and the leaders who are chiefs of a thousand: Gidaijal, Keel, and Heel. And the name of the additional leader of a thousand is Asfael. The days of his influence are at an end.

Enoch's First Vision

83:1-11.

And now I will show you, my son Methuselah, every sight which I saw prior to your birth. I will relate another vision, which I saw before I was married, they do not resemble each other. The first was when I was learning to write and the other before I married your mother. I saw a terrible vision, and sought the Lord about it. I was lying down in the house of my grandfather Mahalalel, when I saw in a vision the heavens collapse and they were snatched away and fell to the earth. I also saw the earth absorbed by a huge abyss, and mountains suspended over mountains. Hills were sinking on hills, and tall trees were gliding off from their trunks, and were being hurled into the abyss.

Words fell into my mouth and I cried out, "The earth is destroyed!"

Then my grandfather Mahalalel woke me up as I lay near him, and asked me, "Why did you cry out like this, my son, why are you moaning?"

I told him the whole vision which I had seen. He said to me, "My son, you have seen a terrible thing! The vision in your dream concerns every secret wrongdoing of the earth. It will sink into the abyss, and a great destruction will take place. Now, my son, get up, and implore the splendid Lord, for you are faithful, that a remnant may be left on the earth and that he would not completely destroy it. My son, all this disaster on earth comes down from heaven, and great destruction will come on the earth."

Then I got up, prayed, and pleaded, and wrote down my prayer for the generations of the world, explaining everything to my son Methuselah. When I had gone down below, and looked up to heaven, I saw the sun rising in the east, the moon setting in the west, a few scattered stars, and everything which God has known from the beginning, I blessed the Lord of judgment, and praised him, because he had sent the sun from the windows of the east, so that it rose and set and in the face of the heavens, and kept on the pathway appointed for it.

84:1-6.

I lifted up my hands with justice, and blessed the sacred, and the Great One. I spoke with the breath of my mouth, and with a mortal tongue, which God has formed for all the mortal humans, so that they may speak forever and ever. Your dominion lasts for generation after generation. All the heavens are your throne forever, and the whole earth your footstool forever and ever. For you have made them, and you reign over everything. No deed whatsoever is beyond your power. Your wisdom is never changes, nor does it leave your throne or your presence. You know, see, and hear all things; there is nothing that is concealed from you, for you perceive everything.

"The angels of your heavens have misbehaved, and your fury will remain on mortal flesh, until the day of the great judgment. Now then, God, Lord and great King, I entreat you, and implore you to grant my prayer, that a posterity may be left for me on earth, and that the whole human race may not perish, so that the earth will not be left without inhabitants in the face of eternal destruction. My Lord, let the race which has made you angry perish from the earth, but establish a just and honest race for a posterity forever. Lord, do not ignore your servant's prayer!", giving them breath, a mouth, and a tongue to converse with. "Blessed are you, Lord, the King, great and powerful in your greatness, Lord of all the creatures of heaven, King of kings, God of the whole world, whose reign, kingdom, and magnificence last.

Prophecy About the Animals

85:1-9.

After this I saw another dream, and I will explain it all to you, my son. Enoch arose and said to his son Methuselah, "My son, will I speak to you. Hear my words, and listen to the visionary dream of your father. Before I married your mother Edna, I saw a vision in my sleep. A cow (Adam) sprung out of the earth, and this cow was white. After that a female young cow (Eve) sprung out, and other young cows were with it. One of them was black (Cain), and one was red (Abel). The black young cow (Cain) then struck the red one (Abel), and chased it over the earth.

Commentary

Adam, the first human. Adam is a word which simply means "human." The above statement demonstrates the confusion between the English language and the original languages of Scripture. The verse actually reads, "God created *adam* (the word for the race of human beings) in God's image - God created it in the image of God, God

created them male and female." Genesis 5:2 states, "God created them male and female and blessed them and called them human (*adam*) on the day they were created."

The word "Adam" that we see in English translations of Genesis is merely a "transliteration", the result of putting the Hebrew letters into English letters. The translation is "human", person/s of both genders. Hebrew has grammatical gender. Many languages have grammatical gender but English does not. In English, we only use words like "he" and "she" when we are speaking of persons, and we try to find out the biological gender of those persons so we know whether to refer to a particular person as "he" or "she." In languages which have grammatical gender, all nouns, whether or not they refer to persons, have a gender. Hebrew has two genders and Greek has three. These languages use pronouns like "he" and "she" with nouns, such as table, tree, and lake. The pronoun goes with the noun to which it refers.

This is what is meant by "the pronoun agreeing with its antecedent."

We need to learn the grammatical gender of the noun to know which pronoun to use. It is exceptionally important to note that grammatical gender does not match biological gender - it may, but by coincidence only. Thus, in ancient Greek,

the word for "old woman" is neuter gender. Yet if we were translating a Greek sentence about an old woman into English, we would not refer to the old woman as "it," we would refer to the old woman as "she". The Greek word for a trench is feminine gender, but in English it would be silly to refer to the trench as "she." We just don't do that in English. English is different from Hebrew and Greek. In Hebrew, the word *adam* is masculine grammatical gender. That means it has to have a masculine pronoun, just as the word for hand (even a man's hand) in Hebrew is feminine and must have a feminine pronoun. Again, this has nothing to do with biological gender. In the account of the *adam* in Genesis, Genesis 1:27 states, "God created human in God's image. In the image of God, God created *oto*." *Oto* is the singular masculine accusative pronoun agreeing with *adam*, the human. It has to be masculine grammatical gender to agree with the gender of the noun. It simply replaces the word *adam*. In English we say "him" because tradition holds that the biological gender of the *adam* was male and the English language does not refer to a person as "it." The verse continues, "Male and female God created *otam*." *Otam* is the plural gender-unmarked accusative pronoun. Grammatically, this refers to the *adam*, humanity. Thus the verse means, "God created humanity in God's

image. God created it in God's image, God created them male and female." Thus God did not create the male first, God created the human first, humanity. God did not create a male first and identify humanity with that male's name. The previous verse, 26, states, "Let us make *adam* . . . and let them rule." *Adam* is here treated as a collective noun, agreeing with a plural verb, that is, the human race. Again, the account does not mention a singular male.

Genesis1:27 speaks of the creation of the *adam*. If the noun is a collective it could either agree with a plural or singular pronoun. That means that we do not know, from the grammar, whether the noun means "human" and thus the first human was androgynous (as the ancient tradition holds), or whether the noun means "humanity". That is, we do not know whether a single androgynous "human" was created, or whether "humanity", males and females, were created.

Further on, the account consistently refers to males and females under the term *adam*. *Adam* is the general term for humans, both male and female. At the end of 1, all the references to *adam* are in the plural. Genesis 2:5 states that there was no *adam* to cultivate the ground, that humans have not yet been created. The verse makes the point that humans are the only beings on earth that cultivate the soil. There is no reference to

maleness in the verse. Genesis 2:7 tells us that God formed the *adam* from dust, breathed into its nostrils the breath of life, and that the *adam* was a living being. We do not know if the noun is collective or singular (as grammatically it could be either), and no gender is specified. Genesis 2:8 says God put the *adam* in the garden. Again, the masculine pronoun is used as it must agree with the grammatical gender, unlike English, where a masculine pronoun would indicate a male person. In verses 16-17, God speaks to the *adam*. At this point, the term *adam* still encompasses male and female.

In Genesis 2:18-19 God says, "It is not good for the *adam* to be alone, I will appoint a suitable helper for it." Again, the masculine personal pronoun in Hebrew simply agrees with the grammatical gender of the Hebrew noun *adam*. It is usually translated as "he" in English, as people have assumed that the *adam* was a male. There is nothing in the grammar to indicate that the *adam* was a male, and animals are first brought as suitable companions. There was no initial idea that a female of the species was lacking. There is no idea, grammatical or otherwise, that the *adam* is a male. In Genesis 2:20, the *adam* gave names to the animals. The *adam* here is now presented in the Hebrew as a singular person, but still there is nothing to suggest that the *adam* was not both

male and female. In verse 21, God put a deep sleep on the *adam*, and withdrew the female portion from it. (Hebrew *tsal'ot*, Greek *pleura*, referring to the factor, the portion, it was only later Rabbinic tradition that had "rib".) In verse 22, God shaped that which he had taken from the *adam* into an *isha* (female) and brought her to the *adam*. In verses 23 and 24, the word *isha* (female) is distinguished from the *ish* (male). This is the first time the words for female and male have appeared in the account. The *adam* is now an *ish*, and becomes the individual Adam. However, the meaning of the word *adam* has not changed, he is a human. Yes, he is now, at this point, also a male, but the word *adam* means "human." The female portion was taken out of the human, the *adam*, and became an *isha*. That which was left was still called a human, *adam*. Someone can remove a piece of pie from a whole pie, but the remaining pie is still called a pie. It does not have to be renamed just because a piece of it was removed. The following verse refers to the new two individuals as *ish* and *isha*, male and female. However, Adam as a name does not appear until 5. This has similar language to 1, where the *adam* is created in God's image, male and female. However, this is followed by a significant statement. After the male and female are introduced, God blessed them, and named them *adam*: "God

created them male and female and blessed them and called them human (*adam*) on the day they were created." Thus it is clear that the word *adam* bears no connotations of maleness. When the term is finally applied to the individual male Adam, it is the term *ish* which is used to note his maleness. Thus Adam is now a male, but the word "Adam" does not mean male, it still means "human". The Hebrew word *adam* did not refer to male humans in particular: it means "human," "humanity," and did eventually refer to the husband of Eve, but his name was "Human". Yes, at this point, he was a male human being, but his name was not "Male" in Hebrew, it was "Human."

"From then on I could see nothing more of the red young cow (Abel), but the black one (Cain) increased in size, and a female young cow (his wife) went with him. After this I saw many cows coming out (their children), looking like him and following him. The first female young cow (Eve) also went away from the first cow (Adam), and looked for the red young cow (Abel), but did not find him. She was greatly distressed while she was looking for him.

"Then I watched until the first cow (Adam) came to her and calmed her down, and she stopped crying. Afterward she calved another white cow (Seth), and afterward calved many cows and black young cows (more children). In my sleep I also perceived the white bull (Seth), which grew in the same way, and became a large white bull. After him many white cows (his descendants) which looked like him came out. They began to calve many other white cows (his descendants), which looked like them and followed each other."

86:1-6.

Again I looked attentively in my sleep, and surveyed heaven above. And a single star (Azazel) fell from heaven! It got up, and ate and grazed among those cows. After that I perceived the large black cows, and all of them changed their stalls and their young cows, and they began to moan one with another!

Again I looked in my vision, and saw heaven, when I saw many stars (The Watchers), which descended, and projected themselves from heaven to where the first star (Azazel) was! It was the middle of those young cows and cows (women and men), grazing among them. I observed them, and they all acted like stallions ready to serve, and began to mount the young cows (women), all of whom became pregnant, and gave birth to elephants, camels, and donkeys! (Giants, Nephilim, and Elioud.) The cows were alarmed and terrified at this, and began biting with their teeth, devouring, and goring with their horns. And thus they began to eat those cows. All the inhabitants of the earth were terrified, shook with fear at them, and fled away!

87:1-4.

Again I perceived them, how they began to strike

and gore each other, and the earth cried out. Then I lifted my eyes a second time to heaven, and saw in the vision that there came from heaven, beings that looked like white humans. Four (Archangels) came from there, and three (angels) with them. Those three, who came out last, took me by my hand and lifted me from the races of earth, and lifted me to a high place. Then they showed me a tower high above the earth, with all the hills much lower. One said to me, "Stay here, until you see what happens to those elephants, camels, and donkeys (Giants, Nephilim and Elioud), to the stars (the Watchers), and to all the cows (the humans).

88:1-3.

Then I looked at the one of the four white humans, who came out first (Raphael). He seized the first star (Azazel) which had fallen from heaven. He bound it hand and foot and threw it into an abyss, a narrow, deep, terrible, and gloomy abyss. Then one of them drew his sword, and gave it to the elephants, camels, and donkeys (Giants, Nephilim and Elioud), who began to strike each other. And the whole earth shook because of them. And when I looked in the vision, one of those four who had come out threw a line from heaven, and collected all the huge stars, whose penises were like those of horses, and bound them all hand and foot, and threw them into an abyss of the earth.

89:1-78.

Then one of those four went to a white cow (Noah), and taught him a mystery and he was trembling. He was born a bull, and became a human, and he built a large vessel (the Ark). He lived in it, and three cows (Shem, Ham and Japheth) lived with him in that vessel, which covered them.

Again I lifted up my eyes toward heaven, and saw a high roof. Seven channels were above it, and they poured much water on a certain place. Again I looked, and springs opened on the earth in that large place! The water began to bubble up, and rose over the earth, so that the place was not seen, and all its soil was covered with water. There was much water over it, darkness, and clouds. I looked at the height of this water, and it was higher than the place. It flowed over the place, and stood higher than the earth. Then all the cows (humans) which were gathered there, while I looked on them, were drowned, swallowed up, and destroyed in the water. But the vessel (the Ark) floated above it. All the cows, the elephants, the camels, and the donkeys (humans, Giants, Nephilim and Elioud), were drowned on the earth, along with all the animals, so that I could not see them. They were unable to get out, but perished and sank into the deep.

Again I looked in the vision until those water channels were removed from that high roof, and the fountains of the earth became level, while other depths were opened. The water began to go down into them, until dry ground appeared. The vessel (the Ark) settled on the earth, the darkness receded, and it became light. Then the white cow (Noah) which became a human went out of the ship and the three cows (Shem, Ham, and Japheth) with him. One of the three cows was white, resembling that cow, one of them was red as blood, and one of them was black (different human races). And the white cow (Noah) left them. They began to produce wild animals and birds, so from them came different species: lions, tigers, wolves, dogs, hyenas, wild boars, foxes, squirrels, swine, falcons, vultures, kites, eagles, and ravens. Then the white cow (Abraham) was born amongst them. And they began to bite each other, when the white cow (Abraham), which was born among them, fathered a wild donkey (Ishmael) and a white bull (Isaac) at the same time, and after that many wild donkeys (the Ishmaelites). Then the white cow, (Isaac) which was born, gave birth to a black wild sow and a white sheep (Esau and Jacob).

That wild sow also fathered many swine. And that sheep (Jacob) fathered twelve sheep (The Twelve Patriarchs). When those twelve sheep grew up, they handed one of them (Joseph) to the donkeys (the Midianites) and they handed that sheep (Joseph) to the wolves (the Egyptians), and he grew up among them. Then the Lord brought the eleven other sheep (the remaining Patriarchs), to live and graze with him in the middle of the wolves (the Egyptians). They increased, and became many flocks of sheep (had many descendants). But the wolves (the Egyptians) began to frighten them and oppress them, until they took off with their young ones.

And they left their young (the Egyptians' young) in currents of deep water.

Now the sheep (the Hebrews) began to cry out because of their young, and complained to their Lord. One (Moses) which had been saved from the wolves (the Egyptians), escaped, and went away to the wild donkeys (the Ishmaelites). I saw the sheep (the Hebrews) moaning, crying, and petitioning their Lord with all their might, until the Lord of the sheep descended in response to their call from his high dwelling, went to them, and inspected them. He called that sheep (Moses) which had left the wolves (the Egyptians), and told him to make the wolves (the Egyptians) understand that they were not to touch the sheep (the Hebrews). Then that sheep (Moses) went to the wolves (the Egyptians) with the Lord's words, when another sheep (Aaron) met him and went with him.

Both of them together entered the dwelling of the wolves (the Egyptians), and spoke to them to make them understand that from then on they were not to touch the sheep (the Hebrews). Afterward I saw how the wolves (the Egyptians) were acting even more forcefully to the sheep (the Hebrews) with all their might. The sheep (the Hebrews) cried out, and their Lord came to them. He began to strike the wolves (the Egyptians), who began to moan, but the sheep (the Hebrews) kept quiet and from then on did not call out. I then watched them until they left the wolves (the Egyptians). The eyes of the wolves (the Egyptians) were blinded, and they went out and pursued sheep (the Hebrews) with all their might. But the Lord of the sheep went with them and guided them. All his sheep followed him.

His face was terrifying and splendid, and his appearance was superlative. Yet the wolves (the Egyptians) began to chase the sheep (the Hebrews), until they overtook them in a certain body of water (The Red Sea). Then that water became divided, the water standing up on both sides in front of them. And while their Lord was guiding them, he placed himself between them and the wolves (the Egyptians). The wolves (the Egyptians) however had not yet seen the sheep (the Hebrews), but went into the middle of the water after them into the body of water (The Red Sea). But when they saw the Lord of the sheep, they turned to flee from him. Then the water returned, and suddenly went back to its natural state. It became full, and swelled up until it covered the wolves (the Egyptians). And I saw that all the wolves (the Egyptians) which had followed the sheep (the Hebrews) perished and drowned.

But the sheep (the Hebrews) passed over this water, and went to a wilderness, which was without both water and grass. And they began to open their eyes and see. Then I saw the Lord of the sheep inspecting them, and giving them water and grass. The sheep (Moses) already mentioned was going with them and guiding them. And when he had ascended the top of a tall rock, the Lord of the sheep sent him to them. Afterward I saw their Lord standing in front them, and his face was terribly severe.

When they all saw him, they were frightened by his appearance. All of them were alarmed, and trembled. They cried out after that sheep (Moses), and to the other sheep (the Hebrews) who had been with him, and who was in among them, "We are unable to stand in our Lord's presence, or look at him!"

Then that sheep (Moses) who guided them went away, and ascended the top of the rock (Mount Sinai). Then the rest of the sheep (the Hebrews) began to grow blind, and to wander from the pathway that had been shown them, but he was unaware of it. Their Lord however was extremely angry with them, and when that sheep (Moses) had learned what had happened, he came down from the top of the rock (Mount Sinai), and coming to the sheep (the Hebrews), found that there were many which had become blind, and had wandered off the path. As soon as they saw him, they were afraid and trembled and wanted to return to their pens.

Then that sheep (Moses), taking with him other sheep (Hebrews), went to those which had gone astray and began to kill them. They were terrified by his appearance. Then he caused those which had gone astray to come back, and they went back to their pens. I also saw there in the vision, that this sheep who became a man (Moses), built a house (the desert Tabernacle) for the Lord of the sheep, and made them all stand in the house. I looked until the sheep (Hebrews) which had met this sheep, their guide (Moses), died. I also looked until all the large sheep perished, while smaller ones rose up in their place, and came to grazing land, and approached a river of water (The River Jordan).

Then that sheep, their guide, who became a human (Moses), separated from them and died. All the sheep missed him, and cried for him bitterly. I also watched until they stopped crying for that sheep (Moses), and passed over the river of water (The River Jordan). And there arose other sheep (The Judges of Israel), all of whom guided them, instead of those who had previously conducted them but who now were dead. Then I watched until the sheep (the Hebrews) came to a good place, a luscious and magnificent land (Canaan). I also saw that they became satisfied, that their house (the Tabernacle) was in the middle of them in a wonderful land. Sometimes their eyes were opened, and sometimes they were blind, until another sheep (Samuel) arose and guided them. He brought them all back, and their eyes were opened.

Then dogs, foxes, and wild boars began to devour the sheep (the Hebrews), until again another sheep (Saul) arose, the master of the flock, one of themselves, a ram (Saul), to guide them. This ram (Saul) began to butt on every side those dogs (the Philistines), foxes, and wild boars, until they all perished. The eyes of the sheep were opened, and saw the ram (Saul) in the middle of the sheep (Hebrews), how it had abandoned its splendor, and had begun to strike the sheep (Hebrews), trampling them, and behaving without decorum. Then their Lord sent the former sheep (Samuel) again to a different sheep (David), and raised him up to be a ram, and to guide them instead of that sheep (Saul) which had abandoned its splendor. That sheep went to him (David) and speaking with him alone, raised up that ram, and made him a prince and leader of the flock (Hebrews).

All the time that the dogs (the Philistines) troubled the sheep, the first ram (Saul) paid respect to this latter ram (David). Then the latter ram (David) got up and fled away from him. And I saw that those dogs (the Philistines) caused the first ram (Saul) to fall. But the latter ram (David) arose, and guided the smaller sheep (the Hebrews). That ram (David) likewise fathered many sheep, and then died. Then there was a smaller sheep (Solomon), which became a ram (king) instead of him, a prince and leader, guiding the flock (Hebrews). And the sheep (Hebrews) grew and increased in number. And all the dogs (the Philistines), foxes, and wild boars were afraid, and ran away from him. That ram (Solomon) also struck and killed all the wild animals, so that they could not again triumph over the sheep (Hebrews), nor at any time ever snatch anything from them.

And that house was made large and wide, and a high tower (Temple) was built on it for the sheep (Hebrews), for the Lord of the sheep. The house was low, but the tower (Temple) was elevated and very high. Then the Lord of the sheep stood on the high tower (Temple), and they spread a full table to in front of him. Again I saw those sheep (Hebrews) who went astray, and went various ways, and abandoned that their house. The Lord of the sheep called some of the sheep (Hebrews) among them, whom he sent to the sheep (prophets), but the sheep (the Hebrews) began to kill them. But one of them (Elijah) was saved from slaughter. He sprang up and cried out against the sheep (the Hebrews) who wanted to kill him. But the Lord of the sheep saved him from them, and brought it up to me, and made it stay. He also sent many others to them (prophets), to bear witness, and to complain about them. Again I saw, when some of them abandoned the house of their Lord, and his tower (Temple), they went astray with everything, and their eyes were blinded. I saw that the Lord of the sheep did much slaughter among them in their pasture, until they invited that slaughter, and betrayed his place. Then he handed them over to lions, tigers, wolves, hyenas, to the power of foxes, and to all animals (all human races).

And the wild animals began to tear the sheep (Hebrews). I also saw that he abandoned the house of their ancestors (the Levites took the Ark), and their tower (Temple), and handed them over to the power of lions (the Assyrians) to tear them up and devour them, and handed them over to the power of all animals (all human races). Then I began to cry out with all my might, pleading with the Lord of the sheep, and showing him how the sheep (Hebrews) were devoured by all the animals. But he looked on in silence, happy that they were devoured, swallowed up, and carried away, and leaving them in the power of all the animals (all human races) for food.

He called also seventy shepherds, and designated the care of the sheep (the Hebrews) to them, that they would care for them. He said to them and to their associates, "Every one of you from now on is to take care of the sheep (the Hebrews), and you are to do whatever I order you to do, and I will hand them over to you properly numbered. I will tell you which of them is to be slain, and you are to destroy these ones." And he handed the sheep over to them.

Then he called another, and said, "Observe, and watch everything that the shepherds do to these sheep, because many more of them than I have commanded will be destroyed. Make an account of every excess of slaughter which the shepherds commit, of how many have perished by my order, and how many they may have destroyed by their own decision. There will be an account of all the destruction brought about by each of the shepherds, and according to the number, I will have a record made for evidence as to how many they have destroyed by their own decision, and how many they have handed over for destruction. This is so that I may have this evidence against them, and so that I may know all their dealings, and that I may see what they will do in handing the sheep over to them, whether or not they will act as I have ordered them.

"However, they are to be unaware of this. You are

not to make any explanation to them, and you are not to reprimand them, but there will be an account of all the destruction done by each individual in their respective times."

Then they began to kill, and destroy more than they were ordered to. They left the sheep (Hebrews) in the power of the lions (the Assyrians), so that very many of them were eaten and swallowed up by lions and tigers, and wild boars preyed on them. They burnt that tower (Temple), and overthrew that house. Then I was extremely upset because of the tower (Temple), and because the house of the sheep was overthrown. Afterward I was unable to perceive whether they entered that house again. The shepherds and their associates handed them over to all the wild animals, so that they could eat them. Each of them in their own time, according to their number, was delivered up, and it was recorded in a book how each of them was destroyed. However, more than ordered were killed and destroyed. Then I began to cry, and I was extremely upset because of the sheep.

In the same way too I saw in the vision the one who wrote, how daily he wrote down each one destroyed by the shepherds. He brought up and showed each of his books to the Lord of the sheep. His books contained everything they had done, and everything each of them had made away with, and everything which they had handed over to be destroyed. The Lord of the sheep took the book up in his hands, read it, sealed it, and put it down.

After this, I saw shepherds pasturing sheep for twelve hours. And three of the sheep (Ezra, Haggai, and Zechariah) returned (the return after exile), arrived, went in, and began building everything that had fallen from that house! But the wild boars (the Samaritans) tried to prevent them, but they were not able to. Again they began to build as before, and raised up that tower, which was a high tower (the second Temple). And again they began to place a table in front of the tower (the second Temple) which had every impure and unclean kind of food on it. In addition to this, all the sheep were blinded and could not see, as was also the case with the shepherds. Thus they handed more over to the shepherds to be destroyed, and they trampled them underfoot and ate them up.

Yet their Lord stayed silent, until all the sheep were all mixed with the wild animals, but the shepherds did not save them from the power of the wild animals. Then he who wrote the book went up and showed it, and read it out at the residence of the Lord of the sheep. He petitioned him for them, and prayed, pointing out every act of the shepherds, and testifying against them all in his presence. Then he took the book, and deposited it with their Lord, and left.

90:1-42.

I looked until the time that 35 shepherds were pasturing the sheep in the same way as the first shepherds. Others then received them into their hands to pasture them in their respective times, each shepherd in his own time. Afterward I saw in the vision that all the birds of sky arrived, eagles, vultures, kites, and ravens. The eagles (the Romans) led them all. They began to devour the sheep, to peck out their eyes, and to eat up their bodies. The sheep cried out because their bodies were devoured by the birds. I also cried out, and groaned in my sleep because of the shepherd which pastured the flock.

And I looked, while the sheep were eaten up by the dogs, by the eagles, and by the kites. They did not leave them flesh or skin, or their muscles, until only their bones remained, until their bones fell on the ground. And the sheep became few. I also observed during that time that 23 shepherds were pasturing, and they completed, each in their time, 58 times. Then small lambs were born from those white sheep, and they began to open their eyes and see, crying out to the sheep. The sheep, however, did not cry out to them, nor did they hear what they said to them, but they were deaf, blind, and stubborn to the utmost. I saw in the vision that ravens flew down on those lambs, and took one of them, and tore the sheep in pieces, and devoured them. I watched until horns grew on those lambs, and that the ravens knocked down their horns. I also saw that a large horn sprouted out on one of the sheep, and their eyes were opened. He looked at them and their eyes were opened. He called out to them and they ran to him.

And besides this, all the eagles, the vultures, the ravens and the kites were still carrying off the sheep, flying down on them and devouring them. The sheep were silent, but the rams lamented and called out. Then the ravens battled and grappled with them. They wished to break his horn, but they did not triumph over him. I looked on until the shepherds, the eagles, the vultures, and the kites came and called out to the ravens to break the horn of the ram, to fight him and kill him. But he struggled with them, and called out for help.

Then I watched until that man, who had written down the names of the shepherds, and who had ascended into the Lord of the sheep's presence, arrived. He brought assistance, and showed the ram that help was on its way. I also watched until the Lord of the sheep came to them angrily, while all those who saw him fled away, all fell down in his presence. All the eagles, the vultures, ravens, and kites assembled, and brought with them all the wild sheep. They all came together and tried to break the ram's horn. Then I saw that the man, who wrote the book at the order of the Lord, opened the book of destruction that the last twelve shepherds had made. He pointed out in the presence of the Lord of the sheep that they had destroyed more than had those who preceded them.

I also saw that the Lord of the sheep came to them, and took the scepter of his anger in his hand. He struck the earth, which split open. All the animals and birds of the sky fell from the sheep and sunk into the earth, which closed over them. I also saw that a large sword was given to the sheep, and they went out against all the wild animals to kill them. All the beasts and birds of the sky fled from them.

I watched until a throne was erected in a lovely land. The Lord of the sheep sat on it. They took all the sealed books and opened them in front of him. Then the Lord called the first seven white ones, and commanded them to bring before him the first (Azazel) of the first stars, which preceded the stars whose penises were like horses, and they brought them all before him. And he spoke to the man who wrote in his presence, who was one of the seven white ones, "Take those seventy shepherds, to whom I handed over the sheep, and who killed more of them than I ordered."

I saw them all bound, and standing in front of him. The judgment was held, first on the stars (The Watchers), which were judged and found guilty, and they went to the place of punishment. They were thrown into a deep place which was full of flaming fire, and full of pillars of fire. Then the seventy shepherds were judged and found guilty, and they were thrown into the fiery abyss. At that time I also saw that one abyss was opened in the middle of the earth which was full of fire. The blind sheep were brought there, and were judged and found guilty, and were thrown into that abyss of fire on the earth, and burnt. The abyss was on the right side of that house. And I saw the sheep burning, and their bones dissolving.

I stood watching him folding up that ancient house, and they removed all its pillars and all the beams and ornaments in it. They removed it and put it in a place on the right side of the earth. I also saw that the Lord of the sheep produced a new house, bigger and taller than the former, and he set it up on the site of the first one which had been folded up. All its pillars were new, and its ornaments were new and more plentiful than the former ancient one, which had been removed, and all the sheep were in it. All the beasts of the earth, and all the birds of heaven, fell down and worshipped them, petitioning them, and obeying them in everything. And the Lord of the sheep was in the middle of it. And I saw all the sheep that were left, all the animals of the earth, and all the birds of the sky, falling down and worshipping those sheep, and begging them and obeying their every command.

Then those three, who were dressed in white, and who had taken hold of my hand, the ones who had previously caused me to ascend, and with the hand of him who spoke holding me, raised me up, and placed me among the sheep, before the judgment took place. The sheep were all white and their wool was long and pure. Then all who had perished and had been destroyed, all the wild animals, and every bird of the sky, assembled in that house, while the Lord of the sheep celebrated greatly because they were all good, and had returned to his dwelling. And I watched until they put down the sword which had been given to the sheep, and returned it to his house, sealing it up in the Lord's presence. All the sheep were enclosed in that house, but it was not capable of containing them, and the eyes of all of them were opened. There was not one among them who did not see. I also saw that the house was large, wide, and extremely full. I also saw that a white cow was born, and its horns were big, and that all the wild animals, and all the birds of the sky, were afraid of it, and continually begged him. Then I saw that the nature of all of them was changed, and that they became white cows. The first among them was a lamb. It was large and on its head were large black horns. While the Lord of the sheep celebrated about them and about all the cows, I lay down among them. I woke up and saw everything. This is the vision which I saw when I was asleep. I woke up and blessed the just Lord, and praised him. Afterward I cried profusely, and my tears did not stop, until I could no longer stand it. While I was looking, they flowed on account of what I saw, for everything will come to pass and be fulfilled, all the deeds of humankind in their order were seen by me. That night I remembered my previous dream, and so I cried and I was troubled, because I had seen that vision.

Prophecy of the Ten Weeks.

91:1-19.

And now, my son Methuselah, call all your siblings to me, and assemble your mother's children for me, for a voice calls me, and a spirit is poured out on me, so that I may show you everything which will happen to you forever. Then Methuselah went and called all his siblings to him, and gathered his relatives. He spoke to all his children truthfully, and said, "My children, hear every word of your father, and listen properly to the voice of my mouth, as I wish to have your attention while I address you. My beloved, have integrity, and behave justly! Do not approach integrity in a deceitful way, and do not associate with deceitful people, but behave justly, my children, and this will guide you in good pathways, and truth will be your companion. "For I know that oppression will continue and prevail on the earth and that great punishment will in the end take place on earth, and all wrongdoing will come to an end. It will be cut off from its root, and its whole structure will pass away. However wrongdoing will be renewed, and completed on earth. Every criminal act, and every act of oppression and wickedness, will prevail a second time. So then when injustice, wrongdoing, blasphemy, tyranny, and every evil work increase, and when wrongdoing, impiety, and uncleanness increase, then great punishment be inflicted on them all from heaven.

"The sacred Lord will go out angrily, and great punishment will be inflicted on them all from heaven. The sacred Lord will go out angrily, in order to execute judgment on earth. In those days oppression will be cut off from its roots, and iniquity with fraudulent crime will be destroyed from under heaven. Every strong place will be surrendered with its inhabitants, and burnt with fire. They will be brought from every part of the earth, and be cast into a fiery judgment. They will perish by being angrily overpowered forever. Justice will be raised up from sleep, and wisdom will get up and be given to them. Then the roots of wrongdoing will be cut off, wrongdoers and blasphemers will perish by the sword. And now, my children, I will describe and point out to you the pathway of justice and the pathway of oppression. I will point them out to you again, so that you may know what is to come. Listen to me now, my children, and behave justly! Do not behave in an oppressive way, for all who behave wickedly will perish forever."

92:1-5.

That which was written by Enoch. He wrote this complete instruction of wisdom which is praised by people and a judge of the whole earth, for all my children who will live on earth, and for subsequent generations who will conduct themselves in a just and peaceful manner. Do not let your inner self worry on account of the times, for the sacred Great One has prescribed a time for all things.

The just one will awake from sleep, will arise, and proceed along the way of justice, in all its pathways which will be good and compassionate forever. He will be compassionate to the just person, and give them integrity and power forever. He will behave well and justly forever, and will walk in eternal light, but wrongdoing will perish in eternal darkness, and from that time on will never be seen again.

93:1-14.

After this, Enoch began to speak from a book. Enoch said, "About the just people, about the chosen of the world, and about the plant of justice and integrity, about these things will I speak, and these things will I explain to you, my children, I, Enoch, according to that which has been shown to me, from my heavenly vision and from the words of the sacred angels and understanding from the tablet of heaven."

Commentary

A Qumran text reads, "Watchers and Sacred Ones," that is, Watchers who were not among the wicked ones, cf. J.T. Milik, *Books of Enoch*, Oxford, 1976, p. 264. Some differentiate "Watchers" and "holy ones" ("sacred ones") in Daniel 4:13 (and 4:17): "a watcher and a sacred one came down from heaven", but the translation there is likely "a sacred Watcher came down from heaven." (Literally, "a Watcher, sacred, came.")

Enoch then began to speak from a book, and said, "I was born the seventh, in the first week, while judgment and justice waited patiently. But after me, in the second week, great wickedness will arise, and fraud will spring out. In that week the end of the first will happen, in which humankind will be safe. But when the first week comes to an end, wrongdoing will spring up, and during the second week he will execute the decree on wrongdoers. Then after that, at the end of the third week, a just person will be selected as the plant of just judgment, and after him the just plant will come forever.

"Then after that, at the end of the fourth week, the visions of the sacred and the just will be seen, and the law of generation after generation, and a living place will be made for them. Then after that, at the end of the fifth week, the splendid and masterful house will be erected forever. Then after that, in the sixth week, all those who are in it will be darkened, and the hearts of all of them will forget wisdom. In it, a person will get up and come out. At its end he will burn the masterful house with fire, and the whole race of the chosen root will be dispersed.

"Then after that, in the seventh week, a rebellious generation will arise. It will do many rebellious deeds. At its end, the just will be selected from the eternal just plant, and they will be given seven portions of the teaching of his whole creation. Then after that, there will be another week, the eighth of justice, and a sword will be given to execute judgment and justice on all oppressors. Wrongdoers will be handed over to the just, and at its end they will acquire dwellings because they are just, and the dwelling of the splendid great king will be established forever. Then after that, in the ninth week, the just judgment will be revealed to the whole world. All the deeds of the ungodly will disappear from the whole earth, the world will be marked for destruction, and all people will look for the just pathway.

"And after this, on the seventh day of the tenth week, there will be an eternal judgment that will be executed on the Watchers, and a spacious eternal heaven will spring out amongst the angels. The former heaven will vanish and pass away, and a new heaven will appear, and all the heavenly powers will shine forever with seven times the light. Afterward there will be many weeks, which will exist forever with integrity and justice. From then on wrongdoing will not be named there forever and ever.

"Who of all the humans is capable of hearing the voice of the Sacred One without emotion? Who is capable of thinking his thoughts? Who is capable of understanding all the workings of heaven? Who is capable of understanding the actions of heaven? They may see its workings, but not how it works. They may be capable of speaking about it, but not of ascending to it. They may see all the boundaries of these things, and think on them, but not understand them. What human is able to understand the breadth and length of the earth? And to whom have all its measurements been shown? Is any human capable of understanding the extent of heaven, what its height is, and by what it is supported, or the numbers of the stars, and where all the luminaries rest?"

Enoch's Message

94:1-11.

Now, my children, let me urge you to love justice, and to behave justly, for the pathways of justice are worthy to be accepted, but the paths of wickedness will suddenly fail and fade away. To certain people of a future generation the pathways of oppression and death will be revealed, but they keep far away from them, and will not follow them. Now I urge you who are just, not to behave in an evil or oppressive manner, or in a manner which causes death. Do not approach these pathways so that you will not be destroyed. And choose for yourselves justice, and a good life. Walk along the peaceful pathways, so that you may live and be found worthy. Keep my words in your innermost thoughts, and do not let them leave your hearts, for I know that wrongdoers cunningly advise people to commit crimes. No place will be found for wisdom, and wrongdoing will increase. Woe to those who build evildoing and oppression, as they will suddenly be undermined, and will never find peace. Woe to those who build up their houses with wrongdoing, for from their very foundations they will be demolished, and they themselves will fall by the sword. Those who acquire gold and silver will justly and suddenly be destroyed in the judgment. Woe to you who are rich, for you have trusted your riches, but your riches will be removed from you, because you have not remembered the Most High in the days of your prosperity.

You have committed blasphemy and wickedness,

and are destined for the days of the outpouring of blood, for the day of darkness, and for the day of the great judgment. This I will declare and point out to you, that he who created you will destroy you, and when you fall, he will not show you any compassion, but your Creator will celebrate over your destruction. Your just ones in those days will be a reproach to the wrongdoers and the ungodly.

95:1-7.

If only my eyes were clouds of water, so that I might weep over you, and pour out my tears like rain, and rest from the sorrow of my heart! Who permitted you to hate and to do wrong? Judgment will come on you, you wrongdoers! The just will not fear the wicked, because God will give them over to your hands, so that you may avenge yourselves on them as you wish. Woe to you who pronounce curses that you cannot remove; healing will be far removed from you because of your wrongdoings! Woe to you who repay your neighbor with evil, for you will be repaid according to your actions! Woe to you, false witnesses, you who do evil, for you will suddenly perish! Woe to you, wrongdoers, for you persecute the just, for you yourselves will be handed over and maltreated, and their yoke will be heavy on you!

96:1-8.

Be hopeful, you just, for wrongdoers will suddenly perish in front of you, and you will exercise power over them, as you like. In the day of the sufferings of wrongdoers your offspring will be lifted up like eagles. Your nest will be higher than that of the vultures. You will go up, and enter the openings in the earth and the clefts of the rocks, forever, like the lawless, but they will groan and weep over you, like mountain goats. You will not be afraid of those who trouble you, for healing will be yours, a splendid light will shine around you, and the tranquil voice will be heard from heaven. Woe to you, wrongdoers, for your wealth makes you appear sacred, but your hearts prove you to be wrongdoers! This word will testify against you as a reminder of your crimes.

Woe to you who feed on the best of the grain, and drink the best of the deepest spring, and trample down the humble with your power! Woe to you who drink water when you wish to, for suddenly you will be repaid, worn out and withered, because you have left the foundation of life! Woe to you who act wickedly, deceitfully, and blasphemously, for there will be a reminder of evil against you! Woe to you, you powerful, you who powerfully strike down justice, for the day of your destruction will come, while at that time many good days will be the allotment of the just at the time of your judgment!

97:1-10.

Believe, you just ones, that wrongdoers will be disgraced, and perish in the day of judgment. You wrongdoers will be aware of it, for the Most High will remember your destruction, and the angels will celebrate it. What will you do, you wrongdoers? And where will you flee in the day of judgment when you hear the words of the just prayer? You are not like those against whom this word bears witness, "You are associates of wrongdoers!"

In those days the prayers of the just will come up in the Lord's presence and the day of your judgment will arrive, and every detail of your wrongdoing will be related in the presence of the great sacred one. Your faces will be covered with shame, while every deed founded on crime will be discarded. Woe to you, wrongdoers, who are in the middle of the sea, or on dry land, their memory will prove harmful to you! Woe to you who amass silver not obtained by honest means, and say, "Our barns are full, and our house's servants are as abundant as overflowing water."

Like water your life will pass away, for your wealth will not be permanent, but will suddenly leave you, because you have obtained it all dishonestly, and you will be handed over to extreme denunciation.

98:1-16.

And now I swear to you, the crafty, as well as the foolish, that you will see many things on the earth. You men will clothe yourselves more elegantly than a woman, and with more ornaments than a girl, dressing yourselves magnificently, ornamentally, powerfully, and in silver - but gold, purple, honor, and wealth flow away like water. Because of this, they do not have knowledge or wisdom. Thus they will perish because of this, together with their riches, all their splendor, and their honor, but their spirits will be thrown into a fiery furnace with disgrace, with slaughter, and in extreme poverty. I have sworn to you, you wrongdoers, that just as a mountain or hill has not been a woman's maid, nor was wrongdoing sent down to earth, but humans themselves created it, and those who commit it will be cursed.

Barrenness has not been inflicted on a woman, but because of her actions she will die childless. I swear to you, wrongdoers, by the sacred great one, that all your wrongdoings are revealed in heaven, and that none of your oppressive acts are hidden or secret. Don't let your inner self think, and don't say to yourself, that every crime is not clearly seen. In heaven it is written down daily in the presence of the Most High. From now on it will be made clear, for every wrongful act you commit will be recorded daily, until the time of your judgment.

Woe to you, you fools, for you will perish because of your foolishness! You will not listen to the wise, and you will not obtain anything good. So then now know that you are ready for the day of destruction. Have no hope that wrongdoers will live, but in the process of time you will die eventually, for you are not marked for ransom. Instead, you are destined for the day of the great judgment, for the day of distress, and the extreme shame of your lives. Woe to you who are stubborn, who commit crimes, and feed on blood! From where do you feed on good things to eat and drink, and be satisfied? Is it not because our Lord, the Most High, has placed abundance on the earth? You will find no peace.

Woe to you who love wrongful acts! Why do you

hope for good to happen to you? Know that you will be given over to the hands of the just ones, who will cut your throats and kill you, and will not show you any compassion. Woe to you who celebrate the troubles of the just, for a grave will not be dug for you! Woe to you who frustrate the words of the just, for there will be no hope of life for you! Woe to you who write down lying words, and the words of the wicked, for they record their lies, so that people will hear and not forget their foolishness! They will not find any peace, but they will certainly die suddenly.

99:1-16.

Woe to those who act wickedly, who praise and honor false words! You will be lost, and will not have a good life Woe to you who change truthful words! They contravene the eternal decree, and consider themselves not to be wrongdoers. They will be trampled down on the earth. You just ones, in those days you will be considered worthy to have your prayers rise up in remembrance. They will have them put as evidence in front of the angels, so that they can record the wrongdoers' acts in the presence of the Most High.

In those days the nations will be overthrown, but the races of the nations will rise again in the day of destruction. In those days women who become pregnant will abort their children, and leave them. Their offspring will slip from them, and they will leave their nursing babies. They will never return to them, and will not show compassion to their loved ones. Again I swear to you, wrongdoers, that crime is ready for the day of blood which never ceases.

They will worship stones, and carve golden, silver, wooden and clay images. Some, with no knowledge, will worship unclean spirits, demons, and all kinds of idols, in temples, but will get no help from them. They will become ungodly through their foolishness, and their eyes will be blinded through the fear in their hearts and through visions in their dreams. Through these they will become ungodly and fearful, lying in all their actions, and worshipping stones. They will be destroyed at the same time. But in those days blessed will be those who accept words of wisdom, and understand and follow the paths of the Most High, who behave justly, and who do not act wickedly with the wicked. They will be saved. Woe to you who extend crime to your neighbor, for you will be killed in Sheol!

Woe to you who lay the foundations of wrongdoing and deceit, and who cause bitterness on earth, because you will be consumed by it! Woe to you who build your houses by the labor of others, and construct them with the stones of crime, I tell you, you will not find peace! Woe to you who despise the extent of the eternal inheritance of your ancestors, and whose lives follow idols, for you there will be no peace! Woe to those who do wrong and help blasphemy, who kill their neighbor until the day of the great judgment, for he will throw down your splendor! You put evil in your hearts, and stir up the spirit of his anger and consequently he will destroy every one of you by the sword. Then all the just and the sacred will remember your crimes.

100:1-12.

In those days fathers will be struck down with their children in front of each other, and siblings will fall dead with their siblings until their blood flows like a river. For a man will not withhold his hand in mercy from his children, nor from his children's children - he will kill them. The wrongdoer will not restrain his hand from his honored brother. From the dawn of day to the setting of the sun they will kill each other. The horse will wade up to its chest, and the chariot will sink to its axle, in the blood of wrongdoers.

In those days the angels will come down into the hidden places, and collect in one spot all who have assisted in crime. On that day the Most High will rise up to execute the great judgment on all wrongdoers, and to set guards from the sacred angels, over all the just and sacred, that they may protect them like the apple of an eye, until every evil, and every crime is wiped out. Even though the just sleep a long sleep, they have nothing to fear. The wise will see the truth, and the inhabitants of the earth will understand every word of this book, knowing that their riches cannot save them or wipe out their crimes.

Commentary

The word translated "sons" with a place name,

indicates inhabitants of that place and should not be translated as "son/child of..." The Benai Israel, translated in the KJV as "children/sons of Israel" actually means "members of the class of people called Israel" and should be translated "Israelites."

Woe to you, wrongdoers, when you afflict the just on the day of the great trouble, and burn them with fire, you will be paid back for your actions! Woe to you who have stubborn hearts, who watch in order to devise evil! You will be afraid and no one will help you. Woe to you, wrongdoers, for with the words of your mouths, and with the work of your hands, you have acted wickedly! You will be burnt in the flames of a blazing fire. And now know, that the angels will inquire into your conduct in heaven, from the sun, the moon, and the stars, will they inquire about your crimes, for on earth you execute judgment on the just. Every cloud, the snow, the dew, and the rain will bear witness against you, for all of them will be withheld from you so that they will not fall on you, and they will think about your crimes. Now then bring gifts to the rain so that it will not be withheld and will descend on you, and to the dew, which will fall on you if it has received gold and silver from you. But when the frost, snow, cold, every snowy wind, and all their irritations fall on you, in those days you will not be able to stand in front of them.

101:1-9.

Consider heaven, all you inhabitants of heaven, and all the works of the Most High, and respect him, and never do evil in his presence. If he shut up the windows of heaven and withheld the rain and dew, so that it did not fall on the earth because of you, what will you do? And if he sends his anger on you and all your deeds, will you not appeal to him? You speak against his justice in arrogant and powerful language. To you there will be no peace.

Do you not see ships' captains, how their vessels are tossed about by the waves, torn to pieces by the winds, and exposed to the greatest danger? For this reason they are afraid, because all their possessions are at sea with them, and they only think negatively, because the sea may swallow them up, and they may perish in it. Is not the whole sea, all its waters, and all its movement, the work of the Most High, he who has sealed up all its workings, and girded it on every side with sand? Does it not dry up at his rebuke and become afraid, while all its fish and everything in it die? But you wrongdoers on the earth are not afraid of him. Is he not the maker of heaven and earth and of everything that is in them? And he who has given knowledge and wisdom to all things that move on the earth and in the sea? Don't the ships' captains fear the ocean? Yet wrongdoers are not afraid of the Most High.

102:1-11.

In those days, when he directs a severe fire at you, where will you flee, and where will you be safe? And when he sends his word against you, will you not be afraid and terrified? All the luminaries are shaken with great fear, and all the earth will be terrified, and will tremble and be anxious. All the angels will carry the commands they received, and will want to hide from the presence of the one who is greatly splendid, while the inhabitants of the earth are afraid and terrified. But you, wrongdoers, are accursed forever, you will not find peace.

Do not be afraid, souls of the just, but be hopeful, you who were just when you died. Do not grieve, because your souls descend to Sheol with sadness, and because in your lifetime your bodies did not receive a reimbursement in proportion to your goodness, but when you die the wrongdoers will say about you, "As we die, the just die. What use to them were their actions? Like us, they die with sorrow and in darkness. What advantage do they have over us? From now on we are equal. What will be within their grasp, and what will they see forever? For they too are dead, and they will never again see the light." I say to you, wrongdoers, "You have been satisfied to eat and drink, strip people naked, commit crimes, acquire wealth, and see good days. Have you not seen the just, how their end is peaceful? For no oppression is found in them up until the day of their death. They perish, and are as if they were not, while their souls went down with sadness to Sheol.

103:1-15.

But now I swear to you, the just, by his great splendor and his magnificence, by his superb sovereignty and by his majesty, I swear to you, that I understand this mystery, that I have read the tablet of heaven, and have seen the writing of the sacred ones, and have discovered what is written and engraved on it about them. I have seen that all good, happiness, and honor has been prepared for you, and has been written down for the spirits of those who died justly. Much good will be given to you in return for your troubles, and your allotment of happiness will far exceed the allotment of the living.

The spirits of you who died justly will live and celebrate and be happy, and their memory will remain in the presence of the Mighty One from generation after generation. Do not be afraid of their abuse. Woe to you, wrongdoers, when you die committing wrong, and those who are like you say about you, "Blessed are these wrongdoers. They have lived out their whole time, and now they die with prosperity and wealth. They did not see distress and slaughter while they were alive, and they have died with honor, and judgment did not come upon them in their lifetime!"

When their souls will do down to Sheol they will be miserable and greatly tormented. In darkness, in chains, and in the flames, your spirits will come to the great judgment which will last forever and ever. Woe to you, for you will find no peace! Do not say to the just and the good who are alive, "We were afflicted during the days of our trouble, and we have seen all kinds of trouble and have suffered many evil things. Our spirits have been exhausted, lessened, and diminished. We were destroyed, and there was no one to help us with words or actions. We were tormented and destroyed and did not expect to live day after day.

"We hoped to have been the head but we have become the tail. We worked hard and exerted ourselves, but we have been devoured by wrongdoers and the lawless, and their yoke has been heavy on us. Those who exercised authority over us hate us and goad us, and we bowed down to those who hate us, but they have shown no compassion to us. We wished to escape from them, so that we could flee and find rest, but we have found no place to flee or be safe from them. In our distress we complained to the rulers, and have cried out against those who were devouring us, but our cry has been disregarded, and they would not listen to our voice. Instead, they helped those who robbed and devoured us, those who decreased our numbers, and they concealed their oppression, and did not remove their yoke from us, but they devoured, weakened, and killed us. They concealed our slaughter, and did not remember that they have lifted up their hands against us."

104:1-13.

I swear to you, you just ones, that in heaven the angels record your good in the splendid presence of the Mighty One. Be hopeful, for formerly you were disgraced with evils and afflictions, but now you will shine like the heavenly luminaries. You will be seen, and the portals of heaven will be opened for you. Cry out for judgment, and it will appear for you, for an account of all your sufferings will be required from the rulers and from every one who helped those who robbed you.

Be hopeful, and do not abandon hope, for great happiness will be yours, like that of the angels in heaven. What do you have to do? You will not have to hide in the day of the great judgment and you will not be found to be wrongdoers. Eternal judgment will be far from you, for all the generations of the world. Do not be afraid, you just ones, when you see wrongdoers flourishing and prospering in what they do. Do not associate with them, but keep yourselves at a distance from their wrongdoing, for you will become associates of the hosts of heaven.

You wrongdoers say, "They won't find out about all our crimes and record them!" but all your crimes will be recorded daily. And I assure you that light and darkness, day and night, see all your crimes. Do not be irreverent, do not lie, do not alter truthful words, do not say that the words of the sacred mighty one are lies, do not praise your idols, for all your lies and all your irreverence do not lead to justice, but to great crime. Now will I point out this hidden truth: many wrongdoers will alter and misrepresent truthful words. They will say evil things, they will tell lies, make up great falsehoods, and write books in their own words. But when they write all my words correctly in their own languages, they will not change them or omit anything, but will write them all correctly, everything that I previously testified about them. Now will I point out another hidden truth: books which are a source of happiness, of reliability, and of great wisdom will be given to the just and the wise. Books will be given to them, and they will believe them and be happy about them. All the just ones who have learnt all truthful pathways from them will be rewarded.

105:1-2.

In those days, says the Lord, they will call to the inhabitants of the earth, and make them listen to their wisdom. Show it to them for you are their leaders, and the rewards will be over the whole earth, for my son and I will be united with them throughout their lives in the pathways of justice, forever. Peace will be yours! Be happy about the truth, you who have integrity!

The Book of Noah - a fragment

106:1-19.

After a time, my son Methuselah chose a wife for his son Lamech and she became pregnant by him, and gave birth to a child. His body was as white as snow, and as red as a rose, and his hair was as white as wool, and long, and his eyes were beautiful. When he opened them, he illuminated the whole house like the sun, so that the whole house was extremely bright.

When he was taken from the midwife's hands, his father Lamech was afraid of him, and fled away to his own father Methuselah, and said, "I have fathered a son, who is not like other children. He isn't human, but looks like offspring of the angels of heaven! He has a different nature to ours, and is completely unlike us! His eyes are as bright as the sun's rays, his appearance is splendid, and he looks like he belongs to the angels and not to me! I'm afraid that something miraculous will happen on earth in his time. And now, my father, I beg and request you to go to our ancestor Enoch, and find out the truth from him, for he lives amongst the angels."

When Methuselah heard his son's words, he came to me at the extremities of the earth, for he had been informed that I was there. He called out, and I heard his voice. I went to him and said, "My son, I'm here, since you've come to me!"

He answered, "I've come about an important event! I've approached you about a disturbing sight! My father, listen to me, my son Lamech has fathered a child who doesn't resemble him, and whose nature isn't like a human's. His color is whiter than snow, he is redder than a rose, the hair of his head is whiter than white wool, his eyes are like the sun's rays, and when he opened his eyes he lit up the whole house! Also, when he was taken from the midwife's hands, his father Lamech was afraid and fled to me, because he didn't believe that the child was his, because he looked like the angels of heaven. And now I've come to you to find out the truth!"

Then I, Enoch, answered him, "The Lord will do a new thing on the earth. I have seen this in a vision and already explained it to you. In Jared my father's generation, some of those from heaven disregarded the Lord's word. They committed crimes, laid aside their race, and were promiscuous with women. They committed wrong, slept with them, and produced children with them. There will be great destruction on the earth, a deluge, a great destruction for one year. This child who is born to your son will survive on the earth, and his three sons will be saved with him. When all humans on the earth die, he and his sons will be safe. His descendants will produce giants on the earth, not spiritual giants, but bodily giants. A great punishment will be inflicted on the earth, and all dishonesty will be washed from the earth. So then inform your son Lamech, that the child who is born is in fact his child, and he is to call him Noah, for he will be left to you. He and his children will be saved from the destruction that is coming on the earth because of wrongdoing and because of all the wickedness which will be committed on the earth in his days. Afterward there will be greater wickedness than that which was committed on the earth before. For I know the sacred secret hidden truths, which the Lord himself showed and explained to me, and which I have read in the tablets of heaven."

Commentary

After, "and produced children with them,"one Greek papyrus adds, "who are not like spiritual

beings, but creatures of flesh," cf. Milik, *opt.cit.*, p. 210.

107:1-3.

"In them I saw it written that generation after generation will disobey, until a just race arises, until wrongdoing and crime perish from off the earth, and all manner of good comes on it. And now, my son, go tell your son Lamech, that the child who is born is truly his child, and that this is no lie."

When Methuselah heard the words of his father Enoch, who had shown him every secret thing, he returned with understanding, and gave the child the name Noah, because he was to comfort the earth after all its destruction.

Enoch's Concluding Words

108:1-15.

Another book which Enoch wrote for his son Methuselah, and for those who would come after him, and keep the law in the last days. You, who have watched and are waiting in those days, until the evil doers are consumed, and the power of the guilty is destroyed, wait until wrongdoing passed away, for their names will be blotted out of the sacred books, their offspring will be destroyed, and their spirits slain. They will cry and grieve in a chaotic wasteland, and they will burn in the bottomless fire. There I saw something like a cloud which I could not see through, as I was unable to look through it because of its depth. I also saw a flame of fire burning brightly, and things like sparkling mountains whirling around, and shaking from side to side.

Then I asked one of the sacred angels, who was with me, "What is this shining object? It is not the sky, but a flame of fire alone which blazes, and in it there are the sounds of shrieks, of anguish, and of great misery."

He said, "Into the place which you see, will be thrown the spirits of wrongdoers and blasphemers, of those who do evil, and who will alter everything which God has said through the mouths of the prophets about things that will happen. There will be writings and records about these things in heaven, so that the angels can read them and know what will happen both to wrongdoers and to the spirits of the unassuming, those whose bodies have suffered but have been rewarded by God, those who have been treated badly by wicked people, those who have loved God, those who have not loved gold or silver or other good things on the earth, but who gave their bodies over to torture, those who from the time of their birth have not coveted earthly riches, but have considered themselves to be a breath passing away. Such has been their behavior, and the Lord examined them and found their spirits to be pure, so that they might praise his name. I have recorded all their blessings in a book, and he has rewarded them, for they were found to love heaven more than their earthly life."

God said, "They were trampled underfoot by wicked

people, and heard their abuse and blasphemies, and were treated shamefully, while they were blessing me. Now will I call the spirits of the good who are from the generation of light, and I will change those who were born in darkness, whose bodies were not rewarded as splendidly as they deserved

"I will bring those who love my sacred name into the shining light and I will place each of them on their own splendid throne, and they will shine for unnumbered times." God's judgment is just. He gives faith to the faithful where justice lives. They will see those who were born in darkness thrown into darkness, while the just will be shining. Wrongdoers will cry out when they see them shining, but they go where the days and times have been prescribed for them.

CHAPTER 4: SECOND BOOK OF ENOCH: INTRODUCTION

As the whole text of the *Second Book of Enoch* was found in Slavonic, the *Second Book of Enoch* is often called the *Slavonic Enoch*. To date, over twenty Slavonic manuscripts have come to light. In 2009, four fragments in Coptic were discovered.

The *Second Book of Enoch* was originally written in Greek at Alexandria, although some parts of the text were written in Hebrew in Palestine.

Scholars cannot agree on the dating. However, the *Second Book of Enoch* is generally dated to the Second Temple Period on the basis that Enoch encourages his children to bring gifts to the Temple for the forgiveness of sins, a practice of the Second Temple Period. This is supported by the fact that there is no evidence from the text to suggest that the Temple had already been destroyed. The Temple was destroyed in 70 CE.

The *Second Book of Enoch* is quoted by name in the

Testament of Naphtali, the Testament of Daniel, and the Testament of Levi. It was referred to by Origen and referred to by Irenaeus. It was used by the writer of the Letter to Barnabas.

Melchizedek

Chapters 69-73 of *Second Book of Enoch* are often referred to as *The Exaltation of Melchizedek*. This section is for your reference after you read *The Exaltation of Melchizedek*.

As Melchizedek predates Aaron, he cannot be a descendant of Aaron from whom the priesthood must descend. Several Rabbis advanced theories to get around this problem. In the Midrash, the Rabbis identified Melchizedek with Shem, Noah's son. Although Shem was not a descendant of Aaron, he was believed to have officiated as a priest. (See, for example, Genesis Rabbah 46:7, 56:10; Leviticus Rabbah 25:6; Numbers Rabbah 4:8; Babylonian Talmud Nedarim 32b.) Rabbi Isaac the Babylonian *Genesis Rabbah* 43:6 said that Melchizedek was born circumcised. Rabbi Zechariah *Babylonian Talmud Nedarim* 32b said on Rabbi Ishmael's authority that God had intended to bring the priesthood through Melchizedek's descendants, but instead brought it through Abram's descendants after Melchizedek blessed Abram before he blessed God. Rabbi Eleazar *Babylonian Talmud Makkot* 23b said that

Melchizedek's school was one of three places where the Holy Spirit manifested.

Rabbi Hana bar Bizna *Babylonian Talmud Sukkah* 52b, citing Rabbi Simeon Hasida, said that Melchizedek was one of the four craftsmen about whom Zechariah wrote. Zechariah 1:21-22: *Next Yahweh showed me four craftsmen. I asked, 'What are they going to do?' He answered, 'These military powers are the ones that have scattered Judah so that there was no hope. The craftsmen have come to terrify and strike down the military powers of the nations that have come against the land of Judah to scatter it.'*

Old Testament/Hebrew Bible

Genesis 14:18-20.

Melchizedek, the king of Salem, brought out bread and wine. He was a priest of El Elyon. He blessed Abram, and said, "Blessed be Abram by El Elyon, creator of heaven and earth! Blessed be El Elyon Elohim, who handed your enemies over to you!"

Abram gave him one tenth of everything.

Psalm 110.

1 Here is Yahweh's word to my master:

"Sit down at my right hand until I make your enemies your footstool!"

2 Yahweh extends your strong scepter from Zion,

rule in the midst of your enemies.

3 Your people freely follow you on the day of battle.

In sacred splendor, from dawn's womb the dew of your youth is yours.

4 Yahweh swears this promise on oath and will not rescind it:

"You are a priest forever, after the manner of Melchizedek."

5 Adonai is at your right hand,
he strikes down kings in the day of his anger.
6 He judges the nations,
he heaps up corpses,
he crushes their heads over a large land.
7 They drink from a stream along the road,
then they lift up their head.

New Testament.

In the New Testament, references to Melchizedek appear only in the Letter to the Hebrews. Hebrews was written between 49 and 70 CE, most likely between 64 and 70 CE. It is (clearly) prior to its citation by Clement of Rome c. CE AD, and so is prior to the destruction of the Temple in Jerusalem. Another clue to the date is that the Levitical system was still in place when Hebrews was written. Further, Hebrews 13:23 is the only mention in the whole New Testament of Timothy being imprisoned, which has led some to conclude that Hebrews must be after Paul's death. In all his frequent mentions in the Pauline letters Timothy is shown to be a free man, and is in Ephesos at the time of Paul's final imprisonment.

Hebrews 5:5-10.

5 So too the Anointed One did not do himself the honor of becoming a high priest. But God said to him,

"You are my Son, today I have conceived you." 6 And he
says in another place, "You are a priest forever, in the
succession of Melchizedek."

7 During the days when Jesus was of the earthly life,
with loud shouts and tears he offered up earnest
requests as well as prayers claiming the right of help and
protection to him who was able to save him from death.
His precaution was listened to. 8 Although he was a
Son, he learnt to pay attention from the things that
happened to him. 9 And when he had been brought to
maturity, he became the cause of salvation to all who
pay attention to him. 10 This was after he had been
proclaimed as high priest by God "in the succession of
Melchizedek."

Commentary

Verse 5. Psalm 2:7.
Verse 6. Psalm 110:4.
Verse 7.
***Hiketeria*, literally, an olive branch which the suppliant held their hand as a symbol of their condition and as a claim for help and protection, cf. Aesch. Supp. 192, Hdt. 5.51., 7.141, Ar. Pl. 393, Andoc. 15.2, Dem. 262.16. Jesus offered up earnest requests as well as prayers claiming the right of help and protection. These prayers were called here in the New Testament, *hiketeria*. In**

pagan terms it was always honored. If all else failed, the *biketeria* could be offered.
See for example Aeschylus, *The Suppliant Maidens*, 192. The daughters of Danaus are fleeing from Egypt. When they see armed crowds coming as well as horses and chariots, their father advises the *biketeria*, to be on the safe side.
See also Herodotos 7.141: the Athenians sent their envoys to Delphi to consult the oracle. The priestess foretold a terrible fate. They were about to give up in dismay, when someone suggested they should approach the oracle the second time as suppliants, holding the olive branch. The priestess then gave a more favorable prophecy. The Greek in these examples is the same as in verse 7. See also Soph. *OT*, 911-923.

***Eulabeia*, means "precaution", not "reverent submission". The word for "submission" does not appear here in the Greek, nor does "godly fear" or "fear". This noun is not to be confused with the noun *eulabes*, which can mean "reverent", "pious" or "religious", particularly hundreds of years after the New Testament was written. For the cognate verb of *eulabeia*, see for example, *P.Oxy.Hels*. 23 (Oxyrhynchos, April 23, 212.) A man called Theon is taking legal action to restrain his former employee from carrying out unspecified threats against him. He writes,**

"Therefore, I am presenting this petition by way of safe-guarding myself, taking the precaution lest what he threatened should actually come about." Occurs only here and in Hebrews 12:28 in the New Testament.

Verse 10. Psalm 110:4.

Hebrews 6:19 - 7:21.

19 We have this hope as an anchor of the soul,
unfailing and trustworthy. It enters the inner sanctuary
behind the veil, 20 where Jesus, our forerunner, has
entered on our behalf. He has become a high priest
from the line of succession of Melchizedek.

Ch.7:1-3 This Melchizedek was the king of Salem
and a priest of the Most High God. He went out to
meet Abraham, who was returning from the slaughter
of the kings, and blessed him. 2 Abraham gave him a
tenth of everything. Firstly, his name means "king of
righteousness", and secondly, "king of Salem" means
"king of peace". He remains a priest continually forever,
like the Son of God. 3 There is no record of his father
or recorded mother, he has no genealogy. There is no
record of his beginning of days or end of life.

4 Now think about what a great person he was –
even the patriarch Abraham gave him a tenth of the
best plunder of war. 5 Now on the one hand the law
requires the descendants of Levi who hold the office of
priest to receive the one-tenth from the people –that is

to say, their fellow believers – even though their fellow believers are descended from Abraham. 6 But on the other hand, this person has not traced his descent to Levi, but he has collected the one-tenth from Abraham and has blessed the one (Abraham) who had the promises.

7 Without any dispute whatsoever, the lesser is blessed by the more important. 8 In the one case, the one-tenth keeps being collected by people who die, but in the other case, it keeps being collected by him who is witnessed as being alive. 9 It could even be said that Levi, who is the receiver of the one-tenths, paid the one-tenths through Abraham, 10 for he was still in the body of his father when Melchizedek went out to meet him.

11-17 Therefore, if then there had been completion through the Levitical priesthood (for under the Law it was given to the people), why was there still a need for a different priest to come – one from the line of succession of Melchizedek, not from the line of succession of Aaron? 12 For when there's a change of priesthood, it's necessary that there be a change of the law. 13 The One about whom these things are said participated in a different tribe, and no one from that tribe has ever devoted themselves to sacrificial duties. 14 For it is clear that our Lord descended from Judah, and Moses didn't speak anything about that tribe with regard to the priesthood. 15 And it is even more obvious if another priest like Melchizedek arises, one who has become a priest 16 not on the basis of the Law's command about selection due to ancestry, but on the basis of power of indissoluble life. 17 For it is testified, "You are a priest forever, from the line of succession of Melchizedek."

18-22 For on the one hand there is an annulment of the previous command because of its weakness and uselessness – 19 as the Law did not bring anything to completion – but on the other hand there is the introduction of a superior hope, through which we draw near to God. 20 And it was not without an oath being sworn! 21 Indeed others became priests without any oath being sworn, but he became a priest with an oath being sworn through God saying to him, "The Lord has sworn and will not change his mind. 'You are a priest forever.'"

Commentary

Verse 20. *Prodromos*, "forerunner", one who goes first. See Delos inscription *BCH* 29. Occurs only here in the New Testament.

Verse 2. *Dienekes*, "continually forever". The adjective occurs only in Hebrews in the New Testament , 7:3; 10:1, 12, 14). *P.Mich*. 659.201-2 (Aphrodite, VI) has the similar phrase *hapanta kai dieneke khronon*, "for all continually succeeding time." The text describes the use of a land holding. Similar phrases occur in two documents of land sale from Aphrodite, *P.Mich*.

662.15 (VII) and 664.10, 19 (585 or 600). The adverb occurs at *P.Mich*. 659.271, and in an honorific inscription for a benefactor from Ainos (in Turkish Thrace), *BE*.275.

Verse 6. *Genealogeo*, to trace one's descent from (someone). Occurs only here in the New Testament. A rare word. See *SB* 5.7835.15 (Philadelphia, I BC), "and let none of them be permitted to lead a conspiracy or cause divisions..., or for one person to trace another's pedigree at the banquet, or for one person to disparage another at the banquet..."
Verse 7. *Antilogia*, "dispute." This is a formula in loan contracts whereby the debtor agrees to repay the loan "without any dispute". See *P.Mich*. 669 (Aphrodite, 12-3/9/529 or 514); *BASP* 17.145-154. The term occurs elsewhere in the New Testament in Hebrews 7:7; 12:3; Jude 11.

Verse 17. Psalm 110:4.

Verse 21. Psalm 110:4.

Later Times.

The 5th century theologian, Marcus Eremita, in *Against the Melchizedekites*, states that a new sect is making Melchizedek an incarnation of the Logos. They appear to have been otherwise orthodox. Jerome *Ep*. 73, rebuts a work which wrote that Melchizedek was the Holy Spirit. In the 7th century CE, Timotheus, Presbyter of Constantinople, *De receptione Haereticorum*, mentions a sect of Phrygian Melchizedekites whom he states are referred to as "Untouchables." They are not Jews or pagans. Although they keep the Sabbath, they are not circumcised. They refrain from touching another human, and will not take food from the hand of another.

Today, the Church of Jesus Christ of Latter Day Saints (LDS Church Section 84:14; Community of Christ Section 83:2e) believes that Melchizedek was a righteous man ordained as a high priest, a king of Salem, and a descendant of Noah.

CHAPTER 5: SECOND BOOK OF ENOCH: TRANSLATION

I. There was a wise person, a great craftsperson, and the Lord loved him and received him so that he would see the uppermost dwellings and be an eye witness to the wise, great, unimaginable and undeniable realm of the Almighty God, to the very wonderful, splendid, bright and many-eyed situation of the Lord's servants, and to the Lord's inaccessible throne, and to the degrees and manifestations of the spiritual hosts, and to the indescribable administration of the multitude of the elements, and to the various spirits and inexpressible singing of the host of the Cherubim, and to the limitless light.

At the time, he said, that I was 165 years old, I conceived my son Methuselah.

Commentary

This is following Enoch's age given in the (Greek) *Septuagint*, as in the Hebrew he was said to be 65. Enoch was the son of Jared, great grandfather of Noah, and father of Methuselah, not to be confused with the Enoch who was the eldest son of Cain.

After that I lived for 200 years and lived out all the years of my life which amounted to 365 years.

On the first day of the month I was alone in my house and was resting on my bed, sleeping. While I was asleep, I became greatly distressed and I was crying while asleep. I could not understand what this distress was, or what would happen to me.

Two people appeared to me. They were huge, the like of which I had never seen on the earth. Their faces were shining like the sun, their eyes were like a burning light, and fire came out of their mouths. The fire was arrayed with and resonated with various kinds of purple. Their wings were brighter than gold and their hands were whiter than snow. They were standing at the head of my bed and began to call me by my name.

I woke up from my sleep and saw clearly those two people standing in front of me. I greeted them. I was gripped with fear and the appearance of my face changed with shock. Those people said to me, "Enoch, don't be afraid, the everlasting God has sent us to you, and today you certainly will ascend with us into heaven! You will tell your children and your whole household everything they need to do without you on earth in your house, and no one is to look for you until the Lord returns you to them."

I hurried to obey them. I left my house, and made to the doors, as I was ordered to do, and summoned my sons Methuselah, Regim, and Gaidad, and related to them all the amazing things those people had told me.

2.

"My children, listen to me, I don't know where I'm going, or what will happen to me. Now then, my children, mark my words: do not turn away from God to the useless, who did not make heaven and earth, for these will perish and so will those who worship them! May the Lord make your hearts secure in the fear of him! And now, my children, see to it that no one looks for me, until the Lord returns me to you."

3.

After Enoch had told his children, the angels took him on their wings and carried him up to the first heaven and placed him on the clouds.

And there I looked, and again I looked higher and saw the ether. They placed me on the first heaven and showed me an enormous sea, far larger than the earthly sea.

4.

They brought into my presence the elders and rulers of the star orders, and showed me 200 angels who rule the stars, and their services to the heavens. They fly with their wings and come around all those who sail.

5.

I looked down here and saw the storehouses of the snow, and the angels who keep their amazing storehouses, and the clouds from which they come out, and into which they return.

6.

They showed me the storehouse of the dew, which looked very much like olive oil and all the earth's flowers. They showed me many angels guarding the storehouses of these things, and how they are made to open and shut.

7.

Those people took me and led me up onto the second heaven, and showed me darkness, far darker than earthly darkness. There I saw prisoners hanging, watched, awaiting the vast limitless judgment, and these angels were dark looking, far darker than earthly darkness, and they were constantly crying all the time.

I said to the people who were with me, "Why are these ones constantly tortured?"

They answered, "These are God's renegades, who did not obey God's commands, but took their own advice, and turned away with their prince, who also is bound in the fifth heaven."

I felt extremely sorry for them. They greeted me, and said to me, "Man of God, pray for us to the Lord!"

I answered to them, "Who am I, a human being, to pray for angels? Who knows where I'm going, or what will happen to me? Who will pray for me!"

8.

Those people took from there, and led me up onto the third heaven, and placed me there. I looked downwards, and saw the produce of these places, the beauty of which has never been seen! I saw all the sweet flowering trees and saw their fruits, which were sweetly scented, and all the foods they bore which were sparkling with fragrant scents.

In the midst of the trees that live there, in that place where the Lord rests when he goes Paradise, there is a tree of indescribable beauty and fragrance, and embellished more than everything that exists. On every side it has a golden appearance and it is covered with a fiery golden red color, and carries produce from all types of fruits. Its roots are in the garden at the earth's end.

Paradise is between Perishable and Non Perishable. Out of it come two springs which send out milk and honey. Their springs send out oil and wine. They separate into four parts, and go around quietly down into the Garden of Eden, between Perishable and Non Perishable. From there they go out along the earth, and have a revolution to their cycle just like other elements. There is no unfruitful tree here, and every place is blessed.

There are 300 very bright angels who keep the garden, and they serve the Lord with constant sweet singing and never silent voices throughout all the days and hours.

I said, "This place is very charming!"

Those people said to me,

9.

"Enoch, This place is prepared for the just, who put up with all sorts of offense from those who frustrate their lives. They turn away from wrongdoing, they make just judgments, they give food to the hungry and clothes to those who need clothing, they lift up the fallen, they help injured orphans, and they live blameless lives in front of the Lord, and serve him alone. This place of eternal inheritance is prepared for them."

10.

Those two people led me up onto the northern side. There they showed me there a very dreadful place, and there were all types of tortures in that place: cruel darkness and shadowy gloom. There is no light there, only murky fire constantly flaming high. There is a fiery river coming out, and fire is everywhere over the whole place, and everywhere over the whole place there is frost and ice, thirst and shivering. The bonds are very cruel, and the angels are terrifying and merciless, and carry frightening weapons and merciless torture.

Commentary

Jude 4 (New Testament) states, "God didn't spare the Messengers who sinned but handed them over to Tartarus in ropes in the underworld's gloom where they are firmly held for judgment."

I said, "Alas, alas, how very dreadful is this place!"

Those people said to me, "Enoch, this place is prepared for those who dishonor God, those who on earth practice wrongdoing other than nature, which is ritually unclean child-corruption, magic-making, enchantments and witchcrafts, and who boast of their wrongdoings, stealing, lies, slanders, resentment, malice, idol worshiping, murder. These are the accursed ones who steal people's livelihoods, and take away the possessions of the poor while they themselves grow rich. They cause harm in getting other people's possessions. Although they had the means to feed the hungry, they caused the hungry to die. Although they were able to clothe people, they stripped the naked. They did not know their creator, and worshiped lifeless gods which cannot see or hear. They built carved images and worshipped ritually unclean workings. This place is prepared for their eternal inheritance."

Commentary

This passage is echoed by Romans 1:18-29.
18-23 From heaven, God's anger is continually being revealed against every form of ungodliness and wrongdoing of people who suppress the truth by unjust means. 19 The reason for the revealing of God's anger is this: all that may be realized and known about God is evident to people - as God made it evident to them. 20 This

**knowledge is derived from the creation. The
invisible things of God - his eternal power and
divinity - are clearly seen in the world, in the
creation. Thus the mind sees the visible, the
creation of the world, and understands the invisible, the things of God. So these people don't have
an excuse, 21 and this is why. Although they
perceive God, they didn't praise him as God, or
even thank him. Rather, their reasoning became
useless and their stupid minds were darkened
and obscured. 22 They alleged that they were
wise, but they became fools! 23 They exchanged
the splendor of the imperishable God for an
image made like a perishable person – not to
mention images of birds, and four-legged
animals, and even reptiles!**

**24-25 So for this reason God handed them over to
ritual uncleanness, in their minds' wants and
wishes, so that their bodies would be dishonored
with each other. 25 They exchanged God's truth
for the lie, the idol, and worshipped and served
the creation other than the Creator, who is
blessed for the ages! Amen!**

**26-32 Because of this, God handed them over to
experiences of public stigma, for the females
exchanged natural sex for what is other than
nature. 27 And the same goes for males too. The
males got rid of natural sex with the female and
burned with their mutual yearning – males**

producing indecency with one another, and as a result got what was coming to them for their mistake. 28 They didn't think it fit to acknowledge God, so he gave them an unfit mind, to do things that are not appropriate. 29 They have been filled with every kind of wrongdoing, evil, greedy grasping behavior, malice - full to the utmost with jealousy, murder, quarrels, deceit, nasty dispositions. They are people who give out information, whether true or false, which is detrimental to the character or welfare of others. 30 They are slanderers, God haters, insolent, arrogant, boastful, inventors of bad deeds. They are not obedient to parents, 31 they don't have intelligence, they do not keep covenant, they do not have natural affection, they do not have mercy. 32 Although they are fully aware of God's decree, which is that those who do such things deserve death, not only do they do these things, but also they are in agreement with those who do them!

11.

Those two people led me up onto the fourth heaven, and showed me all the successive courses, and all the rays of the light of the sun and the moon. I measured their courses and compared their light, and found that the sun's light is greater than the moon's. Its circle and the wheels on which it constantly goes are like the wind going past with incredible speed, and it has no rest day and night. Its passage and return are accompanied by four immense stars. Each star has a thousand stars under it, to the right of the sun's wheel, and four to the left, each having under it a thousand stars. There are altogether eight thousand stars coming out with the sun continually.

By day, fifteen myriads of angels attend it, and by night a thousand myriads of angels attend it. Six-winged ones come out with the angels in front of the sun's wheel into the fiery flames, and one hundred angels kindle the sun and set it alight.

12.

I looked and saw other flying elements of the sun, whose name is the bronzed snake-like Phoenix. They were spectacular and astonishing, with feet and tails in the form of a lion, and a crocodile's head. Their appearance is colored like the rainbow. Their size is nine hundred measures. Their wings are like those of angels. Each has twelve wings. They attend and accompany the sun, bearing heat and dew, as God has ordered them to do so. Thus the sun revolves and goes, and rises under the heaven. Its course goes under the earth and the light of its rays is continual.

Commentary
The bronzed snake-like Phoenix

The Roman poet Ovid said that the phoenix

reproduces itself, and lives on frankincense and fragrant gum. In the 1st century CE, Clement of Rome *First Clement* 25 stated that the phoenix lives 500 years and reproduces itself, and goes to Heliopolis very 500 years.
This was echoed in the next century by Tertullian *The Resurrection of the Flesh* 13 yet had been stated hundreds of years earlier by Herodotus 2. 73 who reports that the people of Heliopolis say the phoenix comes to Egypt only once every 500 years. This was also reported by the 2nd century writer Philostratus. Herodotos noted that the plumage is gold and red, and resembles an eagle. Pliny *Natural History*, 10.2 also says the bird is the size of an eagle. Herodotos states that the plumage around the neck is golden, and the rest of the body is purple except for the tail which is blue. Pliny describes it as a famous Arabian bird considered sacred to the sun and says that it lives 540 years. Pliny *Natural History*, 10.2 states that a phoenix was brought to Rome under the censorship of the Emperor Claudius and was displayed publicly in the Comitium, and that this fact is recorded by the public Annuls.

13.

Those people took me away to the east, and placed me at the sun's gates, where the sun goes out in accordance with the regulation of the seasons and the circuit of the months of the whole year, and the number of the hours of day and night.

I saw six open gates. Each gate was 61 ¼ stadia. I measured them accurately, and determined that this was their size. Through these gates the sun goes out, and goes to the west, and is made even, and rises throughout all the months, and then returns from the six gates according to the progression of the seasons. In this way the period of the whole year is made complete after the progression of the four seasons.

14.

Those people again led me away to the west, and showed me six immense open gates corresponding to the eastern gates, opposite to where the sun sets, for 365 ¼ days. Again it goes down to the western gates, taking away its light, its great brightness, under the earth. Its shining crown is in heaven with the Lord, and is guarded by 400 angels. While the sun goes around on its wheel under the earth, it stands for seven great hours in the night, and spends half its course under the earth. However, when it comes to the eastern approach in the eighth hour of the night, it brings its lights, and its shining crown, and the sun shines more brightly than fire.

15.

Then the elements of the sun, called the bronzed snake-like Phoenixes, burst into song. Every bird flutters its wings, happy at the giver of light, and they break into song at the Lord's command. The giver of light comes to give brightness to the whole world. The morning guard, which is the rays of the sun, takes shape. The sun of the earth goes out, and receives its brightness to light up the whole face of the earth. They showed me this calculation of the sun's course.

The gates through which the sun enters are the great gates of the calculation of the hours of the year. This is why the sun is a great creation. The sun's circuit lasts 28 years, then starts again from the beginning.

16.

Those people showed me the other course, that of the moon. They showed me twelve great gates, crowned from west to east, by which the moon goes in and out at the routine times. The moon goes in at the first gate to the western places of the sun, by the first gates with 31 days exactly, by the second gates with 31 days exactly, by the third with thirty days exactly, by the fourth with 30 days exactly, by the fifth with 31 days exactly, by the sixth with 31 days exactly, by the seventh with 30 days exactly, by the eighth with 31 days perfectly, by the ninth with 31 days exactly, by the tenth with 30 days perfectly, by the eleventh with 31 days exactly, by the twelfth with 28 days exactly.

It goes through the western gates in the order and number of the eastern, and accomplishes the 365 ¼ days of the solar year, while the lunar year has 354, and there are twelve days of the solar circle lacking, which are the lunar days necessary to bring the solar calendar into harmony with the lunar calendar of the whole year.

Thus the great circle is 532 years. The quarter of a day is omitted for three years, but the fourth completes it exactly. So then they are taken outside of heaven for three years and are not added to the number of days, because they change the time of the years to two new months toward completion, to two others toward dwindling.

When the western gates are finished, it returns and goes to the eastern to the lights. Therefore it goes day and night around the heavenly circuits, lower than all circles, and faster than the heavenly winds, spirits, elementals, and angels flying. Each angel has six wings. The moon has a sevenfold course in nineteen years.

17.

In the midst of the heavens I saw armed soldiers serving the Lord with a kettledrum and pipes, with never-ending sweet incessant voice and various types of song, which it is impossible to describe, and which amazes every mind, so superb and awe-inspiring is the singing of those angels! I was delighted to listen to it.

18.

The people took me onto the fifth heaven and placed me there. I saw countless soldiers, called Watchers. They had human appearance, and their size was larger than that of big giants. Their faces were shriveled, and their mouths were continually silent. There is no service in the fifth heaven. I said to the people who were with me, "Who are these ones with very shriveled miserable faces and silent mouths, and why is there no service on this heaven?"

Commentary
Watchers, in the Greek, "Grigori."

They answered me, "These are the Watchers, who with their chief Satanail rejected the Lord of light, and after them are those who are held in the great darkness on the second heaven, and three of them went down on earth to the place Hermon, and broke their vows on the shoulder of the Mount Hermon and saw the human women, and slept with them, and contaminated the earth with their deeds. In their times they caused lawless mixing, and Nephilim were born, amazing big people, and great hostility. So God judged them strongly, and they weep for their associates. They will be punished on the Lord's great day."

Commentary
In 1 Enoch, the leader of the Watchers was called Semjaza.

I said to the Watchers, "I saw your associates and their works, and their great torments. I prayed for them, but the Lord has condemned them to be under earth until the end of the existing heaven and earth."

I said, "Why do you wait, associates, and do not serve in the presence of the Lord, and do not serve him?

You are in danger of making your Lord extremely angry!"

They listened to my reproach, and spoke to the four ranks in heaven, and look! As I stood with those two people, four trumpets trumpeted together very loudly, and the Watchers broke into song in unison. Their voice went up in the presence of the Lord pitifully and touchingly.

Commentary

Here is a cross reference to the account in The First Book of Enoch.
6:1-8.
It happened after the humans had multiplied, that in those times daughters were born to them, and they were attractive and beautiful.
When the angels, the inhabitants of heaven, saw them, they lusted after them and said to each other, "Come on, let's choose consorts for ourselves from the humans, and let's produce children!" Then their leader Semjaza said to them, "I'm concerned as I fear that perhaps you won't agree to carry out this venture, and that I alone will have to pay the penalty for such a serious crime."
But they answered, "Let's all swear an oath, and bind ourselves by mutual curses, that we will not

change our minds but carry through this venture."

So they swore all together and bound themselves by mutual curses. They were two hundred in number, they descended in the time of Jared, on the top of Mount Hermon. They called it Mount Hermon because they had sworn an oath on it and bound themselves by mutual curses.

These are the names of their leaders: Semjaza, who was their leader, Arakiba, Rameel, Kokaqbiel, Ramuel, Tamiel, Ramiel, Danel, Ezeqeel, Baraqijal, Asael, Armaros, Batarerl, Ananel, Zaqiel, Samsapeel, Satareil, Turel, Jomjael, Sariel. These were the leaders of the groups of ten.

7:1-6.

They and the rest took consorts. Each one chose their own. They had sex with them and defiled themselves with them. They taught them charms and sorceries, the cutting of roots, and the uses of plants.

The women got pregnant and gave birth to Nephilim whose height was three hundred cubits. They consumed everything humans produced. When humans could no longer sustain them, they turned against them, in order to consume them. They began to do wrong against birds, beasts, reptiles, and fish, and to eat each

other's flesh, and to drink their blood. Then the earth laid accusation against the lawless ones.
Account in the Book of Jubilees
"And in the second week of the tenth jubilee Mahalalel took Dinah as a wife. She was the daughter of Barakiel, the daughter of his father's brother, and she bore him a son in the third week of the sixth year. He named him Jared, and in his days the Lord's angels named the Watchers came down to the earth, in order to instruct the humans, and so that they could carry out judgment and justice on the earth." (Jubilees 4:15)
God was exceedingly angry with the angels he had sent upon the earth. (Jubilees 5:6)

19.

From there those people took me up onto the sixth heaven. There I saw seven bands of angels, very bright and splendid. Their faces shone more brightly than the sun, and glistened. There is no difference in their faces, behavior, or type of dress. These make the orders, and learn the courses of the stars, and the variation of the moon, revolution of the sun, and the good administration of the world. When they see wrongdoing, they make directives and instructions. They sing loud and sweetly, and sing all types of praise songs.

These are the archangels who are above angels. They measure all life in heaven and on earth. They are the angels who are appointed over seasons and years, who are over the rivers and the seas, who are over the earth's produce, who are over all pasture and the giving of food to every living thing, the angels who write all about the lives of humans and everything they do in the presence of the Lord. In their midst are six Phoenixes and six Cherubim and six six-winged ones continually singing in unison. It is not possible to describe their singing! They celebrate in the Lord's presence at his footstool.

20.

Those two people lifted me up from there onto the seventh heaven. There I saw a very vast light, and fiery troops of great archangels, spiritual forces, and authorities, orders and administrations, cherubim and seraphim, thrones and many-eyed ones, nine regiments, the orbital stations of light. I became dreadfully afraid, and shook with great terror! Those people took me, and led me after them, and said to me, "Take heart, Enoch! Don't be afraid!" They showed me the Lord afar off, sitting on his very high throne. For what is there on the tenth heaven, as the Lord dwells there? God is in the tenth heaven. In the Hebrew language he is called "Father of Creation."

All the heavenly troops would come and stand on the ten steps according to their rank, and would bow down to the Lord, and would again go to their places very happily and blissfully, singing songs in the limitless light with soft affectionate voices, splendidly serving him.

21.

The cherubim and seraphim stand about the throne, and the six-winged and many-eyed ones do not leave. They stand in the Lord's presence doing what he wants, and they cover his whole throne, singing softly in the Lord's presence, "Sacred, sacred, sacred, Lord Ruler of Sabaoth, the heavens and earth are full of your splendor!"

After I saw all those things, those people said to me, "Enoch, we have been commanded to travel with you this far." At that, those people left me and I did not see them.

I remained alone at the end of the seventh heaven and so became afraid. I fell on my face and said to myself, "Woe is me, what has happened to me!"

The Lord sent one of his splendid ones, the archangel Gabriel, who said to me, "Take heart, Enoch! Don't be afraid! Arise in the Lord's presence into eternity, arise, come with me!"

Commentary

"One of splendid ones." Variation, "One of the seven highest angels by the name of Gabriel."

I answered him, and said to myself, "My Lord, my life is leaving me as I'm so afraid and terrified!" I called to the people who led me up to this place, as I had relied on them, and had gone up with them into the Lord's presence.

Gabriel caught me up, as a leaf caught up by the wind, and placed me in the Lord's presence. I saw the eighth heaven, which is called Muzaloth in the Hebrew language, the changer of the seasons, of drought, and of wet, and of the twelve constellations of the circle of the firmament, which are above the seventh heaven. I saw the ninth heaven, which is called Kuchavim in Hebrew language. There are the heavenly homes of the twelve constellations of the circle of the firmament.

22.

On the tenth heaven, which is called Araboth, I saw the appearance of the Lord's face. The Lord's face was like an iron made to glow in fire, and brought out, emitting sparks, and burning. Thus in a moment of eternity I saw the Lord's face, but the Lord's face is inexpressible, spectacular and very dreadful, and very, very terrible.

Commentary

Araboth. The semantic range includes desert region, the heavens, the plains.

Who am I to tell of the Lord's unspeakable being, and of his very astonishing face? I cannot tell the quantity of his many instructions, and various voices! The Lord's throne is very impressive and not made with hands! I cannot tell of the quantity of those standing round him, the troops of cherubim and seraphim, nor their constant singing, nor his indisputable beauty, and who shall tell of the inexpressible greatness of his splendor!

I fell prone and bowed down to the Lord, and the Lord said to me with his lips, "Take heart, Enoch! Don't be afraid! Arise and stand in my presence into eternity!"

The chief general Michael lifted me up, and led me to the Lord's presence. The Lord said to his servants, persuading them, "Let Enoch stand in my presence into eternity!"

The splendid ones bowed down to the Lord and said, "Let Enoch go according to your command."

The Lord said to Michael, "Go and take Enoch out of his earthly clothing, and anoint him with my sweet ointment, and put him into my splendid clothing."

Michael did as the Lord told him. He anointed me, and dressed me. The appearance of that ointment is stronger than the great light, and is like sweet dew, and has a gentle fragrance, and shines like the sun's ray. I looked at myself, and I was like one of his splendid ones.

Commentary

"And I was like one of his splendid ones." Variation, "Like one of the seven highest angels."

The Lord summoned one of his archangels by the name of Pravuil, whose knowledge was faster and wiser than the other archangels, and who wrote down all the Lord's actions. The Lord said to Pravuil, "Bring out the books from my storehouses, and a fast writing reed, and give it to Enoch. Give him the best and most comforting books."

23.

He told me about all the works of heaven, earth and sea, and all the elements, their passages and goings, and the thundering of the thunders, the sun and moon, the goings and courses of the stars, the seasons, years, days, and hours, the risings of the wind, the numbers of the angels, and the formation of their songs, and all human things, the language of every human song and life, the commandments, instructions, and sweet singings, and everything that it is fitting to learn.

Pravuil said to me, "All the things that I have told you, we have written. Sit and write down all the souls of humankind, however many of them are born, and the places prepared for them to eternity; for all souls are prepared for eternity from before the formation of the world."

For double thirty days and thirty nights, I wrote out everything exactly, and I wrote 366 books.

Commentary

Cf. Philo, *de somno*, 1.22.

24.

The Lord summoned me, and said to me, "Enoch, sit down on my left with Gabriel."

I bowed down to the Lord, and the Lord said to me, "Beloved Enoch, everything that you see, all things that are completed I will tell you even before the very beginning, everything that I created from non-being, and visible things from invisible. Enoch, listen and take in my words, for I have not even told them to my angels in secret. I have not told them about their rise, or about my endless realm. They have not understood my creating, which I tell you today. For before all things were visible, I alone used to go about in the invisible things, like the sun from east to west, and from west to east. But even the sun has peace in itself, I found no peace, because I was creating all things, and I devised the thought of placing foundations, and of creating visible creation.

Commentary

"Everything that I created from non-being, and visible things from invisible." Cf. Philo, *de Justit*, 7.

25.

"I commanded in the very lowest parts, that visible things should come from the invisible, and Adoil came down very grand, and I observed him, and look! He had a belly of great light!

Commentary

"Visible things should come from the invisible."
Cf. Philo, *de Justit*, 7.
Adoil. "Light of creation."

"I said to him, 'Become undone, Adoil! Let the visible come out of you!'

"He came undone, and a great light came out. I was in the middle of the great light, and as there is born light from light, there came out a great age, and showed all creation, which I had thought to create. And I saw that it was good.

"I placed a throne for myself, and sat on it, and said to the light, 'Go up higher over there and fix yourself high above the throne, and be a foundation for the highest things.'

"Above the light there is nothing else, and then I bent up and looked up from my throne.

26.

"I summoned the very lowest a second time, and said, 'Let Archas come out hard!' and he came out hard from the invisible. He came out hard, heavy, and very red.

Commentary

Archas "Spirit of creation."

"I said, 'Be opened, Archas, and let there be born from you!' and he came undone, and an age came forth, very great and very dark, bearing the creation of all lower things, and I saw that it was good. I said to him, 'Go down below, and make yourself firm, and be a foundation for the lower things!' It happened. He went down and fixed himself, and became the foundation for the lower things, and below the darkness there is nothing else.

27.

"I commanded that there should be taken from light and darkness. I said, 'Be thick!' and it became that way. I spread it out with the light, and it became water, and I spread it out over the darkness, below the light. Then I made the waters firm, that is to say the bottomless, and I made a foundation of light around the water, and created seven circles from inside. I made the water like wet and dry crystal, that is to say like glass, and the intertwining of the waters and the other elements. I showed each one of them its course. I showed the seven stars their course in heaven. I saw that it was good.

"I separated light and darkness, that is to say, in the midst of the water here and there. I told the light that it should be the day, and I told the darkness that it should be the night, and there was evening and there was morning on the first day.

28.

"Then I made the heavenly circle firm, and made the lower water which is under heaven collect itself together into one whole, so that the emptiness became dry, and that happened.

"I created big hard rock out of the waves, and from the rock I piled up the dry. I called the dry 'earth,' and I called the middle of the earth 'abyss,' that is to say, the bottomless. I collected the sea in one place and bound it together with a yoke.

"I said to the sea, 'I certainly give you your eternal limits, and you shall not break loose from your component parts.'

"In this way I made the firmament fast. I called this day the first-created.

Commentary

Sunday.

29.

"I imaged the image and essence of fire for all the heavenly troops. I observed the hard, firm rock. From the gleam of my eye the lightning received its amazing nature, which is both fire in water and water in fire, and one does not put out the other, nor does the one dry up the other, and so the lightning is brighter than the sun, softer than water and firmer than hard rock.

"I cut off a great fire from the rock, and from the fire I created the orders of the spiritual ten troops of angels. Their weapons are fiery and their clothing a burning flame. I commanded that each one should stand in their order.

"One of the order of angels turned away with the order that was under him, and had the impossible thought to place his throne higher than the clouds above the earth, so that he would become equal in rank to my power. I threw him out from the height with his angels, and he was flying in the air continuously above the bottomless.

30.

"On the third day I commanded the earth to grow large fruitful trees, and hills, and seed to sow. I planted the Garden, and enclosed it, and placed as flaming angels as armed guardians, and thus I created regeneration.

"Then came the evening, and then came the morning of the fourth day. On the fourth day I commanded that there should be great lights on the heavenly circles.

Commentary

I planted the Garden, Equally, "paradise."
The morning of the fourth day: Wednesday.

"On the first uppermost circle I placed the stars, Kronos, and on the second Aphrodite, on the third Aries, on the fifth Zeus, on the sixth Hermes, on the seventh lesser the moon, and adorned it with the lesser stars. On the lower I placed the sun to light up the day, and the moon and stars to light up the night.

"I made the sun go according to each constellation, of which there were twelve, and I appointed the succession of the months and their names and lives, their thundering, and their hourly movements, and how they should accomplish their courses.

"Then evening came, and then the morning of the fifth day came. On the fifth day I commanded the sea to produce fish, and feathered birds of many varieties, and all animals that went over the earth, on four legs, and soaring in the air, male and female, and every soul breathing the spirit of life.

"Then evening came, and then the morning of the sixth day came. On the sixth day I commanded my wisdom to create a human from seven consistencies: one, its flesh from the earth; two, its blood from the dew; three, its eyes from the sun; four, its bones from stone; five, its intelligence from the swiftness of the angels and from cloud; six, its veins and its hair from the grass of the earth; seven, its soul from my breath and from the wind.

Commentary

The morning of the fifth day: Thursday.
The morning of the sixth day: Friday.

"I gave it seven natures: hearing for the flesh, sight

for the eyes, smell for the soul, the veins for touch, the blood for taste, the bones for endurance, and enjoyment for the intelligence.

Commentary

For the seven natures, see Philo, *de mundi op*, 40.

"I conceived a cunning saying which is: I created humankind from invisible and from visible nature, of both are its death and life and image. It knows speech like some created thing, insignificant in significance and yet significant in insignificance, and I placed it on earth, a second angel, honorable, great and splendid. I appointed it as a ruler to rule on earth and to have my wisdom, and there was none like it of all my existing creatures on the earth.

"I appointed it a name, from the four component parts, from east, from west, from south, from north. I appointed four special stars for it. I called gave it the name "Adam"/"Human," and showed it the two ways, the light and the darkness. I told it, "This is good, and that is bad," so that I would learn whether it had love or hatred toward me, so that it would be clear which in the human race loved me.

Commentary

This shows itself to be Greek. The name "Adam"

simply means "Human" in Hebrew, but here is treated as a proper name. "Adam" is said to be an acrostic, and Enoch is said to appoint the name from the north, south, west and eastern regions, which are in Greek, Anatole (eastern), Dusis (western), Arktos, (northern) and Mesembria (southern).

As stated earlier, *Adam* is the Hebrew word for "human." Genesis 1:27 reads (with the correct words for the deity), "Elohim created *adam* (the word for the race of human beings) in Elohim's image, in the image of Elohim, male and female Elohim created." Genesis 5:1 states, "This is the genealogy of the human race. At the time Elohim created the human race, Elohim made the human race in the likeness of Elohim. Elohim created them male and female and blessed them and called them human (*adam*) at the time they were created." The word "Adam" that we see in English translations of Genesis is merely a "transliteration," the result of putting the Hebrew letters into English letters. The translation is "human," person/s of both genders. In Genesis 2:21, Yahweh Elohim put a deep sleep upon the *adam*, and withdrew the female portion from it. (Hebrew *tsal'ot*, Greek *pleura*, referring to the factor, the portion; not "rib".)

In verse 22, Yahweh Elohim shaped that which Yahweh Elohim had taken from the *adam* into an

isha (female) and brought her to the _adam_. In verses 23 and 24, the word _isha_ (female) is distinguished from the _ish_ (male). This is the first time the words for female and male have appeared in the account. The _adam_ is now an _ish_, and becomes the individual Adam. However, the meaning of the word _adam_ has not changed, he is a human. Yes, he is now, at this point, also a male, but the word "Adam" means "human." The female portion was taken out of the human, the _adam_, and became an _isha_. That which was left was still called a human, _adam_. It now becomes a proper name, Adam.

"For I have seen its nature, but it has not seen its own nature, so through not seeing it will do more wrong, and I said, 'After wrongdoing what is there but death?' I put sleep into it and it fell asleep. I subtracted a portion from it, and created woman, so that death should come to it by woman. I took his last word and gave her the name 'Mother,' that is to say, 'Eve.'

31.

"Human has life on earth, and I created a garden in Eden in the east, so that the Human that could observe the decree and keep the command. I made the heavens open to the Human, so that the Human would see the angels singing the victory song, and the gloomless light.

"The Human was continuously in the Garden, and the diabolos understood that I wanted to create another world, because the Human was ruler on earth, to rule and control it. The diabolos is the evil spirit of the lower places. As a fugitive he made Sotona from the heavens as his name was Satanail. So he became different from the angels, but his nature did not change his intelligence as far as his understanding of just and wrongful things.

Commentary

Sotona is a Slavonic transliteration from the Greek, and refers to Satanail, who loses his suffix when spoken of after he has fallen. In Old Church Slavonic texts, Sotona is used to translate both *diabolos* and *satanas*.

"He understood his denunciation and the wrong which he had committed before; therefore he conceived an idea against the Human. In this form he entered and beguiled Eve, but did not touch Adam.

Commentary

In Revelation 12:7:9, the dragon is said to be called an adversary and a slanderer-liar. It says he was hurled to earth with one third of his angels. There was more than one *diabolos* or adversary in the Bible. These are general terms that are applied to more than one person or entity. The

Book of Enoch names Gadreel as the one who tricked Eve, and says the whole blame for evil in the world rests on Azazel. The Book of Jubilees names Mastema, which it also calls an adversary, as the one thrown to earth with his angels.

"I cursed ignorance, but what I had blessed previously, those I did not curse. I did not curse humankind, nor the earth, nor other creatures, but humanity's evil produce and actions.

32.

"I said to humankind, 'You are earth, and you will go into the earth from where I took you. I will not destroy you, but send you from where I took you. Then I can again receive you at my second presence. I blessed all my creatures both visible and invisible. Human was five and half hours in the Garden. I blessed the seventh day, which is the Sabbath, on which he rested from all his works.'

33.

"I also appointed the eighth day, so that the eighth day should be the first created after my work, and that the first seven revolve in the form of the seventh thousand, and that at the beginning of the eighth thousand there should be a time of not counting, endless, with neither years nor months nor weeks nor days nor hours.

"And now, Enoch, all that I have told you, all that you have understood, all that you have seen of heavenly things, all that you have seen on earth, and all that I have written in books by my great wisdom, all these things I have devised and created from the uppermost foundation to the lower and to the end, and there is no adviser to nor inheritor of my creations. I am self-eternal, not made with hands, and without change. My thought is my advisor, my wisdom and my word are made, and my eyes observe how everything stands here and trembles with terror. If I look away, then everything will be destroyed. Enoch, apply your mind, and know him who is speaking to you, and take the books which you yourself have written.

"I give you Sariel and Raguel who led you up, and the books. Go down to earth, and tell your children everything that I have told you, and everything that you have seen, from the lower heaven up to my throne, and all the troops. For I created all forces, and there is nothing that resists me or that does not subject itself to me. Everything subjects itself to my monarchy, and works for my sole rule.

Commentary

Sariel is named in 1 Enoch 6 as one of the leaders of the Watchers: "These are the names of their leaders: Semjaza, who was their leader, Arakiba, Rameel, Kokaqbiel, Ramuel, Tamiel, Ramiel, Danel, Ezeqeel, Baraqijal, Asael, Armaros, Batarerl, Ananel, Zaqiel, Samsapeel, Satarei,

Turel, Jomjael, Sariel. These were the leaders of the groups of ten."
Raguel is named in 1 Enoch 20 as one of the Watchers who did not fall. "Raguel, one of the sacred angels, who inflicts punishment on the world and the luminaries."

"Give them the handwritten books, and they will read them and will know that I am the creator of all things, and will understand how there is no other God but me. They are to distribute your handwritten books - children to children, generation to generation, nations to nations.

"I will give you, Enoch, my intercessor, the chief general Michael, for the handwritings of your fathers Adam, Seth, Enos, Cainan, Mahalaleel, and Jared your father.

34.

"They have rejected my commandments and my yoke! Worthless seed has come up! They do not fear God, and they would not bow down to me, but have begun to bow down to useless gods, and denied my unity! They have laden the whole earth with lies, offences, unclean practices, unjust deeds, harlotries and services of idols. For this reason I will bring down a flood upon the earth and will destroy all humans, and the whole earth will crumble together into great darkness.

35.

"Another generation will arise from their seed a considerable time later, but many of them will be very unsatisfied. He who raises that generation will reveal to them the handwritten books of your fathers. He must point out to them the guardianship of the world, to the faithful people and those who carry out my wishes, who do not acknowledge my name uselessly. They shall tell another generation, and those others having read shall be praised afterward, even more than the first.

36.

"Now, Enoch, I give you a period of thirty days to spend in your house, and tell your children and your whole household, that all may hear direct from me what you tell them, so that they may read and understand how there is no other God but me, and so that they may always keep my commandments, and begin to read and take in your handwritten books.

"After thirty days I will send my angel for you, and he will take you from earth and from your children to me.

37.

The Lord called on one of the older angels, dreadful and menacing, and placed him by me. His appearance was as white as snow, and his hands were like ice, and looked like a heavy frost. He froze my face, because I could not endure the terror of the Lord, just as it is not possible to endure a stove's fire and the sun's heat, and the frost of the air.

The Lord said to me, "Enoch, if your face is not frozen here, no one will be able to look at your face."

38.

The Lord said to those people who first led me up, "Enoch is to go down to earth with you, and wait for him till the determined day."

They put me on my bed at night.

Methuselah had been expecting my coming, and had kept watch night and day at my bed. He was filled with awe when he heard my coming. I told him, "Get my whole household together, so I can tell them everything."

39.

"My children, my loved ones, hear the warning of your father, which is according to the Lord's will. I have been allowed to come to you today, and to announce to you, not from my lips, but from the Lord's lips, all that is and was and all that now is, and all that will be until judgment day.

"The Lord has let me come to you, so then listen to what I have to say! I am one who has seen the Lord's face, which sends out sparks and burns like iron made to glow from fire. You look now at my eyes, the eyes of a man with meaning for you, but I have seen the Lord's eyes, shining like the sun's rays and filling human eyes with awe. You see now, my children, the right hand of a man who helps you, but I have seen the Lord's right hand filling heaven as he helped me. You see the extent of my work like your own, but I have seen the Lord's limitless and complete work, which has no end. You hear my words, as I heard the words of the Lord, like unremitting powerful thunder with hurling clouds. And now, my children, hear the communication from the father of the earth! How fearful and dreadful it is to come before the face of the ruler of the earth! How much more terrible and dreadful it is to come before the face of the ruler of heaven, the controller of the living and the dead, and of the heavenly troops. Who can endure that endless pain?

40.

"And now, my children, I know all things, for this is from the Lord's lips, and this my eyes have seen, from beginning to end. I know all things, and have written everything down in books, the heavens and their end, and their abundance, and all the armies and their goings. I have measured and described the stars, the great countless multitude of them. What human has seen their revolutions, and their entrances? Not even the angels see their number, while I have written all their names. I measured the sun's circle, and measured its rays, and counted the hours. I also wrote down everything that goes over the earth. I have written the things that are nourished, and all seed both sown and unsown which the earth produces as well as all plants, every grass and every flower, and their fragrances, and their names, and the habitations of the clouds, and their composition, and their wings, and how they bear rain and raindrops.

"I investigated all things, and wrote about the pathway of the thunder and of the lightning, and they showed me the keys and their guardians, their rise, and the way they go, for it is let out gently in a measure by a chain, otherwise if by a heavy violent chain it would hurl down angry clouds and destroy everything on earth.

"I wrote about the storehouses of the snow, and the storehouses of the cold and the frosty airs, and I observed their season's keyholder, for he fills the clouds with them, and does not drain the storehouses.

"I wrote about the resting places of the winds, and observed how their keyholders bear weighing scales and measures. First, they put them in one weighing scale, then in the other weighing scale they put the weights. They take them out in careful measure over the whole earth, otherwise by heavy breathing they would make the earth shake.

"I measured out the whole earth, its mountains, and all hills, fields, trees, stones, rivers. I wrote down all existing things, the height from earth to the seventh heaven, and downwards to the very lowest pit, and the judgment place, and the very great, open Sheol.

"I saw how the prisoners are in pain, expecting the boundless judgment. I wrote down all those being judged by the judge, and all about their judgment, sentences, and all their actions.

41.

"I saw all the ancestors from all time with Adam and

Eve, and I sighed and broke into tears and said of their dishonorable ruin, 'Woe is me for my condition and for that of my ancestors!' I thought to myself, 'Blessed is the one who has not been born, or who has been born and will not do wrong in the Lord's presence, that they will not come into this place, nor bring the burden of this place.'

42.

"I saw the key-holders and guards of the gates of Sheol standing like great serpents. Their faces were like extinguishing lamps, and their eyes were like fire. Their teeth were sharp. I saw all the Lord's actions, how they are just, while as for the actions of humans - some are good, and some are bad. Amongst them are those who do evil things.

43.

"I, my children, measured and wrote out every work and every measure and every just judgment. As one year is more honorable than another, so is one person more honorable than another - some for great possessions, some for wisdom, some for particular intellect, some for astuteness, one for silence, another for cleanliness, one for strength, another for beauty, one for youth, another for sharp wit, one for a good figure, another for awareness. Let it be heard everywhere, that there is none better than the one who fears God, this one shall be more splendid in the time to come.

44.

"The Lord himself created humans in the likeness of

his own face. The Lord made humans both insignificant and significant. Whoever berates the ruler's face, has despised the Lord's face, and whoever vents anger on any person without reason, will be cut down by the Lord's great anger. Whoever who spits on the face of someone with accusation, will be cut down at the Lord's great judgment.

"Blessed is the person who is not malicious to any other person, and helps the hurt and condemned, and raises up the broken down, and does charitable things for the needy, because on the day of the great judgment every weight, every measure, and every balance will be as in the marketplace. That is to say, they are hung on scales and put in the market, and every one shall learn their own measure, and will be rewarded according to their own measure.

45.

"Whoever hurries to make offerings in the Lord's presence, the Lord for his part will hurry along that offering by granting his work. However, whoever increases their lamp in the Lord's presence dishonestly, the Lord will not increase their treasure in the realm of the highest.

"When the Lord demands bread, or candles, or the flesh of beasts, or any other sacrifice, then that is nothing; but God demands pure hearts, and with that tests people's intentions.

46.

"Hear, my people, listen to what I have to say. If

someone brings gifts to an earthly ruler, and has disloyal thoughts in their heart, and the ruler knows this, will he not be angry with him, and not only refuse his gifts, but also give him over to judgment? Or if someone makes themselves appear good to another by deceitful words, and has evil intent, then won't the other understand the deceitful intent, and they will be condemned, as their lies were clear to all?

"And when the Lord sends a great light, then there will be judgment for the just and the unjust, and no one will be overlooked and escape.

47.

"And now, my children, consider well, and mark the words of your father, which have all come to you from the Lord's lips. Take these books of your father's handwriting and read them. There are many books, and in them you will learn all the Lord's works, all that has been from the beginning of creation, and will be until the end of time.

"If you will observe my handwritten words, you will not do wrong against the Lord; because there is no other except the Lord, neither in heaven, nor in earth, nor in the very lowest places, nor in the one foundation. The Lord has placed the foundations in the unknown, and has spread the heavens both visible and invisible. The Lord fixed the earth on the waters, and created innumerable creatures. Who has counted the water and the foundation of the unfixed, or the dust of the earth, or the sand of the sea, or the drops of the rain, or the morning dew, or the wind's breathings? Who has filled earth and sea, and the enduring winter? I cut the stars out of fire, and decked out heaven, and put it in their midst.

48.

"The sun goes along the seven heavenly circles, which are the appointment of 182 thrones. It goes down on a short day, and again 182, and goes down on a big day. He has two thrones on which he rests, revolving here and there above the thrones of the months. From the seventeenth day of the month Tsivan it goes down to the month Thevan, from the seventeenth of Thevan it goes up. And so it goes close to the earth, then the earth is happy and makes its produce grow, and when it goes away, then the earth is sad, and trees and all fruits have no radiation.

"He measured all this, with a good measurement of hours, and fixed a measure of the visible and the invisible by his wisdom. He made all things visible from the invisible, and he himself is invisible.

"This I make known to you, my children. Distribute the books to your children, for all your generations, and distribute the books among the nations who have the sense to fear God. Let them receive them, and may they come to love them more than any food or earthly sweets, and to read them and apply themselves to them.

"As for those who do not understand the Lord, who do not fear God, who do not accept, but reject, who do not receive the books, a terrible judgment awaits them.

Blessed is the person who bears their burden and drags them along, for that person will be released on the day of the great judgment.

49.

"I swear to you, my children, but I do not swear by any oath, neither by heaven nor by earth, nor by any other creature which God created. The Lord said, 'There is no oath in me, nor injustice, but truth.' If there is any truth in people, let them swear by the words, Yes, yes, or No, no.

Commentary

Compare Matthew 5:33-37: *33* "You have heard the ancient saying, 'You must not swear an oath that you don't intend to keep. You must keep your oaths to the Lord.' *34* Listen to it! In fact, don't swear an oath at all! Don't swear by heaven, as it is God's throne. *35* Don't swear by the earth, as it is his footstool. Don't swear by Jerusalem, as it is the city of the great King. *36* And what's the point of swearing by your head, because you can't make one hair white or black! *37* But when you say 'Yes,' mean it! When you say 'No,' mean it! Anything more than that is from the evil one!

"And I swear to you, yes, yes, that everyone who has been in their mother's womb, already has had a place prepared for their soul's rest, and a measure fixed as to how much it is intended that a person be tried in this world.

"Children, do not deceive yourselves, for a place for the soul of every person has previously been prepared.

50.

"I have put every person's work in writing and no one born on earth can stay hidden nor do their works stay concealed. I see all things.

"So then, my children, spend your lives tolerantly and respectfully, so that you will inherit endless life. Endure every wound, every injury, every evil word and attack for the sake of the Lord.

"If bad things happen to you, do not return them either to your neighbor or enemy, because the Lord will return them to you and take revenge on you on the day of great judgment. Let there be no avenging here among people.

"Whoever of you spends gold or silver for their fellow's sake, will receive ample treasure in the world to come.

"Do no wrong to widows, orphans, or strangers, so that God's anger does not come upon you.

51.

"Give to the poor according to your ability to do so. Do not hide your silver in the earth. Help the faithful person who is having difficulty, and difficulty will not find you in a time of trouble. Put up with every awful and unkind burden that comes upon you for the sake of the Lord, and you will find your reward in the day of judgment. It is good to go morning, midday, and evening to the Lord's dwelling, for the glory of your creator. Every breathing thing eulogizes him, and every creature both visible and invisible praises him.

52.

"Blessed is the person who opens their mouths to praise the God of Sabaoth and praises the Lord with their whole heart. Cursed is the person who opens their mouths to bring disrespect and slander to their neighbor, because they bring God into disrespect.

"Blessed is the person who opens their lips to bless and praise God. Cursed all the days of their life is the person who opens their lips to curse and abuse in the Lord's presence.

"Blessed is the one who blesses all the Lord's works. Cursed is the one who brings the Lord's creation into disrespect.

"Blessed is the one who looks down and lifts up the fallen. Cursed is the one who is eager for the destruction of what they do not own.

"Blessed is the one who firmly keeps the foundations of their ancestors from the beginning. Cursed is the one who goes away from the decrees of their ancestors.

"Blessed is the one who passes on peace and love. Cursed is the one who upsets those who love their neighbors.

"Blessed is the one who speaks nicely to everyone and means it. Cursed is the one who speaks peace with words alone while in their heart is not peace but a sword.

"All these things will be laid bare in the weighing scales and in the books, on the day of the great judgment.

53.

"And now, my children, do not say, 'Our father is standing in God's presence, and is praying for our sins,' for there is no helper for any person who has sinned.

"You see how I wrote all actions of every person before their creation! You see how I wrote everything that is done among all people for all time! No one can tell or relate my handwriting, because the Lord sees all human thoughts, how useless they are, and where they lie in the storehouses of the heart.

"And now, my children, pay close attention to the words of your father that I have told you, so that you don't regret it and say, 'Why didn't our father tell us?'

54.

"Let these books which I have given you be a peaceful inheritance for you. Hand them to all who want them, and instruct them, so that they may see the Lord's amazingly vast and awe-inspiring works.

55.

"My children, look! My time is up. The angels who are to go with me are standing in front of me and urge me to leave you. They are standing here on earth, awaiting what has been told them. Tomorrow I will go up to heaven, to the uppermost Jerusalem to my eternal inheritance. So then I bid you to do everything the Lord wants in his presence."

56.

Methuselah responded to his father Enoch, "Father, what is agreeable to you, that I may do while you are here, so that you will bless our dwellings, and your children, and that your people may be celebrated through you, and then after that you may leave, as the Lord said?"

Enoch answered his son Methuselah, "Listen, my child. From the time when the Lord anointed me with his splendid ointment, I have not eaten, and my soul does not remember any earthly pleasure, and I do not want to remember anything earthly."

57.

"Methuselah, my child, summon all your kin and all your household and the elders of the people, so that I may talk to them and then leave, as is planned for me."

Methuselah hurried, and summoned his siblings, Regim, Riman, Uchan, Chermion, Gaidad, and all the elders of the people to his father Enoch.

Enoch blessed them, and said to them,

58.

"My children, listen to me today. In those days the Lord came down to earth for humanity's sake, and visited all his creatures which he himself had created prior to creating humanity. The Lord called all the animals of the earth, all the reptiles, and all the birds that fly in the air, and brought them all to the face of our ancestor Human. Human gave the names to all things living on earth. The Lord appointed the Human ruler over everything, and subjected all things to the Human's power, and made them silent and dull so that they could be commanded by Human, and be in subjection and to be obedient to Human. The Lord created every human master to be lord over all their possessions.

"The Lord will not judge a single soul of an animal for humanity's sake, but judges human souls with regard to their animals in this world, as humans have a special place. Just as human souls will not perish, neither will animals perish. Animals' souls will not perish, nor will any soul of an animal which the Lord created. At the great judgment, they will accuse people, if they have not fed them well.

59.

"Whoever defiles the soul of animals, defiles their own soul. People bring ritually clean animals to make sacrifice for sin, in order to have a cure for their own soul. If they bring ritually clean animals and birds for sacrifice, then the person has a cure, they cure their soul.

"Everything is given you for food, so bind it by the four feet to make good the cure, they cure their soul. But whoever kills an animal without wounds, kills his own soul and defiles his own flesh. The person who secretly harms any animal whatsoever, is committing an evil act, and they defile their own soul.

60.

"The person who kills someone else, kills their own soul, and kills their own body, and there is no cure for them for all time. The person who puts another person in any trap, will themselves be caught in it, and there is no cure for them for all time.

"The person who puts another person in any vessel, will surely get what's coming to them at the great judgment for all time. The person who does criminal things or speaks evil against someone else, will never receive justice.

61.

"And now, my children, turn away from every injustice, as the Lord hates this. Just as a person asks something for their own self from God, so let them do this for every living soul, because I know all things, that in the great time to come there is a great inheritance prepared for people, good for the good, and bad for the bad. Blessed are those who enter the good houses, for in the bad houses there is no peace or way out.

"My children, big and small, listen to my words! When someone brings gifts into the Lord's presence but that person did not make those gifts, then the Lord will turn his back on that person's work. If the person did make the gifts, but their heart is not in it, this will bring no advantage.

62.

"Blessed is the person who patiently and faithfully brings gifts into the Lord's presence, because they will find forgiveness of sins. But if they take back their words before the time, there is no changing their mind, and if time passes and they do not freely do what is promised, there is no changing their mind after death. Every work which a person does before the time, is considered deceitful by humans, and sinful by God.

63.

"When someone clothes the naked and feeds the hungry, they will receive a reward from God. But if their heart is not in it, they commit a double evil - ruin for themselves and for that which they give. There is no reward for that. If their own heart is filled with their food, and their own body is clothed with their own clothing, they have committed a contemptible act, and will lose all that keeps poverty from them. There is no reward for that.

"Every arrogant and boastful person is hateful to the Lord, and so is every false speech which clothed with lies - it will be cut with the blade of the sword of death and thrown into the fire, and will burn for all time."

64.

After Enoch had spoken these words to his children, all people far and near heard how the Lord was calling Enoch. They took counsel together and said, "Let's go and kiss Enoch." So two thousand people gathered and came to the place Akhuzan where Enoch was, and his sons.

All the elders of the people, the whole assembly, came and bowed down and started kissing Enoch. They said to him, "Our father Enoch! May the Lord, the eternal ruler, bless you, and now bless your children and all the people, so that we may be exalted today in your presence! You will be exalted in the Lord's presence for all time, since the Lord chose you over all the people on earth, and designated you as the writer of all his creation, both visible and invisible, and fixed the wrongdoings of humans.

65.

Enoch answered all his people, "My children, listen! Before all creatures were created, the Lord created the visible and invisible things. And as for the amount of time that went past, understand that after all that, he created humanity in the likeness of his own form. He gave humanity eyes to see, and ears to hear, and heart to reflect, and the intellect with which to deliberate. The Lord saw all humanity's deeds, the Lord created all creatures, and the Lord divided time. The Lord made the years, and from the years he appointed the months, and from the months he appointed the days, and there were seven days. In those days he appointed the hours, and measured them out exactly, so that humans could consider time and count years, months, and hours, and consider their progression, beginning and end, so that humans could calculate their own life, from the beginning until death, and reflect on their wrongdoing and calculate their actions both bad and good. There is nothing that is hidden before the Lord. Every person would know their own actions and not stray from the

Lord's decrees, and would keep my handwriting from generation to generation.

"When all creation, both visible and invisible, as the Lord created it, ends, then every human goes to the great judgment. Then all time will pass away, and so will the years, and from then on there will be no months, days or hours, as they will be stuck together and will not be counted.

"There will be one age, and all the just who escape the Lord's great judgment, will be collected in the great age. The great age will begin for the just, and they will live eternally. For them will be no work, sickness, disgrace, anxiety, need, rough treatment, night, darkness, but there will be great light. They will have a great indestructible wall, and a bright, imperishable garden, for all perishable things will pass away, and there will be eternal life."

Commentary

Garden or paradise. (Same word.)

66.

"And now, my children, turn away from injustice, which the Lord hates. Live your lives in the Lord's presence with fear and trembling and serve him alone. Bow down to the true God, not to silent idols, but bow down to his likeness, and bring all just offerings before the Lord's face. The Lord hates what is unjust.

"The Lord sees all things. When someone has thoughts and takes advice, all these thoughts are clear to the Lord, who made the earth firm and put all creatures on it. If you look to heaven, the Lord is there. If you think about the sea's deep and the whole sub-earth, the Lord is there. The Lord created all things. Do not bow down to things made by humans, thus leaving the Lord of all creation, because no action can remain hidden from the Lord.

"My children, behave patiently, humbly, honestly, while you are being provoked and upset, behave faithfully and truthfully and honor your promises when you are ill, mistreated, injured, oppressed, lacking enough clothes, in hardship, and love one another until you leave this unpleasant age, so that you will become those who inherit endless time.

"Blessed are the just who will escape the great judgment. They will shine more than the sun sevenfold, for in this world the seventh part is taken away from all light, darkness, food, pleasure, sadness, gardens, torture, fire, frost, and other things. He put this all down in writing, so that you could read it and understand."

67.

After Enoch had talked to the people, the Lord sent darkness onto the earth. The darkness covered those people standing with Enoch. They took Enoch up onto the highest heaven, where the Lord is. The Lord received Enoch and placed him in his presence. The darkness left the earth, and the light returned.

The people saw it but did not understand how Enoch had been taken, and they praised God. They found a roll in which was written, "The Invisible God." Then they all went back home.

68.

Enoch was born on the sixth day of the month Tsivan, and lived for 365 years. He was taken up to heaven on the first day of the month Tsivan and stayed in heaven for 60 days. He wrote about all these signs of all creation, which the Lord created, and wrote 366 books. He and handed them over to his children and remained on earth for 30 days, after which he was again taken up to heaven on the sixth day of the month Tsivan, on the very day and hour when he was born.

As every person's nature in this life is dark, so are also his conception, birth, and departure from this life. At what hour he was conceived, at that hour he was born, and at that hour too he died.

Methuselah and his siblings, all Enoch's children, hurried to erect an altar at that place called Akhuzan, from where Enoch had been taken up to heaven. They took sacrificial oxen. They summoned all the people and sacrificed the sacrifice in the Lord's presence. All the people, the elders of the people, and the whole assembly came to the feast and brought gifts to Enoch's children. They made a great feast, celebrating and partying for three days, praising God, who had given them such a sign through Enoch, who had found favor with him. They would hand it onto their children from generation to generation, from age to age.

The Exaltation of Melchizedek

Commentary

There is no scholarly agreement as to whether this section (known as 2EM) belongs to 2 Enoch or is a very early addition. Sacchi and Short suggest it is an addition, but a very early addition and written by someone of the same sect as the rest of the text. Sacchi, P., Short, W.J., *Jewish Apocalyptic and Its History, Jsp Supplement Series*, No. 20, 1996, *passim*. Sacchi and Short suggest that the reason it did not survive in later editions as part of 2 Enoch is due to Christian copyists' objection to the virgin birth of Melchizedek. Vaillant, A., "Le livre des secrets d'Henoch," *Texte slave et traduction francaise*, Paris, 1952, could find no evidence to suggest that this section was ever separate from the rest of the text. See also Schmidt, N., "The two recensions of Slavonic Enoch," *Journal of the American Oriental Society*, 41(1921) 307ff.

69.

On the third day the people spoke to Methuselah and said, "Stand in the presence of the Lord, the prince of all people, and in the presence of the altar of the Lord, and you will be exalted among the people."

Methuselah answered his people, "People, wait, until the Lord God of my father Enoch raises up for himself a priest over his people."

The people waited all night for no reason at the place Akhuzan. Methuselah was near the altar and prayed to the Lord, and said, "Only the Lord of the whole world who has taken my father Enoch, will raise up a priest for my people and teach them to respect your splendor, and to do what you wish."

Methuselah slept and the Lord appeared to him in a night vision, and said, "Listen Methuselah, I am the Lord God of your father Enoch! Listen to what these people have to say, and stand before my altar. I will exalt you in the presence of all the people, and you will be exalted all the days of your life."

Methuselah awoke from his sleep, and blessed the Lord who had appeared to him.

The elders of the people hurried to Methuselah. The Lord God influenced the heart of Methuselah to hear the voice of the people, and he said, "The Lord God does what he considers to be a good thing to these people."

And Sarsan and Kharmisa and Zazus, the elders of the people, hurried and dressed Methuselah in beautiful clothes and put a shining crown on his head. All the people hurried and bought sheep, cattle, and birds such as were appropriate for Methuselah to sacrifice in the presence of the Lord, and in the presence of the people.

Methuselah went out to the presence of the Lord, and his face shone like the sun when it rises in the morning, and all the people followed him. Methuselah stood in front of the altar of the Lord, and all the people stood around the altar.

The elders of the people took sheep and oxen and bound their four feet, and put them on top of the altar. They said to Methuselah, "Lift the knife. Kill them by the proper way in the Lord's presence."

Methuselah stretched out his hands to the heavens and called to the Lord, "Alas, Lord! Who am I to stand at the head of your altar and at the head of these people! Now, Lord, look down on your servant and on all these people. Do not let the things which have been sought after come to pass, and give blessings to your servant in the presence of all the people, so that they will understand that you have appointed a priest over your people."

And it turned out that when Methuselah had prayed, the altar shook, and a knife rose from the altar and leaped into Methuselah's hand in the presence of all the people. All the people were afraid and praised the Lord.

From that day on, Methuselah was honored in the presence of the Lord and in the presence of all the people.

70.

For the next ten years, Methuselah continued to stand at the altar in the presence of the Lord and all the people, trusting in an eternal inheritance. He taught all the people in the whole land well. There was not one person who was found to turn arrogantly from the Lord in the whole time in which Methuselah lived. The Lord blessed Methuselah and was pleased with his sacrifices, his gifts, and his services which he served in the presence of the Lord.

When the time came for Methuselah to leave, the Lord appeared to him in a night vision, and said, "Listen, Methuselah! I am the Lord God of your father Enoch. I order you to see how the days of your life have come to an end, and the day of your rest approaches. Call Nir, the son of your son Lamech, the second born after Noah, and dress him in your consecrated robes. Place him beside my altar and tell him what will happen in his time, because the destruction of the whole earth approaches, as well as the destruction of every human and every living thing on the earth.

For in his time there will be very great confusion on the earth because a person has been envious of their neighbor, and people have become inflamed against people, and nations are stirred up against nations, and the whole earth is filled with foulness and blood, and all kinds of evil.

"Not only that, but they have also deserted their Maker and have worshiped useless idols, to the firmament of heaven, the course of the earth, and the waves of the sea. The adversary is multiplied and is happy with its actions to my great vexation.

The whole earth changes its form and every tree and every fruit changes its seeds, expecting the time of destruction. All people on earth are changing, to my sorrow.

"Then I will command the abysses to put themselves on the earth, the large storehouses of the waters of heaven will come upon the earth by their nature and according to their first nature. The stability of the earth will be lost and the whole earth be shaken and be deprived of its strength from then on.

"I will preserve the son of your son Lamech, his first son Noah, and I will raise up another one from his seed, and his seed will exist from then on until the second destruction when people will also do wrong in my presence."

Methuselah leaped up from his sleep and was greatly troubled by his dream. He called all the elders of the people and told them what the Lord had told him and the whole vision that had appeared to him from the Lord.

The people were upset at his vision, and said to him, "Let the Lord God do what he wants to do! Methuselah, do the things the Lord told you to do!"

Methuselah called Nir, the son of Lamech, the younger brother of Noah, and dressed him in the robes of the priesthood in the presence of all the people, and placed him at the head of the altar, and taught him everything he was to do among the people.

Methuselah called to the people, "Nir will be in your presence from this time on as a prince and leader."

The people said to Methuselah, "May what you have said be the case. May what the Lord has told you come to pass."

After Methuselah had spoken to the people before the altar, his spirit was confused. He bent his knees, and stretched out his hands to the heavens, and prayed to God. As he prayed, his spirit went out to the Lord.

Nir and all the people hurried to make a grave for Methuselah in the place Aruzan. Nir came in splendid clothing in all his priestly robes, with lights and much pomp and ceremony. The people lifted up Methuselah's body, exalted it, and put it in the grave which they had made for him. They buried him and said, "Methuselah was blessed in the presence of the Lord and in the presence of all the people."

When they were about to go back home, Nir said to the people, "Go quickly and bring sheep, heifers, turtle doves, and pigeons, and let us offer them in the presence of the Lord, and then you can go home."

The people listened to Nir the priest and hurried and brought the victims and tied them to the head of the altar. Nir took the sacrificial knife and killed all the victims, and offered them in the presence of the Lord. All the people celebrated in the presence of the Lord, and from that day on praised the Lord of Nir, the ruler of heaven and earth. From that day on there was peace and order over the whole earth in the time of Nir, which was 202 years.

Then the people turned from God and began to be jealous of one another, and people rebelled against each other, and they began to say nasty things about one another. They would say one thing but mean another. Then the diabolos began to reign for the third time, the first time before paradise, the second time in paradise, the third time outside of paradise, and continued until the deluge. A great dispute and confusion arose. When Nir the priest heard it, he was very upset, and said to himself, "I certainly understand that the time has drawn near, the end which the Lord spoke about to Methuselah, the father of my father Lamech.

71.

The wife of Nir by the name of Sopanima was barren and so had no children to Nir. When Sopanima was old, she conceived, but Nir the priest had not slept with her, and had not done so from the day that the Lord appointed him to serve in the presence of the people. When Sopanima knew she was pregnant, she was ashamed, and hid herself away until she gave birth, and none of the people knew.

After she had been pregnant for 282 days, Nir thought of her and called her to his house to talk to her. Sopanima came to her husband Nir and was heavily pregnant. Nir saw her and was very ashamed. He said to her, "My wife, what have you done! You have shamed me in he presence of the people. Leave me now, and go where you started this shameful business, so that I won't defile my hand on you and sin in the presence of the Lord!"

Sopanima said to Nir her husband, "My lord! I am very old and about to die, and I did not know when I stopped being barren!"

Nir did not believe his wife, and said to her, "Get away from me in case I harm you and sin in the presence of the Lord!"

After Nir said that, Sopanima fell at his feet and died.

Nir was very upset and said to himself, "Was this caused by my words, since a person sins by their words and thoughts in the presence of the Lord. Now the Lord is merciful to me, I know truthfully that I did not strike her. So I say, 'Praise you, Lord, as no one on earth knows this deed which the Lord has done!'

Nir hurried and shut the doors of the house and went to his brother Noah and told him everything that had happened concerning his wife.

Noah hurried and went with Nir, his brother, to Nir's house because of Sopanima's death, and they talked to each other and saw how heavily pregnant she was.

Noah said to Nir, "Don't be upset, Nir, my brother. The Lord has today concealed our shame, because none of the people know this. Now let's go quickly and bring her secretly, and may the Lord hide your shame and humiliation."

They laid out Sopanima on the bed and wrapped her with black robes, and shut her in the house ready for burial. They dug a grave secretly. Then a baby came from the dead Sopanima and sat on the bed at her right hand.

Noah and Nir entered and saw the baby sitting by the dead Sopanima wiping its clothes. Nir and Noah were horrified and very afraid, as the child was well grown like a three year old child. The child spoke and blessed the Lord.

Noah and Nir looked at it and saw that the seal of the priesthood was on its chest, and its appearance was splendid. Noah and Nir said, "Look! The Lord renews the consecration along our bloodline, as he wishes! My brother, this is from the Lord, and the Lord renews the consecrated bloodline in us."

Noah and Nir hurried and washed the child, and dressed it in priestly clothes and gave it the blessed bread. They gave it the name of Melchizedek.

Commentary

Hebrews 7:3 says of Melchizedek, "There is no record of his father or recorded mother, he has no genealogy. There is no record of his beginning of days or end of life."

Noah and Nir took Sopanima's body, and took off her black robes, and built a beautiful grave for her. Noah, Nir and Melchizedek buried her publicly.

Noah said to Nir, "Watch this child in secret until the time, as deceitful people will rise over the earth and will begin to reject God. They won't be aware of anything and will put him to death."

Then Noah went home. There was great lawlessness over the earth in the time of Nir.

Nir began to be very anxious, especially about the child. He said, "Alas, Lord! In my time there is much lawlessness over the earth, and I understand how the end is even closer now on the whole earth due to the lawlessness of the people. Lord, what is the vision? What is the solution? What shall I do for the child? Will the child also be destroyed with us?"

The Lord heard Nir. The Lord appeared to him in a night vision, and said, "Nir, I will not put up with the great lawlessness with regard to many things that has been on the earth and Look! I intend to bring a great destruction on the earth, and every earthly creature will die. But don't worry about the child, Nir, for in a short time I will send my chief captain Michael, and he will take him and place him in the garden of Eden, where Adam formerly was for seven years, leaving that heaven always opened until he sinned.

"This child Melchizedek will not die with those who die in this generation, as I have shown, but will be a sacred priest in all things, and I will appoint him to be the chief of the priests who were previously."

Then Nir awoke from his sleep, and blessed the Lord who had appeared to him, and said, "Blessed is the Lord God of my ancestors, who has spoken to me, who made a great priest in the time he spent in the womb of Sopanima.

"Because I had no family, this child will be given to me as family, and will be a son to me, and you will honor him with your servants the priests, with Seth, with Enoch, Tharasidam, Maleliel and Enos, and your servant, and so Melchizedek will be priest in another generation. For I know that this generation will end in confusion, and everyone will perish. But Noah, my brother, will be kept safe at that time.

"Many people will rise up from my race, and Melchizedek will be the chief of priests among the people, ruling alone, serving you, Lord! Because I had no other child in this family who might be a great priest, and me your servant, now great Lord, honor him with your servants and great priests - with Seth, Enos, Eusii, Almilam, Prasidam, Maleleil, Seroch, Arusan, Aleem, Enoch, Methuselah and me, your servant Nir, and Melchizedek will be chief over 12 priests who lived before, and at last will be chief over all. The great high priests and God's Word have the power to work great splendid marvels above all that have been. Melchizedek will be priest and king in the place Akhuzan, that is to say, in the middle of the earth where Adam was created, there will be his grave.

"And it has been written that a chief priest will be buried there, where the middle of the earth is, where Adam buried his son Abel there, Abel who was killed by his brother Cain, where he laid unburied for three years until he saw a bird called a jackdaw burying its fledgling.

"I know that great confusion has come and that this generation will end in confusion and all will die except Noah my brother, who will be preserved, and afterward there will be offspring from his family, and there will be other people, and another Melchizedek will be chief of the priests among the people, ruling, and serving the Lord."

72.

When the child had been under Nir's roof for forty days, the Lord said to Michael, "Go down to earth to Nir the priest, and take my child Melchizedek who is with him, and place him in the Garden of Eden to keep him safe, because the time approaches when I will discharge all the water upon the earth, and everything on the earth will die. I will establish another race, and Melchizedek will be the chief of the priests in that family, just as Seth is to me in this family."

Michael hurried, and came at night. Nir was asleep in his bed. Michael appeared to him and said, "The Lord says to you, Nir, 'Send the child to me, I entrusted him to you.'"

Nir did not realize that the chief captain Michael

was speaking to him, and was confused, and to himself, "If people know about this child and take him, they will kill him. These people are cunning in the presence of the Lord!"

So Nir said to Michael, "The child is not with me, and I do not know who you are, you who are speaking to me!"

Michael answered him, "Don't be afraid, Nir! I am the chief captain of the Lord. The Lord has sent me and Look! I will take the child today, and will go with him. I will place him in the Garden of Eden and he will be there forever. When the twelfth generation comes along, in 1070 years, a just person will be born, and the Lord will tell him to come out to that mountain where the ark of your brother Noah stands, and there he will find another Melchizedek who has lived there for seven years, hiding himself from the people who worship idols so that they will not kill him. He will lead him out and he will be priest, and the first king in the town of Salem after the fashion of this Melchizedek, the commencement of the priests.

"And 3432 years shall pass from that time until the beginning and creation of Humanity/Adam. From that Melchizedek there will be 12 priests in number until the great Igumen, that is to say, Leader, who will bring forth all things both visible and invisible."

So Nir understood his first dream and believed it. After answering Michael, he said, "Blessed is the Lord, who has exalted you today to me, and now bless your servant Nir, as we are approaching our departure from this world. Take the child, and do with him what the Lord has told you to do."

Michael took the child the same night as he had come, and took him on his wings, and placed him in the Garden of Eden.

The next day Nir got up and went to his house, and did not find the child, and was extremely upset as he looked on him as his son.

Then Nir died, and after him there was no priest among the people. From that time, a great confusion arose upon the earth.

73.

God called Noah on the mountain of Ararat, between Assyria and Armenia in the land of Arabia by the sea, and said to him, "Make an ark 300 ells long, 50 ells wide, 30 ells high, of two stories, and the door about an ell, of those, 300 ells, of ours 15,000, of those 50, of ours 2000 and 500, and so those 30, and of ours 900, and of those 1 ell, and of ours, 50."

The Jews consider this to be the measurement of Noah's ark that the Lord gave him, even to the present time.

The Lord God opened the doors of heaven, and rain came on the earth for 150 days, and everything died. Noah was 500 years old and had three sons, Shem, Ham, and Japhet. One hundred years after the birth of his three sons, he went into the month known in the

Hebrew as Itsars, and known in the Egyptian as Famenoth in eighteen days.

The ark floated for forty days. Altogether they were in the ark for 120 days. Noah went into the ark at the age of 600 and came out of the ark at the age of 601 in the month known as Farmut by the Egyptians and in the Hebrew known as Nisan about 28 days. He lived a further 250 years then died. All up he lived for 950 years according to the will of the Lord our God, to him be the splendor from the beginning and now to the end of the world, Amen. Enoch lived until the age of 365.

In another way it is written here about Noah's ark. Of theirs 300 ells, and of ours 15,000, of theirs 100, and of ours 5000, of theirs, 20, and of ours, 1000, of theirs 10, and of ours 500, of theirs 5, and of ours 250, of theirs 1, and of ours 50. This is the truth.

CHAPTER 6: THIRD BOOK OF ENOCH: INTRODUCTION

The *Third Book of Enoch* is also known as the *Hebrew Book of Enoch*, as the evidence suggests it was originally written in Hebrew. The *Third Book of Enoch* is also known as *Sefer Hekhalot*, meaning *Book of Palaces*.

There is evidence that the *Third Book of Enoch* was in part dependent on the *First Book of Enoch*, but scholars are divided as to whether 3 Enoch represents a separate and mystical experience.

The *Third Book of Enoch* claims to be written by Rabbi Ishmael (Ishmael ben Elisha) who lived 90 - 135 CE. Rabbi Ishmael was a Tanna, a rabbinic sage whose views are recorded in the Mishnah. Rabbi Ishmael was a leading proponent of later Merkabah literature.

Scholars cannot agree about the meaning or origin of the name *Metatron*. It appears only in Hebrew writings, but not in the Hebrew Bible and thus not in the Christian Old or New Testaments. Metatron is not mentioned in any Islamic source.

The Alphabet of Ben Sira has Metatron as a heavenly scribe. In Yalkut Hadash, Metatron is said to be appointed over the archangels Michael and Gabriel. The Talmud Avodah Zarah 3b states that Metatron is the teacher of prematurely dead children in Paradise. 117. The Babylonian Talmud also mentions Metatron in Sanhedrin 38b.

The 17th century German anti-Jewish scholar and eminent linguist Johann Andreas Eisenmenger stated that Metatron daily transmitted orders from God to the angels Gabriel and Sammael.

Samael Aun Weor, an early 19th century Columbian (and later Mexican) spiritual leader and founder of the neo-Gnostic Universal Christian Gnostic Movement, stated that Metatron was an archangel who provided humanity with not only the 22 Hebrew letters but also the original Tarot.

Metatron has been variously identified with Mithra (for example King, C.W., *The Gnostics and Their Remains Ancient and Mediaeval*, Second Edition, David Nutt, London, 1887, p.1.) and the Gnostic Horus, and the Targum Yerualmi to Exodus substitutes the name of Michael for Metatron. Hugo Odeberg *3 Enoch, or the Hebrew Book of Enoch*, Cambridge University Press, London, 1928, 1.132, 1.134) lists a number of parallels between Metatron and the Persian Mithras, and states that they have similar celestial functions such as Guardian of the World, Mediator for the Earth, Prince of the World, and the Witness of all thoughts, words, and actions.

However, Odeberg considered that the name Metatron should be considered to be a pure Jewish invention, a metonym for the term "The Lesser Yahweh." Several scholars agree that Metatron may simply be a coined name, and note that several coined names appear in the Hekhalot-Merkabah texts. Philip Alexander, "3 Enoch." In *The Old Testament Pseudepigrapha*, New York: Doubleday, 1983, 243, although putting forth views of the origin of Metatron (see below), states that if indeed the name Metatron did originate in the Hekhalot-Merkabah texts, then it may well be coined.

In the *Third Book of Enoch*, Enoch ascends to heaven and is transformed into the angel Metatron. The Talmud does not state this, but the tradition is found in the earliest Kabbalists. Both the Zohar and 3 Enoch refer to Metatron as "the Youth." The Zohar further claims that Metatron was the angel who went before the Israelites after their exodus from Egypt. Medieval Jewish authorities, such as Eleazar of Worms and Nahmanides, suggested that the name Metatron is derived from the Latin metator, guide, measurer, messenger, leader (cf. Odeberg, *op.cit.,* 1.127–128). Scholem disagreed. (Scholem, G., *Jewish Gnosticism,*

Merkabah Mysticism, and Talmudic Tradition, Jewish Theological Seminary of America,1960, 43.) However, their view was supported more recently by Alexander who suggests that the name Metatron may have been given to the angel who led the Israelites through the wilderness, acting like a Roman army metator, guiding the Israelites. (Alexander, P.S. "From Son of Adam to a Second God: Transformation of the Biblical Enoch," in *Biblical Figures Outside The Bible*, *Edd.* M.E. Stone, T.A. Bergen; Harrisburg, 1998, 107.) Alexander states that the Latin word metator sometimes designates the officer in the Roman army who went ahead of the column on the march in order to strike camp. (*Loc.cit.;* Alexander, P S. "3 Enoch." In *The Old Testament Pseudepigrapha*, New York: Doubleday, 1983, 243.) He further suggests that Enoch himself could be viewed by adepts as metator or forerunner since he showed them the way of escape from the wilderness of this world into the promised land of heaven. (Alexander, P.S. "From Son of Adam to a Second God: Transformation of the Biblical Enoch," in *Biblical Figures Outside The Bible*, *Edd.* M.E. Stone, T.A. Bergen; Harrisburg, 1998, 107.) Alexander cites as evidence that metator is attested as a loanword in Hebrew and Aramaic. (Alexander, P S. "3 Enoch." In *The Old Testament Pseudepigrapha*, New York: Doubleday, 1983, 243.)

Matthew Black suggests that the term *praemetitor*, found in a piece of Philo extant in Armenian, could be the Greek equivalent of the Latin *metator* applied to the

Logos. (Black, M. "The Origin of the Name Metatron," *VT* 1 (1951) 218.)

Joseph Dan proposed that the name "Metatron" may be connected with the function of this angel as the bearer of God's name. In 3 Enoch, Metatron is named as the "Lesser Yahweh." Dan takes the "him" in Exodus 23:21, "because my name is within him," as referring to Metatron, (*b. Sanh.* 38b) suggesting that "he has within himself God's ineffable name, which gives him his power." (Dan, J. *The Ancient Jewish Mysticism*, Mod Books, 1990, 109.) Dan further proposes that, in view of the phrase "my name is within him," the name Metatron might be construed as related to the four letters of the divine Name." (*Ibid.*, 109-110.)

In the introduction to his 1989 French translation of 3 Enoch, Charles Mopsik suggests that the etymology of the name "Metatron" can be linked to the Biblical Enoch references, citing the Septuagint of Genesis 5:24, "Enoch walked with God; then he was no more, because God took him." Mopsik states that the Septuagint of Genesis 5:24 and Sirach 44:16 translates the Hebrew verb "to take" by the Greek verb *metatithemi*, to change the place, to be transferred. He concludes that the three main consonants for the name Metatron are a possible transliteration of the Greek. Mopsik suggests that the name "Metatron" could designate "the one who has been translated" and thus would be in direct relation to the Enoch story and his translation to heaven. (Mopsik, C., and Moché Idel. *Le Livre hébreu d'Hénoch ou Livre des palais.* Paris: Verdier, 1989, 48.)

The word "Metatron" is numerically equivalent to Shaddai (one of the Jewish names for God) in Hebrew gematria (that is, the assigning of numerical values to words, letters and phrases).

CHAPTER 7: THIRD BOOK OF ENOCH: TRANSLATION

I

Rabbi Ishmael said:

I ascended on high to see the vision of the Merkabah and had entered the six Halls, one within the other. As soon as I reached the door of the seventh Hall, I stood still and prayed before the Sacred One - may he be blessed! Then I lifted my eyes high to the Divine Majesty and said, “Lord of the Universe, I pray that the merit of Aaron, the son of Amram, the lover and pursuer of peace, who received the crown of priesthood from your Splendor on Mount Sinai, would be valid for me at this time, so that Qafsiel, the prince, and the angels with him may not gain power over me nor throw me down from the heavens.”

Then the Sacred One - may he be blessed! - sent Metatron, his servant the angel, the Prince of the Presence, to me. He spread his wings and came very happily to meet me to save me from them.

He took me by the hand in front of them and said to me, "Enter in peace before the high and exalted King, and look at the picture of the Merkabah."

Then I entered the seventh Hall, and he led me to the camps of Shekinah and placed me before the Sacred One - may he be blessed! - to look at the Merkabah. As soon as the princes of the Merkabah and the flaming Seraphim noticed me, they fixed their eyes upon me. Immediately, I was seized with trembling and shuddering. I was numbed by the radiance of their eyes and the splendid appearance of their faces, until the Sacred One - may he be blessed! - rebuked them. He said, "My servants, my Seraphim, my Cherubim and my Ophanin! Cover your eyes before Ishmael, my child, my friend, my splendid loved one, so that he does not tremble or shake!"

Commentary

Seraphim

The Ethiopic word is *Ikisat* which means "serpents" and was translated by the Greeks as *drakon*, which means a huge serpent, a python, a dragon. The Hebrew word "Seraphim" can also mean "serpents."

Ophanin

Ophanin, from a root meaning "to revolve." Usually translated as "wheels." 1 Enoch 71 stays, "The Seraphim, the Cherubim, and Ophanin.... These are those who never sleep, but guard his splendid throne."

At once Metatron, the Prince of the Presence, came and restored my spirit and put me back on my feet. After that moment there was not enough strength in me to sing a song before the Splendid Throne of the splendid King, the mightiest of all kings, the most excellent of all princes, until after the hour had passed.

After one hour had passed, the Sacred One - may he be blessed! - opened the gates of Shekinah, the gates of Peace, the gates of Wisdom, the gates of Strength, the gates of Power, the gates of Speech, the gates of Song, the gates of Qedusha, and the gates of Chant for me. He enlightened my eyes and my heart with praise songs, admiration, exaltation, gratitude, worship, adoration, worship song, and eulogy.

As I opened my mouth and sang a song before the Sacred One - may he be blessed! - the Sacred Chayyoth beneath and above the Splendid Throne answered, "Sacred and Blessed be the Splendor of Yahweh from his place!"

Commentary

Chayyoth

Chayyoth: "Living creatures."

The Merkabah

Jewish mysticism traces to the Merkabah practices of the 1st c. CE. The goal of Merkabah Mysticism was to enter a trance-like state by means of fasting, meditation, prayer and incantation, and thus ascend to God's heavenly throne room and experience God's Throne-Chariot (Hebrew: "Merkabah") as described in Ezekiel 1:15-28.

Ezekiel 1.

4) As I watched, I saw a huge windstorm coming from the north – a huge cloud, with lightning flashing, and it radiated a brightness like glowing amber from the middle of a fire.

5) In the middle of the fire were what looked like four living beings. They looked like humans,

6) but each had four faces and four wings.

7) Their legs were straight, but the soles of their feet were like calves' hooves. They gleamed like burnished bronze.

8) They had human hands under their wings on their four sides and each of the four of them had faces and wings.

9) Their wings touched each other; they did not turn as they moved, but went straight ahead.
10) Their faces looked like this. Each of the four had the face of a human, with the face of a lion on the right side, the face of an ox on the left side, and also the face of an eagle at the back.
11) Their wings were outstretched above them. Each had two wings, one touching the wings of the other living creatures on either side, and the other pair of wings covering their bodies.
12) Each moved straight ahead. Wherever the spirit went, they went, without turning as they went.
13) In the middle of the living beings there was something that looked like burning coals of fire or like fiery torches. It moved back and forth among the living creatures. It was bright, and lightning was flashing out of the fire.
14) The living beings moved backward and forwards as quickly as flashes of lightning.
15) Then I looked, and I saw a wheel on the ground beside each of the four living creatures.
16) The appearance of the wheels and their construction was like gleaming Tarshish stone, and all four wheels looked alike. Their structure was like a wheel at right angles to another wheel.
17) When they moved they would go in any of the four directions they faced without turning as they moved.

18) Their rims were high and frightening, and the rims of all four wheels were full of eyes all around.
19) When the living beings moved, the wheels beside them moved; when the living beings rose up from the ground, the wheels rose up too.
20) Wherever the wind/spirit would go, they would go, and the wheels would rise up beside them because the spirit of the living being was in the wheel.
21) When the living beings moved, the wheels moved, and when they stopped moving, the wheels stopped. When they rose up from the ground, the wheels rose up from the ground; the wheels rose up beside them because the spirit of the living being was in the wheel.
22) Over the heads of the living beings was something like a dome, glittering amazingly like crystal, stretched out over their heads.
23) Under the platform their wings were stretched out, each toward the other. Each of the beings also had two wings covering its body.
24) When they moved, I heard the sound of their wings which was like the sound of rushing waters, or the voice of the Shaddai, or the tumult of an army. When they stood still, they lowered their wings.
25) Then there was a voice from above the plat-

form over their heads and when they stood still, they lowered their wings.
26) Above the platform over their heads was something like a sapphire shaped like a throne. High above on the throne was a form that appeared to be a human.
27) I saw an amber glow like a fire enclosed all around from his waist up. From his waist down I saw something that looked like fire. There was a brilliant light around it,
28) like the appearance of a rainbow in the clouds after the rain. This was the appearance of the surrounding brilliant light; it looked like the Splendor of Yahweh. When I saw it, I threw myself face down, and I heard a voice speaking.
Angels also feature prominently in the Sefer Ha-Razim, a collection of Jewish incantation texts. Note also the conventional Roman term *dis minibus*, "to the divine spirits", which occurs in several Jewish inscriptions, e.g., *CIJ* 1.531, 678, the possibly Jewish *CIJ* 1.287, 464, 524 and *AE* 85. It occurs in many pagan texts. Origen *Comm. Joh*. 13.17 and Clement *Strom*. 6.5.41 both mention the Kerygama Petrou, which mentions the Jewish worship of angels. However, in the Jewish and pagan mystical texts, angels are invoked and commanded, usually for protective purposes, rather than worshipped.

To ascend to God's heavenly throne room, the traveler must pass through 7 heavens, and once in the seventh heaven, the traveler must pass through seven concentric palaces. God's Throne-Chariot stands in the innermost of seven palaces, the gate to each place being barred by fierce guard angels. The angels were hostile, and must be placated through worship for the journey to succeed. Once before God's throne, the traveler would worship God side by side with angels and thus observe the innermost secrets of all persons and things, otherwise unsolvable and invisible. The ascent to the highest heaven and the innermost sanctum was most hazardous, so perilous in fact, that there was a Jewish tradition which forbade the study of the beginning and the end of the Book of Ezekiel before the completion of the thirtieth year. (Noted by Jerome, cf. Scholem, G., *Major Trends in Jewish Mysticism*, *op.cit.*, p. 42) The Talmud states of Merkabah Mysticism, "The subject of...the work of the chariot [may not be expounded]...unless one is a sage who has innate understanding of it. Whoever speculates on [the work of the chariot], it would have been better if they had not come into the world." (Mishnah Hagigah 2:1)

Several angels are mentioned in connection with Merkabah Mysticism. Sandalfon was one of the oldest angels of the Merkabah Mysticism. He was an exceedingly tall angel who was said to stand on

the earth. A rabbinical saying said of him: "The angel Sandalfon towers above the rest of the angels the length of a five hundred years' journey; his feet touch the earth while his head reaches the holy *Hayyot*. He stands behind the Throne-Chariot binding wreaths for his Master". (*Hag.* 13b). The angel Hadarniel was said to lead Moses in heaven until he reached the fire of Sandalfon. Sandalfon is not found in non-Jewish sources. He is said to be a fierce fire, situated near God in the seventh hall.

F.F. Bruce notes that a preparatory period of ascetism, estimated variously at 12 or 40 days, was carried out, and that angels acted as meditators. Gershom Scholem called Merkabah Mysticism a form of Jewish Gnosticism, and stated that the Merkabah mystics were similar to the later Gnostics as both sought the ascent of the soul from the earth through the spheres of hostile planet-angels and rulers of the cosmos. Ithamar Gruenwald challenged Scholem's conclusions. (Gruenwald, I., "The Problem of Anti-Gnostic Polemic in Rabbinic literature," in *Studies in Gnosticism and Hellenic Religions, EPRO* 91, FS. G. Quispel; Leiden; Brill, 1981. See discussion in C.E. Arnold, *op.cit.*, pp. 55ff.) A.F. Segal likewise argued that the Merkabah texts were not founded on Gnosticism but on pre-rabbinic apocalyptic Judaism. (Segal, A.F.,

"Heavenly Ascent in Hellenistic Judaism, Early Christianity and Their Environment," *ANRW* II.23.2 (1980).)

2.

R. Ishmael said:

In that hour the eagles of the Merkabah, the flaming Ophanin and the Seraphim of consuming fire asked Metatron, "Youth! Why do you allow one born of woman to enter and see the Merkabah? From which nation, from which tribe is this one? What is his character?"

Metatron answered them, "From the nation of Israel which the Sacred One - may he be blessed! - chose for his people from among seventy people-groups from the tribe of Levi, whom he set aside as a contribution to his name and from among the seed of Aaron whom the Sacred One - may he be blessed! - chose for his servant and put the priesthood of on Sinai on him."

Immediately they said, "This one surely is worthy to look at the Merkabah!" They added, "Blessed are the people of whom this is the case!"

Commentary

See Psalm 144:15.

3.

R. Ishmael said:

At that time I asked Metatron, the angel, the Prince of the Presence, "What is your name?"

He answered, "I have seventy names, corresponding to the seventy languages of the world, and all of them are based on the name Metatron, angel of the Presence. However, my King calls me 'Youth.'"

4.

R. Ishmael said:

I asked Metatron, "Why does your Creator call you by seventy names? You are more important than all the princes, higher than all the angels, more loved than all the servants, more honored than all the mighty, great, and splendid ones in kingly positions, so why do they call you 'Youth' in the high heavens?"

He answered, "Because I am Enoch, the son of Jared. When the people-group of the flood sinned and did confused things, they said to Yahweh, 'Leave us, we don't want to know about you,' (Job 21:14) then the Sacred One – may he be blessed! - removed me from them to be a witness against them in the high heavens to all the inhabitants of earth, so that they wouldn't say, 'The Merciful One is cruel.'

Commentary

Hebrews 11:5, "By faith Enoch was transferred from one place to another so that he didn't experience death, and could not be found, because God had taken him away – since before he was

transferred from one place to another he had the reputation that he had pleased God." Genesis 5:24. "Enoch walked with Elohim, then he vanished, because Elohim took him away."

"What sins had all those multitudes committed, they, their wives, their sons, their daughters, their horses, their mules, their cattle, their property, and all the animals wild and domesticated, and the birds of the world, which the Sacred One - may he be blessed! - destroyed off the face of the earth in the flood waters? What did they do that they would die along with them?

"And so the Sacred One - may he be blessed! - lifted me up in their lifetime before their eyes to be a witness against them to the future world. And the Sacred One - may he be blessed! - assigned me to be a prince and a ruler among the ministering angels.

"At that time three of the ministering angels, Uzza, Azza, and Azazel, came out and brought charges against me in the high heavens. They said in the presence of the Sacred One – may he be blessed! - "Didn't the First Ones rightly say in your presence, 'Do not create humans!'

"The Sacred One - may he be blessed! - answered them, 'I have made you and I will support you. I will carry you and I will rescue you.' (Isaiah 46 4.)

"As soon as they saw me, they said in his presence, 'Lord of the Universe! What right does this one have to ascend to the great heights? Isn't he one from among those who perished in the days of the Flood? What is he doing in the Raqia?'

"Again, the Sacred One - may he be blessed! - answered them, 'Who do you think you are, that you enter and speak in my presence! I am happier with this one than with all of you, and so he will be a prince and a ruler over you in the high heavens!'

"So then they all stood up and went out to meet me. They prostrated themselves before me and said, 'You are blessed and your father is blessed because your Creator favors you!'

"And because I am small and a youth in comparison with them with regard to days, months and years, this is the reason that they call me 'Youth.'"

5.

Ishmael said:

Metatron, the Prince of the Presence, said to me:

From the day when the Sacred One - may he be blessed! - expelled the first human from the Garden of Eden and thereafter, Shekinah was residing upon a Cherub under the Tree of Life, the ministering angels were gathering and going down from heaven in groups, from the Raqia in companies, and from the heavens in camps, to do his will throughout the whole world.

And the first human and the first human's people were sitting outside the gate of the Garden to look at the radiant appearance of the Shekinah. For the splendor of the Shekinah went over the world from one end to the other with a radiance 365,000 times that of the sun's orb.

No flies and no gnats rested on anyone who made use of the splendor of the Shekinah, and they did not become ill nor did they suffer any pain. No demons got power over them and they were not able to injure them.

When the Sacred One - may he be blessed! - went out and in from the Garden to Eden, from Eden to the Garden, from the Garden to Raqia and from Raqia to the Garden of Eden, then certainly everyone saw the splendor of his Shekinah, and they were not harmed, right up to the time of the generation of Enosh who was the chief of all idol worshipers of the world.

And what did the generation of Enosh do? They went from one end of the world to the other, and each one brought silver, gold, precious stones, and pearls in huge heaps like mountains and hills. They made idols out of them throughout the whole world. They erected the idols in every quarter of the world. The size of each idol was 1000 parasangs. They brought down the sun, the moon, planets and constellations, and placed them before the idols on their right hand and on their left, to attend them just as they attend the Sacred One – may he be blessed! - as it is written (1 Kings 22:19), "All the armies of heaven were standing next to him on his right hand and on his left."

What power did they have that they were able to bring them down? They would not have been able to bring them down but for Uzza, Azza, and Azazel, who taught them sorceries, by which means they brought them down and made use of them.

In that time the ministering angels brought charges against them before the Sacred One - may he be blessed! – and said in his presence, "Master of the World! What are you going to do with the humans?" As it is written (Psalm 8:4), "What is humankind, that you should notice them, human beings, that you should pay attention to them." Adam is not written here, but Enosh, for Enosh was the chief of the idol worshipers.

Commentary

"Enosh," humankind.

"Why have you left the Highest of the High heavens which are full of your splendor, and the high exalted Throne in high Abroth, and gone to live with the humans who worship idols and consider idols equal to you! Now you are on earth and so are the idols. What are you going to do with the inhabitants of the earth who worship idols?"

Then the Sacred One – may he be blessed! - took his Shekinah away from the earth, away from them.

At that moment the ministering angels arrived, the troops of armies, and the armies of Araboth. A thousand camps and ten thousand hosts arrived. They fetched trumpets and took the horns in their hands, and surrounded the Shekinah with all types of songs.

He ascended to the high heavens, as it is written (Psalm 47:5), "Elohim ascended amid a shout, Yahweh amid the sound of a ram's horn."

Commentary

Araboth. The semantic range includes desert region, the heavens, the plains.

6.

R. Ishmael said:

Metatron, the angel, the Prince of the Presence, said to me:

"When the Sacred One - may he be blessed! - wished to lift me up on high, he first sent Anaphiel the Prince. He took me from amongst them right in their sight. He carried me with great splendor on a fiery chariot with fiery horses. He lifted me up to the high heavens together with the Shekinah. As soon as I reached the high heavens, the Sacred Chayyoth, the Ophanin, the Seraphim, the Cherubim, the Wheels of the Merkabah (the Galgallim), and the ministers of the consuming fire, becoming aware of my smell from a distance of 365,000 times many thousands of parasangs, said, "What's that smell of one born of woman! What taste of a white drop of semen is this, that he ascends to the high heavens to minister among those who divide flames of fire!"

The Sacred One - may he be blessed! - answered

them, "My servants, my armies, my Cherubim, my Ophanin, my Seraphim! Do not be unhappy about this! Since all the humans have denied me and my great Kingdom and have taken up worshiping idols, I have removed my Shekinah from them and have lifted it up on high. But this one whom I have taken from among them is a chosen one among the inhabitants of the world! He is equal to all of them put together with regard to faith, justice and good deeds, and I have taken him as a tribute from my world under all the heavens."

7.

R. Ishmael said:

Metatron, the angel, the Prince of the Presence, said to me:

When the Sacred One - may he be blessed! - took me away from the generation of the Flood, he lifted me on the wings of the wind of Shekinah to the highest heaven and brought me into the great palaces of the high Araboth Raqia, where are the splendid Throne of Shekinah, the Merkabah, the angry troops, the vehement armies, the fiery flames, the troops of rage, the armies of vehemence, the fiery Shinanim, the flaming Cherubim, and the burning Ophanin, the flaming servants, the flashing Chashmattim and the lightning Seraphim.

He placed me there to attend the splendid Throne day after day.

8.

R. Ishmael said:

Metatron, the Prince of the Presence, said to me:

Before he appointed me to attend the Splendid Throne, the Sacred One - may he be blessed - opened to me

300,000 gates of understanding

300,000 gates of subtlety

300,000 gates of life

300,000 gates of kind favor

300,000 gates of love

300,000 gates of Torah

300,000 gates of gentleness

300,000 gates of protection

300,000 gates of compassion

300,000 gates of the respect for heaven.

At that time the Sacred One - may he be blessed! - added to me great wisdom, great understanding, great subtlety, great knowledge, great compassion, great instruction, great love, great kindness, great goodness, great gentleness, great power, great strength, great force, great brilliance, great beauty, great splendor, and I was honored and decorated with all these good, praiseworthy things more than all the inhabitants of heaven.

9.

R. Ishmael said:

Metatron, the Prince of the Presence, said to me:

After all these things, the Sacred One - may he be blessed! - put his hand on me and blessed me with 5360 blessings. I was lifted up to the size of the length and width of the world. He made 72 wings grow on me, 36 on each side. Each wing was like the whole world. He fixed 365 eyes on me. Each eye was like the great luminary. There was no kind of splendor, brilliance, radiance, or beauty in all of the lights of the universe that he did not fix on me.

10.

R. Ishmael said:

Metatron, the Prince of the Presence, said to me:

All these things the Sacred One - may he be blessed! - made for me: he made me a Throne, similar to the Splendid Throne, he spread over me a splendid curtain of brilliant appearance, of beauty, grace, and compassion, similar to the curtain of the splendid Throne, and on it all kinds of lights in the universe were fixed. He placed it at the door of the Seventh Hall and seated me on it.

The herald went out into every heaven, and said, "This is Metatron, my servant. I have made him a prince and a ruler over all the princes of my kingdoms and over all the inhabitants of heaven, with the exception of the eight great princes, the honored and revered ones who are called Yahweh, by the name of their King. Every angel and every prince who has something to say in my presence will go into his presence and shall speak to him instead. Every command that he gives you in my name, you are to observe and carry out. For I have committed the Prince of Wisdom and the Prince of Understanding to him to instruct him in the wisdom of heavenly things and earthly things, in the wisdom of this world and of the world to come. Furthermore, I have set him over all the treasuries of the palaces of Araboth and over all the stores of life that I have in the high heavens."

11.

R. Ishmael said:

Metatron, the angel, the Prince of the Presence, said to me:

The Sacred One - may he be blessed! - revealed to me all the mysteries of Torah, all the secrets of wisdom, all the depths of the complete Law and all living beings' thoughts in their minds. All the secrets of the universe and all the secrets of Creation were revealed to me just as they are revealed to the Maker of Creation.

I watched intently to observe the secrets of the depth and the wonderful mystery. Before a person thought something, I knew what the person was thinking. There was nothing above and there was nothing in the deep below that was hidden from me.

12.

R. Ishmael said:

Metatron, the Prince of the Presence, said to me:

By reason of the love with which the Sacred One – may he be blessed! - loved me more than all the inhabitants of heaven, he made me a splendid glorious garment and all kinds of lights were attached to it, and he dressed me in it. He made me a noble, honorable robe. All kinds of beauty, splendor, radiance, and magnificence were attached to it. He made me a royal crown, and 49 precious stones like the light of the sun's orb attached to it. Its radiance went out in the four quarters of the Araboth Raqia, and through the seven heavens, and in the four quarters of the world. He put it on my head. He called me "The Lesser Yahweh" in the presence of his entire heavenly household, as it is written (Exodus 23:21), "For my name is in him."

13.

R. Ishmael said:

Metatron, the angel, the Prince of the Presence, the splendor of all heavens, said to me:

By reason of the great love and compassion with which the Sacred One – may he be blessed! - loved and valued me more than all the inhabitants of heaven, he wrote the letters with his finger in a fiery style on the crown on my head by which heaven and earth, the seas and rivers, the mountains and hills, the planets and constellations, the lightning, winds, earthquakes and thunders, the snow and hail, the storms and the hurricanes were created - the letters by which all the earth's needs were created and all the orders of Creation.

Every single letter was sent out time after time as it were lightning, time after time as it were torches, time after time as it were flames of fire, time after time as it were the rising of the sun and the moon and the planets.

14.

R. Ishmael said:

Metatron, the angel, the Prince of the Presence, said to me:

When the Sacred One - may he be blessed! - put this crown on my head, then all the Princes of Kingdoms who are in the height of Araboth Raqia and all the hosts of every heaven trembled before me, and even the princes of the Elim, the princes of the Erellim and the princes of the Tafsarim, who are more important than all the ministering angels who minister before the Splendid Throne, shook with fear and trembled before me when they saw me.

Even Sammael, the Prince of the Accusers, who is more important than all the princes of kingdoms on high, was afraid and trembled before me. Even the angel of fire, the angel of hail, the angel of the wind, the angel of the lightning, the angel of anger, the angel of the thunder, the angel of the snow, the angel of the rain, the angel of the day, the angel of the night, the angel of the sun, the angel of the moon, the angel of the planets, and the angel of the constellations, who rule the world by their power, were afraid and trembled and were frightened of me, when they saw me.

These are the names of the rulers of the world: Gabriel, the angel of the fire, Baradiel, the angel of the hail, Ruchiel who is appointed over the wind, Baraqijal who is appointed over the lightnings, Zamiel who is appointed over the forcefulness, Zaqiel who is appointed over the sparks, Ziel who is appointed over the commotion, Zdaphiel who is appointed over the stormy wind, Ramiel who is appointed over the thunders, Rctashiel who is appointed over the earthquake, Shalgiel who is appointed over the snow, Matarel who is appointed over the rain, Shimshiel who is appointed over the day, Lailiel who is appointed over the night, Galgalliel who is appointed over the sun's orb, Ophanniel who is appointed over the moon's globe, Kokaqbiel who is appointed over the planets, and Rahatiel who is appointed over the constellations.

They all fell prostrate when they saw me. They were unable to look at me because of the majestic splendor and beautiful appearance of the shining light of the splendid crown on my head.

Commentary

Sammael

Alternate spellings: Samael, Samil. Sammael is an important angel in both Talmudic and post-Talmudic literature. Sammael has been regarded as both good and evil and as a seducer, accuser and destroyer. Sammael is said to be Esau's guardian angel, cf. Yalkut I, 110 of the Talmud; Sotah 10b; and also the angel of death. In *The Ascension of Moses* 4 he is described as the one who takes the souls away from people. In the *Sayings of Rabbi Eliezer*, he is said to be the one who tempted Eve. Eve was said to have become

pregnant by him, with the result being Cain. cf. Targ. Yer. to Gen. 4 1. As a good angel, Samael resides in the seventh heaven, and he is also the chief angel of the fifth heaven. See also Brecher, Das Transcendentale, Magie, und Magische Heilarten in Talmud, pp. 40-44, Vienna, 1850.

Baraqijal

Alternate spellings: Baraqiel, Baraqel, Barakiel, Barkiel. Named here as the angel of lightning. Baraqiel is named in the Book of Enoch (1 Enoch) as one of the Watchers who was a leader of a group of Ten Watchers, and was also one of the fallen Watchers. 1 Enoch states that Baraqijal taught humans astrology.

Zaqiel

Zaqiel, alternate spellings: Ziqiel, Zeqiel. Named here as the angel of sparks. Zaqiel is also named in the Book of Enoch (1 Enoch) as one of the Watchers who was a leader of a group of Ten Watchers, and was also one of the fallen Watchers.

Ramiel

Alternate name Remiel. Ramiel is also named in

the Book of Enoch (1 Enoch) as one of the Watchers who was a leader of a group of Ten Watchers, and was also one of the fallen Watchers.

Matariel

Alternate spellings Matarel, Armaros (1 Enoch). Matariel (under alternate spelling Armaros) is also named in the Book of Enoch (1 Enoch) as one of the Watchers who was a leader of a group of Ten Watchers, and was also one of the fallen Watchers.

Lailiel

Alternate spellings Leliel, Layla, Lailah, Lailahel. Layil is the Hebrew word for "night." Book 3, 199 (and 349) of *The Zohar* states that the blossoms on the Tree of Life in Paradise are souls which fall into the Treasury of Souls. The angel Gabriel reaches into the Treasury of Souls and takes out the first soul he comes to. After that Lailah, the Angel of Conception, protects the embryo until it is born. *B. Niddah* 16b.

Kokaqbiel

Alternate spellings Kokbiel, Kokabiel, Kokabel.

Kokaqbiel is also named in the Book of Enoch (1 Enoch) as one of the Watchers who was a leader of a group of Ten Watchers, and was also one of the fallen Watchers. 1 Enoch states that Kokaqbiel taught humans the constellations.

15.

R. Ishmael said:

Metatron, the angel, the Prince of the Presence, the splendor of all heavens, said to me:

As soon as the Sacred One - may he be blessed! - took me in his service to attend the Splendid Throne and the Wheels (Galgallim) of the Merkabah and the needs of Shekinah, at once my flesh was changed into flames, my sinews into flaming fire, my bones into coals of burning juniper, the light of my eyelids into the splendor of lightning, my eyeballs into fire-brands, the hair of my head into flames, all my limbs into wings of burning fire and the whole of my body into glowing fire. On my right were divisions of fiery flames and on my left fire-brands were burning. Around about me storm winds and hurricanes were blowing, and in front of me and behind me thunder roared with an earthquake.

15b – an addition occurring in two texts.

R. Ishmael said,

Metatron, the Prince of the Presence and the prince of all princes, stands before him who is greater than all the Elohim. He goes in under the Splendid Throne. He has a great tabernacle of light on high. He brings out the fire of deafness and puts it into the ears of the Sacred Chayyoth, so that they are not able to hear the voice of the Word (Dibbur) that goes out of the Divine Majesty's mouth.

When Moses ascended on high, he fasted 121 fasts, until the Fragment of habitation of the Chashmal was opened for him, and he saw that it was as white as the heart of the Lion, and he saw the innumerable companies of the hosts around him. They wished to burn him, but Moses prayed for compassion, first for Israel and after that for himself. He who sits on the Merkabah opened the windows that are above the heads of the Cherubim. A host of 1800 advocates and the Prince of the Presence, Metatron, along with them went out to meet Moses. They took the prayers of Israel and put them as a crown on the head of the Sacred One – may he be blessed! - and they said (Deuteronomy 6:4), "Israel, hear this! Yahweh Elohim, Yahweh is one!

Commentary

The Chashmal (Hashmal)

Maimonides stated that the Chashmal is an angel who is sometimes silent but sometimes speaks on the basis that the word Chashmal refers to both silence and speech. Mishneh Torah: Hilchot Yesodei HaTorah 1981. Tr. Eliyahu Touger. New York: Moznaim. 2:7. 166-168. The Book of

Ezekiel mentions Chashmal three times, Ezekiel 1:4, 27; 8:2. Ezekiel 1:4 states, "As I looked, I saw a stormy wind coming out of the north, and a huge cloud, with brightness around it, with continual fire flashing. A radiance was all around it and came out of the midst of the fire like *Chashmal*." (Chashmal in this verse is usually translated in Bible versions as glowing/gleaming amber, gleaming metal.)

The face of Shekinah shone and was happy, and they said to Metatron, "What are these? To whom do they give all this honor and credit?"

They answered, "To the Splendid Yahweh of Israel!"

They said, "Israel, hear this! Yahweh the Living and Eternal!"

At that moment Akatriel Yah Yehod Sebaoth said to Metatron, the Prince of the Presence, "Let no prayer that he prays before me return to him void. Hear his prayer and fulfil his desire whether it be big or small."

At once Metatron, the Prince of the Presence, said to Moses, "Son of Amram! Do not be afraid, for now Yahweh is delighted with you. Ask what you want of the Splendor and Magnificence. Your face shines from one end of the world to the other!"

But Moses answered him, "I am afraid that I may bring guilt upon myself."

Metatron said to him, "Receive the letters of the oath, which preclude any breach of the covenant."

16.

R. Ishmael said:

Metatron, the angel, the Prince of the Presence, the splendor of all heaven, said to me:

At first I was sitting on a great Throne at the door of the Seventh Hall, and I was judging the inhabitants of heaven, the household on high, by the authority of the Sacred One – may he be blessed! - and I divided Greatness, Kingship, Dignity, Rulership, honor and Praise, and Diadem and Splendid Crown to all the princes of kingdoms, while I was presiding in the Celestial Court (Yeshiba), and the princes of kingdoms were standing before me, on my right and on my left by authority of the Sacred One – may he be blessed!

But when Acher came to see the vision of the Merkabah and fixed his eyes on me, he was afraid and trembled before me, and his whole self was afraid to the point that he felt he would die from fear, horror, and dread of me, when he saw me sitting on a throne like a king with all the ministering angels standing by me as my servants and all the princes of kingdoms adorned with crowns surrounding me. At that moment he opened his mouth and said, "Indeed, there are two Divine Powers in heaven!" At once Bath Qol (the Divine Voice) went out from heaven from before the Shekinah and said, "Come back to me, you wayward people." - (Jeremiah 3: 22) except Acher!"

Then Aniyel the Prince came, the honored, adored, loved, wonderful, respected and fearful one, in commission from the Sacred One – may he be blessed! - and gave me sixty strokes with lashes of fire and made me stand on my feet.

Commentary

Acher. 157. "Other." The Talmud states that Elisha ben Abuyah was also called Acher, 'Other," as he became an apostate. The Talmud states that Acher entered Paradise and saw Metatron sitting down in heaven, an act permitted only to the Divine himself. Acher thus considered Metatron to be a deity and exclaimed, "Indeed, there are two powers in heaven!" The rabbis explain that the reason that Metatron was allowed to sit was due to his function as Scribe, writing down Israel's deeds, cf. *Babylonian Talmud*, *Hagiga* 15a.

17.

R. Ishmael said:

Metatron, the angel, the Prince of the Presence, the splendor of all heavens, said to me:

There are seven princes, the great, beautiful, respected, wonderful and honored ones who are appointed over the seven heavens. These are their names: Michael, Gabriel, Shatquiel, Baradiel, Shachaqiel, Baraqiel and Sidril.

Each one of them is the prince of the hosts of one

heaven. Each one of them is accompanied by 496,000 multitudes of ministering angels.

Michael, the great prince, is appointed over the seventh heaven, the highest one, which is in the Araboth.

Gabriel, the prince of the host, is appointed over the sixth heaven which is in Makon.

Shataqiel, prince of the host, is appointed over the fifth heaven which is in Maon.

Shahaqiel, prince of the host, is appointed over the fourth heaven which is in Zebul.

Badariel, prince of the host, is appointed over the third heaven which is in Shehaqim.

Barakiel, prince of the host, is appointed over the second heaven which is at the height of (Merom) Raqia.

Pazriel, prince of the host, is appointed over the first heaven which is in Wilon, which is in Shamayim.

Under them is Galgalliel, the prince who is appointed over sun's orb, and with him are 96 great and honored angels who move the sun in Raqia. Under them is Ophaniel, the prince who is set over the moon's orb. With him are 88 angels who move the moon's orb 354 thousand parasangs every night at the time when the moon stands in the East at its turning point. And when is the moon sitting in the East at its turning point? Answer: in the fifteenth day of every month.

Under them is Rahatiel, the prince who is appointed over the constellations. He is accompanied by 72 great and honored angels. And why is he called Rahatiel?

Because he makes the stars run in their orbits and courses for 339 thousand parasangs every night from the East to the West and from the West to the East. For the Sacred One - may he be blessed! - has made a place for all of them, for the sun, the moon, the planets and the stars in which they travel at night from the West to the East.

Under them is Kokbiel, the prince who is appointed over all the planets. With him are 365,000 multitudes of ministering angels, great and honored ones who move the planets from city to city and from province to province in the Raqia of heavens. Over them are 72 princes of kingdoms on high corresponding to the 72 languages of the world. All of them are crowned with royal crowns, dressed in royal clothes, and wrapped in royal cloaks. All of them are riding royal horses and are holding royal scepters in their hands. And when he is traveling in Raqia, before each one of them royal servants are running with great splendor and magnificence, and in front of every one of them when traveling in Raqia, there are great armies, such as is the custom on earth, with great splendid chariots, and praise, song, and honor.

18.

R. Ishmael said:

Metatron, the angel, the Prince of the Presence, the splendor of all heaven, said to me:

The angels of the first heaven dismount from their horses and fall on their faces, whenever they see their prince. Whenever the prince of the first heaven sees the prince of the second heaven, he dismounts, removes the splendid crown from his head and falls on his face.

When the prince of the second heaven sees the prince of the third heaven, he removes the splendid crown from his head and falls on his face.

When the prince of the third heaven sees the prince of the fourth heaven, he removes the splendid crown from his head and falls on his face.

When the prince of the fourth heaven sees the prince of the fifth heaven, he removes the splendid crown from his head and falls on his face.

When the prince of the fifth heaven sees the prince of the sixth heaven, he removes the splendid crown from his head and falls on his face.

When the prince of the sixth heaven sees the prince of the seventh heaven, he removes the splendid crown from his head and falls on his face.

When the prince of the seventh heaven sees the 72 princes of kingdoms, he removes the splendid crown from his head and falls on his face.

When the 72 princes of kingdoms see the door keepers of the first hall in the Araboth Raqia, they remove the splendid crown from their head and fall on their faces.

When the door keepers of the first hall see the door keepers of the second hall, they remove the splendid crown from their head and fall on their faces.

When the door keepers of the second hall see the

door keepers of the third hall, they remove the splendid crown from their head and fall on their faces.

When the door keepers of the third hall see the door keepers of the fourth hall, they remove the splendid crown from their head and fall on their faces.

When the door keepers of the fourth hall see the door keepers of the fifth hall, they remove the splendid crown from their head and fall on their faces.

When the door keepers of the fifth hall see the door keepers of the sixth hall, they remove the splendid crown from their head and fall on their faces.

When the door keepers of the sixth hall see the door keepers of the seventh hall, they remove the splendid crown from their head and fall on their faces.

When the door keepers of the seventh hall see the four great princes, the honored ones who have been appointed over the four camps of Shekinah, they remove the splendid crown from their head and fall on their faces.

When the four great princes see Tagas, the prince who is greatly honored with praise songs, at the head of all the inhabitants of heaven, they remove the splendid crown from their head and fall on their faces.

When Tagas, the greatly honored prince, sees Baratiel, the great prince of three fingers in the height of Araboth, the highest heaven, he removes the splendid crown from his head and falls on his face.

When Baratiel, the great prince, sees Hamon, the great prince who is frightening and honored, pleasant yet terrible one who causes all the inhabitants of heaven to tremble, when the time is set for the saying of the 'Three-Times Sacred', as it is written (Isa. 33:3), "The nations run away at the sound of a tumult. The nations scatter when you lift yourself up!", he removes the splendid crown from his head and falls on his face.

When Hamon, the great prince, sees Tutresiel, the great prince, he removes the splendid crown from his head and falls on his face.

When Tutresiel, the great prince, sees Atrugiel, the great prince, he removes the splendid crown from his head and falls on his face.

When Atrugiel, the great prince, sees Naaririel, the great prince, he removes the splendid crown from his head and falls on his face.

When Naaririel, the great prince, sees Sasnigiel, the great prince, he removes the splendid crown from his head and falls on his face.

When Sasnigiel sees Zazriel, the great prince, he removes the splendid crown from his head and falls on his face.

When Zazriel, the prince, sees Geburatiel, the prince, he removes the splendid crown from his head and falls on his face.

When Geburatiel, the prince, sees Araphiel, the prince, he removes the splendid crown from his head and falls on his face.

When Araphiel, the prince, sees Ashruylu, the prince, who presides in all the sessions of the inhabitants of heaven, he removes the splendid crown from his head and falls on his face.

When Ashruylu, the prince, sees Gallisur, the prince, who reveals all the secrets of the Torah, he removes the splendid crown from his head and falls on his face.

When Gallisur, the prince, sees Zakzakiel, the prince who is appointed to write down the good points of Israel on the Splendid Throne, he removes the splendid crown from his head and falls on his face.

When Zakzakiel, the great prince, sees Anaphiel, the prince who keeps the keys of the heavenly Halls, he removes the splendid crown from his head and falls on his face.

Why is he called by the name Anaphiel? Because the office of his honor and magnificence and his splendid crown and his brilliance overshadow all the chambers of Araboth Raqia on high just as the Creator of the World overshadows them. Just as it is written with regard to the Creator of the World (Habakkuk 3:3), "His splendor covers the skies, his praise fills the earth," just as the honor and magnificence of Anaphiel cover all the spendors of Araboth the highest.

When he sees Sother Ashiel, the prince, the great, respected, and honored one, he removes the splendid crown from his head and falls on his face. Why is he called Sother Ashiel? Because he is appointed over the four heads of the fiery river over against the Splendid Throne, and every single prince who goes out or enters before the Shekinah, goes out or enters only by his permission, as the seals of the fiery river are entrusted to him. Furthermore, his height is 7000 myriads of parasangs. He stirs up the fire of the river, and he goes out and enters before the Shekinah to explain what is recorded about the inhabitants of the world. As it is written (Daniel 7:10), "The court convened and the books were opened."

When Sother Ashiel, the prince, sees Shoqed Chozi, the great prince, the mighty, terrible, and honored one, he removes the splendid crown from his head and falls on his face. Why is he called Shoqed Chozi? Because he weighs all the merits in a balance in the presence of the Sacred One – may he be blessed!

When he sees Zehanpuryu, the great prince, the mighty and frightening one, honored, praised and feared in the whole heavenly household, he removes the splendid crown from his head and falls on his face. Why is he called Zehanpuryu? Because he rebukes the fiery river and pushes it back to its place.

When he sees Azbuga, the great prince, glorified, revered, honored, adorned, wonderful, exalted, loved, and feared among all the great princes who know the mystery of the Splendid Throne, he removes the splendid crown from his head and falls on his face. Why is he called Azbuga? Because in the future he will clothe the just and dutiful of the world with the garments of life and wrap them in the cloak of life, in order to give them eternal life.

When he sees the two great princes, the strong and exalted ones who are standing above him, he removes the splendid crown from his head and falls on his face. Here are the names of the two princes: Sopheriel the Killer, the great prince, the honored, exalted, blameless, venerable, ancient and mighty one, and Sopheriel the Lifegiver, the great prince, the honored, exalted, blameless, ancient and mighty one.

Why is he called Sopheriel the Killer? Because he is appointed over the books of the dead, and writes the name of the person about to die in the books of the dead.

Why is he called Sopheriel the Lifegiver? Because he is appointed over the books of life, so that every one whom the Sacred One - may he be blessed! - will bring into life - he writes their name in the book of life, by authority of Maqom (the Divine Majesty). You may say, perhaps "Since the Sacred One - may he be blessed! - is sitting on a throne, they also are sitting when writing." This is the answer: The Scripture teaches us (1 Kings 22: 19, 2 Chronicles 18:18), "All the heavenly army are standing behind him."

Even the Great Princes, and there are none like them in the high heavens, only fulfil the requests of the Shekinah when standing. How is it possible that they are able to write, when they are standing? This is how: one is standing on the wheels of the hurricane and the other is standing on the wheels of the stormy wind. The one is dressed in kingly garments, and the other is dressed in kingly garments. The one is dressed in a majestic cloak and the other is wrapped in a majestic cloak. The one is crowned with a royal crown, and the other is crowned with a royal crown. The one's body is full of eyes, and the other's body is full of eyes. The appearance of one is like that of lightning, and the appearance of the other is like that of lightning. The eyes of the one are like the sun at its strength, and the eyes of the other are like the sun at its strength. The one's height is like the height of the seven heavens, and the other's height is like the height of the seven heavens. The wings of the one are as many as the days of the year, and the wings of the other are as many as the days of the year. The wings of the one extend over the breadth of Raqia, and the wings of the other extend over the breadth of Raqia. The lips of the one are like the gates of the East, and the lips of the other are like the gates of the East. The tongue of the one is as high as the waves of the sea, and the tongue of the other is as high as the waves of the sea. From the mouth of the one a flame goes out, and from the mouth of the other a flame goes out. From the mouth of the one lightning goes out and from the mouth of the other lightning goes out. From the sweat of the one fire is kindled, and from the sweat of the other fire is kindled. From the tongue of one a torch is burning, and from the tongue of the other a torch is burning. On the head of the one there is a sapphire stone, and on the head of the other there is a sapphire stone. On the shoulders of the one there is a wheel of a swift cherub, and on the shoulders of the other there is a wheel of a swift cherub. One has in their hand a burning scroll, the other has in their hand a burning scroll. The one has in their hand a fiery stylus, the other has in their hand a fiery stylus.

The length of the scroll is 3000 myriads of parasangs, and the size of the stylus is 3000 myriads of parasangs. The size of every single letter that they write is 365 parasangs.

19.

R. Ishmael said:

Metatron, the angel, the Prince of the Presence, said to me:

Above these three angels, these great princes, there is one Prince, distinguished, honored, noble, exalted, adorned, fearful, courageous, strong, great, praised, splendid, crowned, wonderful, exalted, blameless, loved, lordly, high and superior, ancient and mighty, and there is no one like him among the princes. His name is Rikbiel, the great and revered prince who is standing by the Merkabah.

Why is he called Rikbiel? Because he is appointed over the wheels of the Merkabah, and they are given to his charge. How many wheels are there? Eight; two in each direction. There are four winds encompassing them. Here are their names: "The Stormy Wind," "The Tempest," "The Strong Wind," and "The Earthquake Wind." Under them four fiery rivers are continually running, one fiery river on each side. Around them, between the rivers, four clouds are placed. They are: "clouds of fire," "clouds of lamps," "clouds of coal," "clouds of brimstone," and they are standing against their wheels.

The feet of the Chayyoth are resting on the wheels. Between one wheel and the other, earthquake is roaring, and thunder is thundering. When the time approaches for the recital of the Song, then the multitudes of wheels are moved, the multitude of clouds tremble, all the chiefs are made afraid, all the horse riders rage, all the mighty ones are excited, all the hosts are afraid, all the troops are fearful, all the appointed ones hurry away, all the princes and armies are dismayed, all the servants faint and all the angels and divisions travail with pain.

One wheel makes a sound to be heard to the other and one Cherub to another, one Chayya to another, one Seraph to another saying, (Psalm 68.4), "Sing to Elohim, sing praises to his name. Acclaim the one who rides on the clouds, for Yahweh is that one's name."

20.

R. Ishmael said:

Metatron, the angel, the Prince of the Presence, said to me:

Above these there is one great and mighty prince. His name is Chayyliel, a noble and revered prince, a superb, mighty prince, a greatly respected and revered prince, a prince before whom all the inhabitants of heaven tremble, a prince who is able to swallow up the whole earth in one moment. Why is he called Chayyliel?

Because he is appointed over the Sacred Chayyoth and smites the Chayyoth with lashes of fire, and exalts them, and when they offer magnificent praise and exultation, he causes them to hurry to say "Sacred" and "Blessed be the Splendor of Yahweh from his place!"

21.

R. Ishmael said:

Metatron, the angel, the Prince of the Presence, said to me:

There are four Chayyoth corresponding to the four winds. Each Chayya is like the space of the whole world. Each one has four faces, and each face is like the face of the East. Each one has four wings and each wing is like the roof of the universe. Each one has faces in the middle of faces and wings in the middle of wings. The size of the faces is like the size of 248 faces, and the size of the wings is like the size of 365 wings. Every one is crowned with 2000 crowns on his head. Each crown is like the rainbow in the cloud. Its splendor is like the splendor of the sun's orb. The sparks that go out from every one are like the splendor of the morning star in the East.

22.

R. Ishmael said:

Metatron, the angel, the Prince of the Presence, said to me:

Above these there is one prince, dignified, wonderful, strong, and praised with all kinds of praise. His name is Kerubiel, a mighty prince, full of strength and power, a high prince, and with him is a just prince who is very just, and with him is a sacred prince who is very sacred, and with him is a prince praised by a thousand hosts, praised by ten thousand armies.

At his wrath the earth trembles, at his anger the camps are moved and the foundations are shaken from fear of him, at his rebuke the Araboth tremble. His physique is full of burning coals. The height of his physique is like the height of the seven heavens. The breadth of his physique is like the breadth of the seven heavens and the depth of his physique is like the seven heavens.

The opening of his mouth is like a flaming lamp of fire. His tongue is a consuming fire. His eyebrows are like the splendor of the lightning. His eyes are like brilliant sparks. His appearance is like a burning fire.

There is a sacred crown on his head and on that crown the Explicit Name is engraved, and lightning goes out from it. The bow of Shekinah is between his shoulders. His sword is like lightning, on his hips are arrows like flames, a consuming fire is on his armor, and on his neck are coals of burning juniper, and also coals of juniper are all around him.

The splendor of Shekinah is on his face, the majestic power of magnificence is on his wheels, and a royal circlet is on his skull. His body is full of eyes. Wings cover the whole of his high physique. A flame is burning at his right hand, a fire is glowing at his left hand, and coals are burning from it. Fire-brands go out from his body. Lightnings are cast out from his face. With him there is always thunder upon thunder, by his side there is always earthquake upon earthquake. The two princes of the Merkabah are with him.

Why is he called Kerubiel, the Prince? Because he is appointed over the chariot of the Cherubim. The mighty Cherubim are given to his charge. He decorates the crowns on their heads and polishes the circlets on their skulls.

He praises their magnificent appearance. He praises their majestic beauty. He increases their great honor. He causes the song of their praise to be sung. He intensifies their beautiful strength. He causes their brilliant splendor to shine. He beautifies their goodly compassion and loving kindness. He frames the fairness of their radiance. He makes their merciful beauty even more beautiful. He praises their just magnificence.

He commends the order of their praise, to establish the dwelling place of him who dwells on the Cherubim. Cherubim are standing by the Sacred Chayyoth, and their wings are raised up to their heads. Shekinah is resting upon them, the brilliant Splendor is on their faces, praise song is in their mouth, their hands are under their wings, their feet are covered by their wings and splendid horns are on their heads, the splendor of Shekinah is on their face and Shekinah is resting on them. There are sapphire stones around them, columns of fire on their four sides and columns of fire-brands beside them. There is one sapphire on one side and another sapphire on another side. Under the sapphires are coals of burning juniper.

One Cherub is standing in each direction but the wings of the Cherubim extend above their splendid skulls, and they spread them to sing a song to him that inhabits the clouds and to praise the fearful magnificence of the king of kings.

Kerubiel, the prince who is appointed over them, dresses them in attractive, beautiful, and pleasant orders and praises them with all manner of acclaim, dignity and splendor. He splendidly hurries them along to do the will of their Creator every moment. The splendor of the high king who lives on the Cherubim lives continually above their lofty heads.

22b.

R. Ishmael said to me,

Metatron, the angel, the Prince of the Presence, said to me,

How are the angels standing on high?

He said, "Like a bridge that is placed over a river so that everyone can pass over it, a bridge is placed from the entry to the end. Three ministering angels surround it and sing a song to Yahweh of Israel. Standing in front of it are masters of dread and captains of fear, many tens of thousands in number, and they sing praise songs to Yahweh of Israel, (OR - and there is a court before the splendid Throne, which no seraph or angel can enter, and it is 36,000 myriads of parasangs, and as it is written, "Seraphs stood above him." (Isaiah 6:2.)

Numerous bridges are there - fiery bridges and numerous bridges of hail. There are also numerous rivers of hail, numerous treasures of snow and numerous wheels of fire.

Commentary

Textual variation: There are 36 bridges there.

How many ministering angels are there? 12,000 myriads: 6,000 myriads above and 6,000 myriads below. There are 12,000 myriads of snow, 6,000 above and 6,000 below. There are 24,000 myriads of wheels of fire, 12,000 above and 12,000 below. They surround the bridges and the rivers of fire and the rivers of hail. There are numerous ministering angels forming entries, because all the creatures are standing in their midst, over against the paths of Raqia Shamayim.

Commentary

Textual variation: There are 24 myriads of wheels of fire. There are 12,000 myriads of ministering angels. There are 12,000 rivers of hail, and 12,000 storehouses of snow. In the seven Halls are chariots of fire and flames without number.

Why does Yahweh of Israel, the splendid King, the great fearful God, mightily strong, cover his face? In

Araboth are 660,000 myriads of splendid angels standing over against the Splendid Throne and the divisions of flaming fire. The splendid King covers his face; if he did not, then the Araboth Raqia would be ripped apart in its midst because of the majesty, splendor, beauty, radiance, loveliness, brilliancy, brightness and excellence of the appearance of the Sacred One – may he be blessed!

There are numerous ministering angels performing his will, numerous kings, numerous princes in the delightful Araboth, angels who are revered among the rulers in heaven, distinguished, adorned with song and bringing love to mind, who are frightened of the splendor of the Shekinah, and their eyes are dazzled by the shining beauty of their King. Their faces darken and their strength fails.

From there go out joyful rivers, happy streams, elated rivers, triumphant streams, rivers of love, and streams of friendship. They flow over and go out in front of the Splendid Throne, become larger and go through the gates of the paths of Araboth Raqia at the voice of the shouting and music of the Chayyoth, at the voice of the delight of the timbrels of his Ophanin, and at the melody of the cymbals of his Cherubim. And they become larger and go out with commotion and the sound of the praise song, "Sacred, sacred, sacred is Yahweh who commands armies, the whole earth is full of his splendor!"

22C.

R. Ishmael said:

Metatron, the Prince of the Presence said to me:

What is the distance between one bridge and another? 12 myriads of parasangs. Their ascent is 12 myriads of parasangs, and their descent 12 myriads of parasangs. The distance between the rivers of dread and the rivers of fear is 22 myriads of parasangs; between the rivers of hail and the rivers of darkness 36 myriads of parasangs; between the chambers of lightnings and the clouds of compassion 42 myriads of parasangs; between the clouds of compassion and the Merkabah myriads of parasangs; between the Merkabah and the Cherubim 48 myriads of parasangs; between the Cherubim and the Ophanin 24 myriads of parasangs; between the Ophanin and the chambers of chambers 24 myriads of parasangs; between the chambers of chambers and the sacred Chayyoth 40,000 myriads of parasangs; between one wing of the Chayyoth and another 12 myriads of parasangs; and the breadth of each one wing is of that same measure; and the distance between the Sacred Chayyoth and the Splendid Throne is 30,000 myriads of parasangs. From the foot of the Throne to the seat there are 40,000 myriads of parasangs. The name of him is seated on it: - may the name be praised! The arches of the bow are set above the Araboth, and they are 1000 thousands and 10,000 times ten thousands of parasangs high. Their length is like the length of the Irin and Qaddishin (Sacred Watchers).

Commentary

Irin and Qaddishin, Aramaic, also in Daniel 4:13 and 23. The *Septuagint* translates the word there as *hagion*, "a sacred one." Irin and Qaddishin, "Watchers and Sacred Ones," generally considered to be hendiadys, thus, "Sacred Watchers."

As it is written (Genesis 9:13), "I have placed my bow in the cloud." It is not written here "I will set" but "I have set", that is, already: clouds that surround the Splendid Throne. As his clouds pass by, the angels of hail turn into burning coal. A fire of the voice goes down from by the Sacred Chayyoth. Because of the breath of that voice they run (Ezekiel 1:14) to another place, being afraid that it may command them to go, and they return for fear that it may harm them from the other side. Therefore, "they move backward and forwards." (Ezekiel 1:14).

These arches of the Bow are more beautiful and radiant than the radiance of the sun during the summer solstice. They are whiter than flaming fire and they are very beautiful. Above the arches of the Bow are the wheels of the Ophanin. Their height is 1000 thousand and 10,000 times 10,000 units of measure after the measure of the Seraphim and the troops.

23.

R. Ishmael said:

Metatron, the angel, the Prince of the Presence, said to me:

There are numerous winds blowing under the wings of the Cherubim. There blows "the Incubating Spirit/Breath/Wind," as it is written (Genesis 1:2), "and the spirit/breath/wind of Elohim was incubating over the face of the water."

Commentary

***Ruwach*, spirit, breath, or wind, air. Translated by the Septuagint as *pneuma*, which has the same semantic range as the Hebrew: spirit, breath, wind, air.**

There blows "the Strong Wind," as it is said (Exodus 14:21), "Yahweh drove the sea apart by a strong east wind all that night."

There blows "the East Wind," as it is written (Exodus 10:13), "and the east wind had brought up the locusts".

There blows "the Wind of Quails," "as it is written (Numbers 11:31), "Now Yahweh sent a wind that brought quail."

There blows "the Wind of Jealousy," as it is written (Numbers 5:14), "And the wind of jealousy came over him."

There blows the "Wind of Earthquake," as it is written (1 Kings 19:11), "After the stormy wind there was an earthquake, but the Lord was not in the earthquake."

There blows the "Wind of Yahweh," as it is written (Exodus 37:1), "And he carried me out by the wind of Yahweh and set me down."

There blows the "Evil Wind," as it is written (1 Samuel 16:23), "And the evil wind/spirit would leave him alone."

There blow the "Wind of Wisdom," the "Wind of Understanding," the "Wind of Knowledge," and the "Wind of the respect of Yahweh" as it is written (Isaiah 11:2), "The spirit of Yahweh will rest on him—the spirit of wisdom and understanding, the spirit of guidance and power, the spirit of knowledge and of the respect of Yahweh."

There blows the "Wind of Rain," as it is written (Proverbs 25:23), "A north wind brings rain."

There blows the "Wind of Lightnings," as it is written (Jeremiah 10:13, 51:16), "He sends lightning with the rain and brings out the wind from his storehouses."

There blows the "Wind, Breaking the Rocks," as it is written (1 Kings 19:11), "In the presence of Yahweh a very powerful wind tore away the mountains and broke the cliffs."

There blows the "Wind of Subsiding of the Sea," as it is written (Genesis 8:1), "Elohim made a wind pass over the earth and the waters subsided."

There blows the "Wind of Anger," as it is written (Job 1:19), "Suddenly a powerful wind blew in from the desert and struck the four corners of the house and it collapsed."

There blows the "Stormy Wind," as it is written (Psalm 148:8), "Stormy wind that does Yahweh's word."

The adversary is standing among these winds, for "stormy wind" is nothing else but an adversary, and all these winds only blow under the wings of the Cherubim, as it is written (Psalm 18:10), "He rode upon a cherub and flew, he appeared on the wings of the wind."

And where do all these all these winds go? The Scripture teaches us that they go out from under the wings of the Cherubim and descend on the sun's orb, as it is written (Ecclesiastes 1:6), "The wind goes to the south and circles around to the north. The wind goes round and round continually on its course and returns."

They return from the sun's orb and descend upon the rivers and the seas, upon the mountains and upon the hills, as it is written (Amos 4:13), "The one who formed the mountains and created the wind."

They return from the mountains and the hills and descend to the seas and the rivers; and they return from the seas and the rivers and descend upon the cities and provinces; and they return from the cities and provinces and descend into the Garden, and they return from the garden and descend to Eden, as it is written (Genesis 3:8), "Walking in the garden in the wind of the day." In the middle of the garden they collect and blow from one side to the other, and are perfumed with the spices of the garden even from its most remote parts, until they separate from each other, and, filled with the scent of the pure spices, they bring the scent from the most remote parts of Eden and the spices of the garden to the just and devout who in future times will inherit the Garden of Eden and the Tree of Life, as it is written (Songs 4:16), "Awake, north wind, and come, south wind! Blow on my garden, so that its fragrant spices may flow. May my lover come into his garden and taste its choice fruits."

Commentary

"In the wind of the day." This expression means "cool of the day."

24.

R. Ishmael said:

Metatron, the angel, the Prince of the Presence, the splendor of all heaven, said to me:

The Sacred One – may he be blessed! - has numerous chariots. He has the "Chariots of the Cherubim," as it is written (Psalm 18:10, 2 Samuel 22:11), "He rode upon a cherub and flew."

He has the "Chariots of Wind," as it is written (Psalm 18:10.), "and he flew swiftly upon the wings of the wind."

He has the "Chariots of (the) Swift Cloud," as it is written, (Isaiah 19:1), "The Lord rides on a swift cloud."

He has "the Chariots of Clouds," as it is written

(Exodus 19: 9), "I am going to come to you in a thick cloud."

He has the "Chariots of the Altar," as it is written (Amos 9:1), "I saw Adonai standing by the Altar."

He has the "Chariots of Myriads," as it is written (Psalm 68:17), "Elohim's chariots are tens of thousands, thousands and thousands."

He has the "Chariots of the Tent," as it is written (Deuteronomy 31:15), "Yahweh appeared in the Tent in a pillar of cloud."

He has the "Chariots of the Tabernacle," as it is written (Lev. 1:1), "Yahweh spoke to him from the Meeting Tent."

He has the "Chariots of the Compassion-Seat," as it is written (Numbers 7:89), "He heard the voice speaking to him from above the atonement cover on the ark of the Testimony."

He has the "Chariots of Sapphire Stone," as it is written (Exodus 24:10), "Under his feet was something like a pavement made of sapphire."

He has the Chariots of Eagles," as it is written (Exodus 19:4), "I lifted you on eagles' wings."

He has the "Chariots of Shout," as it is written (Psalm 47:5), "Elohim ascended amid a shout."

He has the "Chariots of Araboth," as it is written (Psalm 68:4), "Sing to Elohim, sing praises to his name. Acclaim the one who rides on the Araboth."

He has the "Chariots of Thick Clouds," as it is

written (Psalm 104:3), "Yahweh makes the thick clouds a chariot."

He has the "Chariots of the Chayyoth," as it is written (Ezekiel 1:14), "The Chayyoth sped backward and forwards." They go backward and forwards by permission, for Shekinah is above their heads.

He has the "Chariots of Whirling Wheels (Galgallim)," as it is written (Ezekiel 10:2), "He said, 'Go in between the whirling wheels.'"

At the time when he rides on a swift cherub, as he sets one of his feet upon him, before he sets the other foot upon his back, he looks through 18,000 worlds at one glance. He discerns and sees into them all. He knows what is in all of them. He then sets down the other foot upon him, as it is written (Ezekiel 48:35), "Around 18,000."

How do we know that he looks through every one of them every day? It is written (Psalm 14:2), "Yahweh looks down from heaven at the human race, to see if there is anyone who acts wisely and seeks Elohim."

He has the "Chariots of the Ophanin," as it is written (Ezekiel 10:12), "The Ophanin were full of eyes all around them."

He has the "Chariots of his Sacred Throne," as it is written (Psalm 47:8), "Elohim sits on his sacred throne!"

He has the "Chariots of the Throne of Yah," as it is written (Exodus 17:16), "For a hand was lifted up to the throne of Yahweh."

He has the "Chariots of the Throne of Judgment,"

as it is written (Isaiah 5:16), "Yahweh who commands armies will be lifted on high when he judges."

He has the "Chariots of the Splendid Throne," as it is written (Jeremiah 17:12), "From the beginning the place of our sanctuary has been the Splendid Throne on high."

He has the "Chariots of the High and Exalted Throne," as it is written (Isaiah 6:1), "I saw Adonai sitting on the high exalted throne."

25.

R. Ishmael said:

Metatron, the angel, the Prince of the Presence, said to me:

Above these there is one great prince, venerated, high, lordly, frightening, ancient, and strong. His name is Ophaniel. He has sixteen faces, four faces on each side, and a hundred wings on each side. He has 8466 eyes, corresponding to the days of the year, 2190, and some say 2116, on each side.

Commentary

2190, and some say 2116, on each side. Textual Variation: "2196 and 16 on each side."

Lightnings are flashing in each one of the two eyes on his face, and from each eye firebrands are burning. No living thing is able to look at them, for anyone who looks at them is instantly burned.

His height is like the distance of 2500 years' journey. No eye can see and no mouth can tell the mighty power of his strength except for the King of Kings, the Sacred One - may he be blessed! - alone.

Why is he called Ophaniel? Because he is appointed over the Ophanin and the Ophanin are given to his charge.

He stands every day and attends to and beautifies them. He praises and orders their residence and polishes their standing-place and makes their abode bright, makes their corners even, and cleans their seats. He waits on them early and late, by day and by night, to increase their beauty, to make their dignity notable, and to make them diligent in praise of their Creator.

All the Ophanin are full of eyes, and they are all very bright. 72 sapphire stones are fixed on their garments on their right side, and 72 sapphire stones are fixed on their garments on their left side. Four carbuncle stones are fixed on the crown of every single one, the splendor of which proceeds in the four directions of Araboth like the splendor of the sun's orb proceeds in all the directions of the universe. Why is it called Carbuncle? Because its splendor is like the appearance of lightning. Splendid tents, brilliant tents, tents as bright as sapphire and carbuncle enclose them because of the shining appearance of their eyes.

26.

R. Ishmael said:

Metatron, the angel, the Prince of the Presence, said to me:

Above these there is one prince, wonderful, noble, great, honorable, mighty, frightening, a chief and leader and a swift scribe, praised, honored and loved. He is filled with splendor, full of praise and shining, and he is full of brilliance, light and beauty. All of him is filled with goodness and greatness.

His appearance is like that of angels, but his body is like an eagle's body. His splendor is like lightning, his appearance like fire-brands, his beauty like sparks, his honor like fiery coals, his majesty like Chashmals, his radiance like the light of the planet Venus. The image of him is like the Greater Light. His height is like the seven heavens. The light from his eyebrows is like the sevenfold light.

The sapphire stone on his head is as big as the whole universe and shines like the splendor of the very heavens. His body is full of eyes like the stars of the sky, innumerable and unsearchable. Every eye is like the planet Venus. However, some of them are like the Lesser Light and some of them are like the Greater Light. From his ankles to his knees they are like stars of lightning, from his knees to his thighs like the planet Venus, from his thighs to his loins like the moon, from his loins to his neck like the sun, from his neck to his skull like the Imperishable Light.

The crown on his head is like the splendor of the Splendid Throne. The length of the crown is the distance of 502 years' journey. There is no kind of splendor, no kind of brilliance, no kind of radiance, no kind of light in the universe but what is fixed on that crown.

The name of that prince is Seraphiel. The name of the crown on his head is "The Prince of Peace." Why is he called Seraphiel? Because he is appointed over the Seraphim. The flaming Seraphim are given to his charge. He presides over them day and night and teaches them song, praise, proclamation of beauty, power and majesty so that they may proclaim the beauty of their King in all manner of praise and the Qedushsha (Sacred Salutation).

How many Seraphim are there? Four, corresponding to the four winds of the world. How many wings does each have? Six, corresponding to the six days of Creation. How many faces do they have? Each one of them has four faces. The length of the Seraphim and the height of each one of them correspond to the height of the seven heavens. The size of each wing is like the measure of all Raqia. The size of each face is like that of the face of the East.

Each one of them radiates light like the splendor of the Splendid Throne, so that not even the Sacred Chayyoth, the honored Ophanin, nor the majestic Cherubim are able to look upon it. The eyes of everyone who looks at it are darkened due to its great splendor.

Why are they called Seraphim? Because they burn (*saraph*) the writing tables of the adversary. Every day the adversary is sitting, together with Sammael, the Prince of Rome, and with Dubbiel, the Prince of Persia, and they write the sins of Israel on writing tables which they hand over to the Seraphim, in order that they may present them to the Sacred One - may he be blessed! - so that he may destroy Israel off the face of the earth. But the Seraphim know from the secrets of the Sacred One - may he be blessed! - that he does not wish the Israelites to perish.

What do the Seraphim do? Every day they accept them from the adversary and burn them in the burning fire over against the high exalted Throne so that they will not come before the Sacred One – may he be blessed! - at the time when he is sitting upon the Throne of Judgment, truthfully judging the whole world.

27.

R. Ishmael said:

Metatron, the angel of H, the Prince of the Presence, said to me:

Above the Seraphim there is one prince, exalted above all the princes, more wonderful than all the servants. His name is Radweriel and he is appointed over the treasuries of the books. He goes and gets the Case of Writings with the Book of Records in it, and brings it before the Sacred One – may he be blessed! He breaks the seals of the case, opens it, takes out the books and delivers them to the Sacred One – may he be blessed!

The Sacred One – may he be blessed! - receives them from him and gives them in his sight to the Scribes, so that they may read them in the Great House of Judgment in the height of Araboth Raqia, before the heavenly household.

Commentary

The Great House of Judgment : The Beth Din.

Why is he called Radweriel? Because an angel is created out of every word that goes out of his mouth, and he stands in the singing group of the ministering angels and sings a song before the Sacred One – may he be blessed! - when the time draws near for the recitation of the Thrice Sacred.

28.

R. Ishmael said:

Metatron, the angel, the Prince of the Presence, said to me:

Above all these there are four great princes, named lrin and Qaddishin (Sacred Watchers), high, honored, revered, loved, wonderful and splendid ones, greater than all the inhabitants of heaven. There is no one like them among all the celestial princes and none their equal among all the Servants. Each one of them is equal to all the rest together. Their residence is over against the Splendid Throne, and their standing place is over against the Sacred One – may he be blessed! - so that the brilliance of their residence is a reflection of the brilliance of the Splendid Throne. Their splendid appearance is a reflection of the splendor of Shekinah. They are glorified by the splendor of the Divine Majesty and praised through the praise of Shekinah.

Commentary

Irin and Qaddishin, Aramaic, also in Daniel 4:13 and 23. The *Septuagint* translates the word there as *hagion*, "a sacred one." Irin and Qaddishin, "Watchers and Sacred Ones," generally considered to be hendiadys, thus, "Sacred Watchers."

Not only that, but the Sacred One - may he be blessed! - does nothing in his world without first consulting them, and he does it only after he consults them. As it is written (Daniel 4:17), "The sentence is by the decree of the Irin and the Qaddishin."

There are two lrin and two Qaddishin. How are they standing before the Sacred One? - May he be blessed! It is to be understood, that one lr is standing on one side and the other on the other side, and one Qaddish is standing on one side and the other on the other side. They always exalt the humble, they abase the arrogant to the ground, and they exalt to the heights those who are humble.

Commentary

Two Irin and two Qaddishin, or, Two Sacred Watchers.

Every day, as the Sacred One - may he be blessed! - is sitting upon the Throne of Judgment and judges the whole world, and the Books of the Living and the Books of the Dead are opened before him, then all the inhabitants of heaven are standing before him in fright, alarm, awe, and trembling. At that time, when the Sacred One – may he be blessed! - is sitting on the Throne of Judgment to execute judgment, his garment is white as snow, the hair on his head is like pure wool, and the whole of his cloak is like the shining light. He is covered with justice all over like with a coat of mail.

Those Irin and Qaddishin are standing before him like court officers before the judge. They raise and argue every case and close the case that comes before the Sacred One – may he be blessed! - in judgment, as it is written (Daniel 4: 17), "The sentence is by the decree of the Ir and the demand by the word of the Qaddishin."

Some of them argue and others pass the sentence in the Great House of Judgment in Araboth. Some of them make the requests in the presence of the Divine Majesty and some close the cases before the Most High. Others finish by going down and executing the sentences on the earth below. As it is written (Daniel 4:13, 14), "A Sacred Watcher was coming down from heaven and called out loudly, 'Chop down the tree and cut off its branches, strip off its leaves and scatter its fruit. Chase the animals flee from under it and shoo the birds from its branches.'"

Why are they called Irin and Qaddishin? Because they make the body and the spirit sacred with lashes of fire on the third day of the judgment, as it is written (Hosea 6:2), "After two days he will revive us; on the third day he will raise us up, so that we may live in his presence."

29.

R. Ishmael said:

Metatron, the angel, the Prince of the Presence, said to me

Each one of them has seventy names corresponding to the seventy languages of the world. All of them are based on the name of the Sacred One – may he be blessed! Every name is written with a flaming style on the Fearful Crown which is on the head of the high exalted King. From each one of them sparks and lightning go out. Each one of them has splendid horns all around. Lights are shining out of each one, and each one is surrounded by brilliant tents so that not even the Seraphim and the Chayyoth who are greater than all the inhabitants of heaven are able to look at them.

30.

R. Ishmael said:

Metatron, the angel, the Prince of the Presence, said to me:

Whenever the Great House of Judgment (Beth Din) is seated in the Araboth Raqia on high no one in the world opens their mouth except for those great princes who are called Yahweh by the name of the Sacred One - may he be blessed! How many princes are there? Seventy two princes of the kingdoms of the world besides the Prince of the World who daily speaks in favor of the world before the Sacred One - may he be blessed! - at the hour when the book, in which is recorded everything that happens in the world, is opened, as it is written (Daniel 7:10), "The court convened and the books were opened."

31.

R. Ishmael said:

Metatron, the angel, the Prince of the Presence, said to me:

At the time when the Sacred One - may he be blessed! - is sitting on the Throne of Judgment, then Justice is standing at his right and Compassion is standing at his left, and truth is standing in front of him.

When a human enters his presence to be judged, then something like a staff comes out from the Splendor of the Compassion and stands in front of him. Immediately the human falls to its face, and all the angels of punishment and tremble before him, as it is written (Isaiah 16:5), "A throne will be established by compassion, and he will rule reliably."

Commentary

A human. Textual variation - "wicked person."

Commentary

The angels of punishment in 1 Enoch 53:1-7

There my eyes saw a deep valley, and its entrance was open.
Everyone who lives on the earth, on the sea, and on islands, will bring him gifts, presents, and offerings, yet that deep valley will not become full. Their hands will commit wrongdoing. Whatever they produce by working, the wrongdoers will devour with crime. But they will be destroyed in front of the Lord of spirits, and from the face of his earth, incessantly, forever and ever. I saw the angels of punishment, who were living there, and preparing every instrument of the adversary.
Then I asked the angel of peace, who went with me, "For whom are they preparing these instruments?"
He said, "They are preparing them for the kings and powerful ones of the earth, so that they will perish. After this the honest and chosen one will cause the house of his worshippers to appear, and from then on they will not be hindered anymore, by the name of the Lord of spirits. In his presence these mountains will not be solid like the earth,

and the hills will be like fountains of water. And the honest will have rest from oppression by wrongdoers."

32.

R. Ishmael said:

Metatron, the angel, the Prince of the Presence, said to me:

"When the Sacred One - may he be blessed! - opens the Book, half of which is fire and half of which is flame, then they go out from his presence in every moment to execute the judgment on the wicked by his sword that is drawn from its sheath. The splendor of his sword shines like lightning and spreads through the world from one end to the other, as it is written (Isaiah 66:16), "Yahweh will execute judgment upon all humankind with fire and his sword."

All those who come into the world are afraid and tremble before him, when they see his sharpened sword like lightning from one end of the world to the other, and sparks and flashes the size of the stars of Raqia going out from it, as it is written (Deuteronomy 32:41), "I will sharpen my lightning-like sword."

33.

R. Ishmael said:

Metatron, the angel, the Prince of the Presence, said to me:

At the time that the Sacred One - may he be blessed! - is sitting on the Throne of Judgment, then the angels of Compassion are standing on his right, the angels of Peace are standing on his left and the angels of Punishment are standing in front of him. One scribe is standing beneath him, and another scribe is standing above him. The splendid Seraphim surround the Throne on its four sides with walls of lightning, and the Ophanin surround them with firebrands around the Splendid Throne.

Commentary

Textual variation - The splendid Seraphim surround them like firebrands around the Splendid Throne.

Clouds of fire and clouds of flames compass them to the right and to the left; and the Sacred Chayyoth carry the Splendid Throne from below, each one with three fingers. The length of each finger is 800,000 and 700 times hundred, and 66,000 parasangs.

Seven fiery rivers are running and flowing underneath the feet of the Chayyoth. The width of each river is 365,000 parasangs and its depth is 248,000 myriads of parasangs. Its length is unsearchable and immeasurable. Each river turns around in a bow in the four directions of Araboth Raqia, and from there it falls down to Maon and is stopped, and from Maon to Zebul, from Zebul to Shechaqim, from Shechaqim to Raqia, from Raqia to Shamayim and from Shamayim on the heads of the wicked who are in Gehenna, as it is written (Jeremiah 23:19), "Look! Yahweh's anger will come like a storm! Like a whirlwind swirling down on the heads of the wicked!"

Commentary

Shechaquim also means "The skies."

34.

R. Ishmael said:

Metatron; the angel, the Prince of the Presence, said to me:

The hoofs of the Chayyoth are surrounded by seven clouds of burning coals. The clouds of burning coals are surrounded on the outside by seven walls of flames. The seven walls of flames are surrounded on the outside by seven walls of hailstones. The hailstones are surrounded on the outside by stones of hail. The stones of hail are surrounded on the outside by stones of the hurricane's wings. The stones of the hurricane's wings are surrounded on the outside by flames of fire. The flames of fire are surrounded by the chambers of the whirlwind. The chambers of the whirlwind are surrounded on the outside by the fire and the water.

Around the fire and the water are those who pronounce the "Sacred." Around those who pronounce the "Sacred" are those who pronounce the "Blessed." Around those who pronounce the "Blessed" are the bright clouds. The bright clouds are surrounded on the outside by coals of burning juniper, and on the outside surrounding the coals of burning juniper there are thousand camps of fire and ten thousand hosts of flames. Between every camp and every host there is a cloud that prevents them being burned by the fire.

35.

R. Ishmael said:

Metatron, the angel, the Prince of the Presence, said to me:

The Sacred One – may he be blessed! - has 506,000 myriads of camps in the height of Araboth Raqia. Each camp is composed of 496,000 angels. As for every single angel, the height of his stature is like the great sea, their appearance is like that of lightning, their eyes are like fiery lamps, their arms and their feet are the color of polished brass, and the roaring voice of their words is like the noise of a crowd.

They are all standing before the Splendid Throne in four rows. The princes of the army are standing at the head of each row.

Some of them pronounce the "Sacred" and others pronounce the "Blessed." Some of them run as angels, others stand in attendance, as it is written (Daniel 7:10), "Many thousands were ministering to him, and many tens of thousands stood ready to serve him. The court was seated, and the books were opened."

At the hour, when the time draws near to pronounce the "Sacred," then firstly a whirlwind goes out from the presence of the Sacred One – may he be blessed! - and bursts upon the camp of Shekinah. A great uproar arises among them, as it is written (Jeremiah 30:23), "Look! Yahweh's whirlwind goes out with fury, a continuing storm."

At that moment thousands upon thousands of them are changed into sparks, thousands upon thousands of them into fire-brands, thousands upon thousands into flashes, thousands upon thousands into flames, thousands upon thousands into males, thousands upon thousands into females, thousands upon thousands into winds, thousands upon thousands into burning fires, thousands upon thousands into flames, thousands upon thousands into sparks, thousands upon thousands into Chashmals of light, until they take the yoke of the kingdom of heaven upon themselves, the high lifted up yoke of their Creator, with fear, dread, awe and trembling, turmoil, anguish, terror and consternation. Then they are changed again into their former shape to have the fear of their King before them always, as they have set their hearts on saying the Song continually, as it is written. (Isaiah 6: 3), "Sacred, sacred, sacred is Yahweh who commands armies."

36.

R. Ishmael said:

Metatron, the angel, the Prince of the Presence, said to me:

At the time when the ministering angels wish to say the Song, then the fiery river rises with many thousands upon thousands and myriads of myriads of angels with the power and strength of fire. It goes along and passes under the Splendid Throne, between the camps of the ministering angels and the troops of Araboth.

All the ministering angels first go down into the fiery river and dip themselves in the fire, and dip their tongue and their mouth seven times, and after that they go up and put on the garment of Machaqe Sama, cover themselves with cloaks of chashmal and stand in four rows over against the Splendid Throne, in all the heavens.

37.

R. Ishmael said:

Metatron, the angel, the Prince of the Presence, said to me:

Four chariots of Shekinah are standing in the seven Halls, and four camps of Shekinah stand before each one. Between each camp a river of fire is continually flowing. Between each river there are bright clouds surrounding them, and between each cloud there are pillars of brimstone. Flaming wheels stand between one pillar and another, surrounding them. There are flames of fire round around between one wheel and another. Between one flame and another there are storehouses of lightning, and the wings of the stormy wind are behind the treasuries of lightnings.

Behind the wings of the stormy wind are the compartments of the storm, and behind the compartments of the storm are winds, voices, thunders, embers upon embers and earthquakes upon earthquakes.

38.

R. Ishmael said:

Metatron, the angel, the Prince of the Presence, said to me:

At the time, when the ministering angels pronounce the three times Sacred, then all the pillars of the heavens and their sockets tremble, and the gates of the Halls of Araboth Raqia are shaken, the foundations of the Shechaqim and the universe are moved, the orders of Maon and the chambers of Makon vibrate, all the orders of Raqia, the constellations and the planets are shocked, and the orbs of the sun and the moon hurry away, flee from their courses and run 12,000 parasangs and wish to throw themselves down from heaven, because of the roaring voice of their chant, the noise of their praise and the sparks and lightnings that go out from their faces, as it is written (Psalm 77:18), "Your thunderous voice was heard in the wind, the lightning lit up the world, the earth trembled and shook."

This happens until the prince of the world calls to them, "Stay in your place! Do not be afraid of the ministering angels who sing the Song before the Sacred One – may he be blessed!" As it is written (Job 38:7), "When the morning stars sang together and all the inhabitants of heaven shouted for joy."

39.

R. Ishmael said:

Metatron, the angel, the Prince of the Presence, said to me:

When the ministering angels pronounce the "Sacred" then all the explicit names that are written with a flaming style on the Splendid Throne fly off like eagles, with sixteen wings. They encircle and surround the Sacred One - may he be blessed! - on the four sides of the place of his Shekinah.

The angels of the host, and the flaming Servants, and the mighty Ophanin, and the Cherubim of the Shekinah, and the Sacred Chayyoth, and the Seraphim, and the Erellim, and the Taphsarim and the troops of consuming fire, and the fiery armies, and the flaming hosts, and the Sacred princes, adorned with crowns, dressed in kingly magnificence, wrapped in grandeur, girded with superiority, fall on their faces three times and say, "May the name of his splendid kingdom be blessed forever and ever!"

40.

R. Ishmael said:

Metatron, the angel, the Prince of the Presence, said to me:

When the ministering angels say "Sacred" before the Sacred One – may he be blessed! - in the proper way, then the servants of his Throne, the attendants of his splendor, go out with great hilarity from under the Splendid Throne. They all carry thousands upon thousands and ten thousand times ten thousand crowns of stars, similar in appearance to the planet Venus, in their hands. They put them on the ministering angels and the great princes who pronounce the "Sacred." They put three crowns on each one of them: one crown because they say "Sacred," another crown because they say "Sacred, Sacred," and a third crown because they say "Sacred, Sacred, Sacred, is the Lord of Hosts."

In the moment that they do not pronounce the "Sacred" in the right order, a consuming fire goes out from the little finger of the Sacred One – may he be blessed! - and falls down in the middle of their ranks and is divided into 496,000 parts corresponding to the four camps of the ministering angels, and consumes them in one moment, as it is written (Psalm 97:3), "Fire goes in front of Yahweh, it burns up Yahweh's enemies on every side."

After that the Sacred One - may he be blessed! - opens his mouth and speaks one word and creates others instead of them, new ones like them. Each one stands before his Splendid Throne, uttering the "Sacred," as it is written (Lamentations 3:23), "They are new every morning; great is your faithfulness!"

41.

R. Ishmael said:

Metatron, the angel, the Prince of the Presence, said to me:

Come and see the letters by which the heaven and the earth were created, the letters by which the mountains and hills were created, the letters by which the seas and rivers were created, the letters by which the trees and herbs were created, the letters by which the planets and the constellations were created, the letters by which the moon's orb and the sun's orb were created, Orion, the Pleiades and all the different luminaries of Raqia were created, the letters by which the Splendid Throne and the Wheels of the Merkabah were created, the letters by which the necessities of the worlds were created, the letters by which wisdom, understanding, knowledge, discretion, gentleness, and justice were created and by which the whole world is sustained.

I walked by his side and he took me by his hand and raised me up on his wings and showed me those letters, all of them, that are written in a flaming style on the Splendid Throne. Sparks go out of them and cover all the chambers of Araboth.

42.

R. Ishmael said:

Metatron, the angel, the Prince of the Presence, said to me:

Come and I will show you where the waters are suspended in the highest, where fire is burning in the midst of hail, where lightning lights up from the midst of snowy mountains, where thunders roar in the celestial heights, where a flame is burning in the middle of the burning fire and where voices make themselves heard in the midst of thunder and earthquake.

Then I went by his side. He took me by the hand and lifted me up on his wings and showed me all those things. I saw the waters suspended on high in Araboth

Raqia by the power of the name "Yah, I am that I am," and their produce going down from heaven and watering the face of the world, as it is written (Psalm 104:13), "Yahweh waters the mountains from the upper rooms, the earth is full of fruit you have made grow."

I saw fire, snow and hailstones that were mingled together yet were undamaged, by the power of the name, "Consuming Fire," as it is written (Deuteronomy 4: 24), "For Yahweh Elohim is a consuming fire."

I saw lightnings that were coming out of mountains of snow yet were not damaged, by the power of the name "Yahweh, the everlasting rock," as it is written (Isaiah 26:4), "Yahweh, the everlasting rock."

I saw thunders and voices that were roaring in the midst of fiery flames and were not damaged, by the power of the name "El Shaddai Rabba," as it is written (Genesis 17:1), "I am El Shaddai."

I saw a flame and glowing flames that were glowing and flaming in the middle of burning fire, and yet were not damaged, by the power of the name "The Hand Upon The Throne of Yahweh," as it is written (Exodus 17:16), "For he said, "A hand was lifted up to the throne of Yahweh."

I saw rivers of fire in the middle of rivers of water and they were not damaged, by the power of the name, "Maker of Peace," as it is written (Job 25:2), "He makes complete peace in his high places." For he makes peace between the fire and the water, between the hail and the fire, between the wind and the cloud, between the earthquake and the embers.

43.

R. Ishmael said:

Metatron said to me:

Come and I will show you where the spirits of the just that have been created and have returned are, and the spirits of the just that have not yet been created.

He lifted me up to his side, took me by the hand and lifted me up near the Splendid Throne by the place of the Shekinah. He revealed the Splendid Throne to me, and he showed me the spirits that have been created and had returned. They were flying above the Splendid Throne in front of the Sacred One – may he be blessed!

After that I went to interpret the following verse of Scripture and I found in what is written, (Isaiah 57:16), "for the spirit would grow faint before me, and the souls which I have made," the wording, "for the spirit would grow faint before me" which means that the spirits that have been created in the chamber of creation of the just and that have returned before One – may he be blessed! - and the wording, "and the souls I which I have made," refers to the spirits of the just that have not yet been created in the chamber.

44.

R. Ishmael said:

Metatron, the angel, the Prince of the Presence, said to me:

Come and I will show you where the wicked spirits

and the intermediate spirits are standing, and where the intermediate spirits go down, and where the wicked spirits go down.

He said to me, "The wicked spirits go down to Sheol by the hands of two angels of punishment. Their names are Zaaphiel and Simkiel. Simkiel is appointed over the intermediate to support them and purify them because of the Prince of the Place's great compassion. Zaaphiel is appointed over the wicked spirits in order to cast them down from the presence of the Sacred One – may he be blessed! - and from the splendor of the Shekinah to Sheol, to be punished in the fire of Gehenna with strips of burning coal.

I went by his side, and he took me by the hand and pointed out all of them with his fingers.

I saw the appearance of their faces and look! They looked like humans, and their bodies were like eagles. And not only that, but also the color of the appearance of the intermediate was like pale gray on account of their deeds, for there are stains upon them which last until they are cleaned from their wrongdoings in the fire. The color of the wicked was like the bottom of a pot on account of their wicked acts.

I saw the spirits of the Patriarchs, Abraham, Isaac, and Jacob, and the rest of the just who they have brought up out of their graves and who have ascended to the Heaven. They were praying before the Sacred One - may he be blessed! - "Lord of the Universe! How long will you sit on your Throne like a mourner in the time of his mourning with your right hand behind you, and not rescue your children and reveal your Kingdom in the world? For how long will you have no pity on your children who are made slaves among the nations of the world? With your right hand that is behind you, you stretched out the heavens and the earth and the skies of heavens! When will you have compassion?"

Then the Sacred One - may he be blessed! - answered every one of them, "Since these wicked do such wrong, and misbehave with such and such wrongdoing against me, how could I rescue them with my great Right Hand from their own downfall which they themselves brought about?"

At that moment Metatron called me and said to me, "My servant! Take the books, and read their evil actions!" At once I took the books and read what they had done and there were to be found 36 wrongdoings written down with regard to each wicked one and furthermore, that they did wrong with respect to all the letters in the Torah, as it is written (Daniel 9:11), "All Israel has broken your Law." It is not written at torateka but et torateka, for they have done wrong from Aleph to Taw, they have disobeyed 40 statutes for each letter."

At once Abraham, Isaac, and Jacob cried.

Then the Sacred One – may he be blessed! - said to them, "Abraham, my beloved, Isaac, my chosen one, Jacob, my firstborn! How can I now rescue them from among the nations of the world?"

At once Michael, the Prince of Israel, cried and

sobbed loudly and said, (Psalm 10:1), "Yahweh, why do you stand far off?"

45.

R. Ishmael said:

Metatron said to me:

Come and I will show you the Curtain of Maqom (the Divine Majesty) which is spread in front of the Sacred One – may he be blessed! - and on which are written all the generations of the world and all their actions, both what they have done and what they will do until the end of all generations.

I went, and he showed it to me, pointing it out with his fingers like a father who teaches his children the letters of Torah. I saw each generation, the rulers of each generation, and the chiefs of each generation, the shepherds of each generation, the drivers of each generation, the keepers of each generation, the terrorizers of each generation, the overseers of each generation, the judges of each generation, the court officers of each generation, the teachers of each generation, the supporters of each generation, the rulers of each generation, the leaders of academies of each generation, the magistrates of each generation, the princes of each generation, the counselors of each generation, the nobles of each generation, and the mighty people of each generation, the elders of each generation, and the guides of each generation.

I saw Adam, his generation, their actions and their thoughts, Noah and his generation, their actions and their thoughts, and the generation of the flood, their actions and their thoughts, Shem and his generation, their actions and their thoughts, Nimrod and the generation of the confusion of languages, and his generation, their actions and their thoughts, Abraham and his generation, their actions and their thoughts, Isaac and his generation, their actions and their thoughts, Ishmael and his generation, their actions and their thoughts, Jacob and his generation, their actions and their thoughts, Joseph and his generation, their actions and their thoughts, the tribes and their generation, their actions and their thoughts, Amram and his generation, their actions and their thoughts, Moses and his generation, their actions and their thoughts, Aaron and Miriam and their works and their actions, the princes and the elders, their works and actions, Joshua and his generation, their works and actions, the judges and their generation, their works and actions, Eli and his generation, their works and actions, Phinehas and their works and actions, Elkanah and his generation, their works and their actions, Samuel and his generation, their works and actions, the kings of Judah with their generations, their works and their actions, the kings of Israel and their generations, their works and their actions, the princes of Israel, their works and their actions; the princes of the nations of the world, their works and their actions, the chiefs of the councils of Israel, their works and their actions; the leaders of the councils in the nations of the world, their generations, their works and their actions; the rulers of Israel and their generation, their works and their actions; the nobles of Israel and their generation, their works and their actions; the nobles of the nations of the world and their generations, their works and their actions; the reputable people in Israel, their generation, their works and their actions; the judges of Israel, their generation, their works and their actions; the judges of the nations of the world and their generation, their works and their actions; the teachers of the Israelites, their generations, their works and their actions; the teachers of children in the nations of the world, their generations, their works and their actions; the interpreters of Israel, their generation, their works and their actions; the interpreters of the nations of the world, their generation, their works and their actions; all the prophets of Israel, their generation, their works and their actions; all the prophets of the nations of the world, their generation, their works and their actions; and all the fights and wars that the nations of the world brought against the Israelites in the time of their kingdom.

I saw Messiah, descendant of Joseph, and his generation and their works and their actions against the nations of the world. I saw Messiah, descendant of David, and his generation, and all the fights and wars, and their works and their actions that they will do with Israel, both good and evil. I saw all the fights and wars that Gog and Magog will fight in the days of Messiah, and all that the Sacred One - may he be blessed! - will do with them in the time to come.

All the rest of all the leaders of the generations and all the works of the generations both in Israel and in the nations of the world, both what is done and what will be done in the future to all generations until the end of time, all were written on the Curtain of Maqom (the Divine Majesty). I saw all these things with my own eyes, and after I had seen it, I opened my mouth to praise Maqom (the Divine Majesty), saying, (Ecclesiastes 8:4, 5), "The king's authority is absolute. No one can say to him, "What are you doing? No harm will come to those who keep the command." I said, (Psalm 104:24), "How many are your works, Yahweh!"

46.

R. Ishmael said:

Metatron said to me:

Come and I will show you the place of the stars that stand in Raqia night by night in fear of Maqom (the Divine Majesty), where they go and where they stand.

I walked by his side, and he took me by the hand and pointed them all out to me with his fingers. They were standing on flaming embers around the Merkabah of the Maqom (the Divine Majesty). What did Metatron do? At that moment he clapped his hands and chased them away from their place. At once they flew off on flaming wings.

They got up and fled from the four sides of the Throne of the Merkabah, and as they flew, he told me the names of every single one. As it is written (Psalm 147:4), "Yahweh counts the number of the stars, and calls each of them by name," teaching that the Sacred One – may he be blessed! - has given a name to each one of them.

They all enter in counted order by the guidance of Rahatiel to the Raqia of Shamayim to serve the world. They go out in counted order to praise the Sacred One – may he be blessed! - with songs and praise songs, as it is written (Psalm 19:1), "The heavens declare El's splendor."

But in the time to come the Sacred One - may he be blessed! - will create them anew, as it is written (Lamentations 3: 23), "They are new every morning." They open their mouths and sing a song. Which is the song that they sing? (Psalm 8:3) "When I see your heavens."

47.

R. Ishmael said:

Metatron said to me:

Come and I will show you the souls of the angels and the spirits of the ministering servants whose bodies have been burnt in the fire of Maqom (the Divine Majesty) that goes out from his little finger. They have been made into fiery coals in the middle of the Fire Stream (Nehar di-Nur). However, their spirits and their souls are standing behind the Shekinah.

Whenever the ministering angels pronounce a song at the wrong time or a time not appointed to be sung, they are burned and consumed in their places by the fire of their Creator and by a flame from their Maker, and a whirlwind blows on them and throws them down into the Fire Stream (Nehar di-Nur). There they are made into numerous mountains of burning coal. But their spirit and their soul return to their Creator, and all are standing behind their Master.

I went by his side, and he took me by the hand and showed me all the souls of the angels and the spirits of the ministering servants who were standing behind the Shekinah on wings of the whirlwind, and with walls of fire surrounding them.

At that moment Metatron opened for me the gates of the walls within which they were standing behind the Shekinah. I lifted up my eyes and saw them, and look! Every one of them looked like angels and their wings looked like birds' wings made out of flames, the work of burning fire. At that moment I opened my mouth to praise Maqom (the Divine Majesty) and said (Psalm 92:5), "How great are your works, Yahweh!"

48a.

R. Ishmael said:

Metatron said to me:

Come and I will show you the Right Hand of Maqom (the Divine Majesty), laid behind him because of the destruction of the Sacred Temple from which all kinds of splendor and light shine and by which the 955 heavens were created, and which not even the Seraphim and the Ophanin are permitted to look at, until the time of rescue arrives.

I went by his side. He took me by the hand and showed me the Right Hand of Maqom (the Divine Majesty), with all methods of praise, jubilation, and song. No mouth can tell of its praise, and no eye can look at it, because of its magnitude, stateliness, magnificence, splendor and beauty. And not only that, but all the souls of the just who are counted worthy to see Jerusalem's joy are standing by it, praising and praying before it three times every day, saying (Isaiah 51:9), "Yahweh's power, awake, awake, be strong!" as it is written (Isaiah 63:12), "He made his splendid power available to Moses."

At that moment the Right Hand of Maqom (the Divine Majesty) was crying. Out of its five fingers, five rivers of tears fell down into the great sea and shook the whole world, as it is written (Isaiah 24:19, 20), "The earth is broken in pieces, the earth is ripped to shreds, the earth shakes violently. The earth will stagger like a drunken person and will be moved to and fro like a hut in a windstorm," five times corresponding to the fingers of his Great Right Hand.

But when the Sacred One - may he be blessed! - sees that there is no just person in the generation, and no devout person on earth, and no justice in the hands of humans, and that there is no one like Moses, and no intercessor like Samuel who could pray before Maqom (the Divine Majesty) for the rescue and deliverance, and for his Kingdom to be revealed in the whole world, and for him to put his great Right Hand to work great rescue for Israel, then at once the Sacred One - may he be blessed! - will remember his own justice, goodwill, compassion and favor, and he will rescue his great Arm by himself, and his justice will support him. As it is written (Isaiah 59:16), "He saw that there was no one, he was appalled that there was no one to entreat, so his own Arm worked rescue for him," and he wondered that there was no intercessor like Samuel who entreated the Sacred One - may he be blessed! - and called to him. He answered him and gave him what he wanted, even if it was not in accordance with the divine plan, as it is written (1 Samuel 12:17), "Is it not wheat-harvest now? I will call Yahweh."

And not only that, but he had fellowship with Moses in every place, as it is written (Psalm 99:6), "Moses and Aaron were among Yahweh's priests."

And again it is written (Jeremiah 15:1), "Even if Moses and Samuel stood before me," (Isaiah 63:5) "My own Arm rescued me."

The Sacred One – may he be blessed! - said at that time, "How long shall I reasonably wait for the humans to rescue themselves! For my own sake and for the sake of my merited justice I will use my power to transfer my children from among the nations of the world." As it is written (Isaiah 48:11), "For my own sake, for my own sake will I act! For how can I allow my name to be dishonored!"

At that moment the Sacred One - may he be blessed! - will reveal his Great Arm (Power) and show it to the nations of the world - for its length is like the length of the world and its width is like the width of the world. Its splendid appearance is like the splendor of the sunshine in its strongest, at the summer solstice.

At once Israel will be rescued from among the nations of the world. Messiah will appear to them and will bring them up to Jerusalem with great joy. Not only that, but they will eat and drink, for they will praise the kingdom of Messiah of the house of David in the four quarters of the world. The nations of the world will not prevail against them, as it is written (Isaiah 52:10), "Yahweh lays bare his sacred Arm in the sight of all the nations; and the whole earth will see the rescue brought about by Elohim." And again, (Deuteronomy 32:12), "The Lord alone guided him, and there was no foreign god with him." (Zechariah 14:9), "Yahweh will be king over all the earth."

Commentary

Arm: "Power" and "Arm" are the same word in Hebrew, but in English they are separate words. The range of meanings possessed by a word is known as the "semantic range." Take, for example, the semantic range of the English word "port": a suitcase, a strong wine, a harbor, the left side of the ship. The English word "bear" can mean a large animal, to put up with something, or carry something. In Hebrew, the word for "arm"

can also mean "power." This does not extend to English. That is why puns do not translate into another language. Likewise, the ancient Greek word *kephale* means a physical head or a source, but cannot mean "leader/chief" as it does in English.

48b.

Here are the names of the Sacred One - may he be blessed! - that go out decorated with numerous crowns of fire, with numerous crowns of flame, with numerous crowns of Chashmal, with numerous crowns of lightning from before the Splendid Throne. And with them are hundreds of thousands of powerful angels who escort them like a king, with honor and pillars of fire and clouds, and pillars of flame, and with lightnings of radiance and with the appearance of the Chashmal.

They praise them and they answer, crying before them, "Sacred, Sacred, Sacred!"

They roll them through every heaven as mighty and honored princes. When they bring them all back to the place of the Splendid Throne, then all the Chayyoth by the Merkabah open their mouth to praise his splendid name, saying: "Blessed be the name of his splendid kingdom forever and ever."

48c.

I seized him, and I took him and appointed him, that is to say, Metatron, my servant who is unique among all the inhabitants of heaven. I made him strong in the generation of the first human. But when I saw that the people of the generation of the flood were corrupt, I removed my Shekinah from among them. I lifted it up on high with the sound of a trumpet and with a shout, as it is written (Psalm 47:5), "Elohim ascended amid a shout, Yahweh amid the sound of a ram's horn."

Commentary

Metatron: Equally here, (textual variation) "Enoch."

I took him, Enoch, the son of Jared, from among them. I lifted him up with the sound of a trumpet and with a shout to the high heavens, to be my witness together with the Chayyoth by the Merkabah in the world to come.

I appointed him over all the treasuries and storehouses that I have in every heaven. I committed the keys of every one to his hand.

I made him the prince over all the princes and a minister of the Splendid Throne and the Halls of Araboth, to open their doors to me, and of the Splendid Throne, to exalt and arrange it, and I appointed him over the Sacred Chayyoth to wreathe crowns upon their heads; the majestic Ophanin, to crown them with glorious strength, the honored Cherubim, to clothe them magnificently; over the radiant sparks, to make them shine with brilliant splendor; over the flaming Seraphim, to cover them with exaltation; Chashmallim of light, to make them radiant with light and to prepare the seat for me every morning as I sit upon the Splendid Throne. I have committed to him the secrets of above and the secrets of below, to exalt and praise my splendor in the height of my power.

I made him higher than all. The height of his physique, in the midst of all who are tall, I made 70,000 parasangs. I made his Throne great by the magnificence of my Throne. I increased its splendor by my glorious honor. I transformed his flesh into fiery torches of fire, and all the bones of his body into fiery coals. I made his eyes appear like lightning, and I made the light of his eyebrows appear like imperishable light. I made his face bright as the sun's splendor, and his eyes as bright as the splendor of the Splendid Throne. I made his clothing honorable and magnificent, his covering cloak beautiful and superb, and a royal crown of a diadem 500 by 500 parasangs.

I put on him my honor, my majesty and my glorious splendor that is on my Splendid Throne. I called him the Lesser Yahweh, the Prince of the Presence, the Knower of Secrets, for I revealed to him every secret as would a father, and I declared to him all mysteries with justice.

I set up his throne at the door of my Hall so that he may sit and judge the heavenly household on high. I placed every prince before him, to receive authority from him, to do his will. I took seventy names from my names and called him by them to increase his splendor. I gave seventy princes over to him, for him to command to them my precepts and my words in every language, and to bring the arrogant to the ground and to exalt by the utterance of his lips the humble to the heights, and to smite kings by his speech, to turn kings away from their paths, to set up rulers over their territories, as it is written (Daniel 2:21), "He changes times and seasons." He gives wisdom to the wise and knowledge to those who have understanding, as it is written (Daniel 2:21), "and knowledge to those that have understanding" and I appointed him to reveal secrets and to teach judgments, as it is written (Isaiah 55:11), "My word that goes out of my mouth will not return to me empty, but will accomplish that which I desire and achieve the purpose for which I sent it."

"I will accomplish" is not written here, but "it will accomplish", which means that whatever word and whatever utterance goes out from the presence of the Sacred One – may he be blessed! - Metatron stands and carries it out. He establishes the decrees of the Sacred One – may he be blessed!

"But will accomplish that which I desire." "I will accomplish" is not written here, but "it will accomplish," which teaches that he will make prosper whatever decree goes out from before the Sacred One - may he be blessed! - concerning a person, as soon as the person is sorry for what they did, they will not execute it upon that person but on some other wicked person, as it is written, (Proverbs 11:8), "The just is rescued from trouble, and it goes to the wicked instead."

And not only that, but Metatron sits for three hours every day in the high heavens, and gathers all the souls of those who died in their mother's womb, and of the nursing babies who died on their mother's breasts, and of the scholars who died over the five books of the Law. He brings them under the Splendid Throne and places them in companies, divisions and classes around the Presence, and he teaches them judgment and justice, Law, and the books of Wisdom, and Haggada and Tradition and completes their instruction for them. As it is written (Isaiah 28:9), "Who is it he is trying to teach? To whom is he explaining a message? To children weaned from their milk, to those just taken from the breast?"

48d.

Metatron has seventy names has Metatron which the Sacred One – may he be blessed! - took from his own name and put on him. Here they are: Yehoel Yah, Yehoel, Yophiel, Yophphiel, Aphphiel, Margeziel, Gipuyel, Paaziel, Aah, Periel, Tatriel, Tabkiel, Ipf, Yahweh, Dhwhyh, Ebed, Isdiburiel, Igaphapiel, Zospiel, Paspasiel, Senegron, Metratron, Sogdin, Adrigon, Asum, Saqpam, Saq, Mitton, Mottron, Rosphim, Tatyah, Degazyah, Pspyah, Bskeyn, Barad, Mkrkk, Msprd, Chshg, Mnrtt, Bsyrym, Mitmon, Titmon, Saphsaphyall, Zrch, Zrchyah, Bsibeyah, Beyah, Pelet, Pltyah, Rabrabyah, Chas, Chasyah, Taphtaphyah, Tamttamyah,

Sehasyah, Jiruryah, Alalyah, Bazridyah, Satsatkyah, Sasdyah, Razrazyah, Bazrazyah, Joarimyah, Sbhayah, Sbibkhyah, Simkam, Yahseyah, Ssbibyah, Sabkasbeyah, Qelilqalyah, Kihh, Hhyah, Wh, Whyah, Zakkyah, Stutrisyah, Suryah, Zeh, Penirhyah, Zizih, Mgal, Razayya, Mamlikyah, Gottyah, Geiemeq, Gzqamyah, Gmekapper, Yah, Gperishyah, Sepham, Gegbir, Gjgbboryah, Gzor, Goryah, Icoziw, Loiokbara, The Lesser Yahweh after the name of his Master, (Exodus 23:21) "For my name is within him," Lozrabibiel, Segansakkiel, the Prince of Wisdom.

Why is he called by the name Sagnesakiel? Because all the storehouses of wisdom are committed to his hand.

All of them were opened to Moses on Sinai, so that he learned them during the forty days, while he was still there: the Torah in the seventy aspects of the seventy languages, the Prophets in the seventy aspects of the seventy languages, the Writings in the seventy aspects of the seventy languages, the Halakas in the seventy aspects of the seventy languages, the Traditions in the seventy aspects of the seventy languages, the Haggadas in the seventy aspects of the seventy languages and the Toseftas in the seventy aspects of the seventy languages.

But as soon as the forty days ended, he forgot all of them in one moment. Then the Sacred One - may he be blessed! - called Yephiphyah, the Prince of the Law, and through him they were given to Moses as a gift. As it is written (Deuteronomy 10:4), "And Yahweh gave them to me." After that it remained with him. And how do we know that he remembered them? Because it is written (Malachi 4:4), "Remember the law of Moses my servant, the decrees and statutes I gave him at Horeb for all Israel."

These seventy names are a reflection of the Explicit Names on the Merkabah which are written on the Splendid Throne. For the Sacred One – may he be blessed! - took from his Explicit Names and put on the name of Metatron, seventy Names of his by which the ministering angels call the King of Kings - may he be blessed! - in the high heavens, and twenty two letters that are on the ring on his finger with which are sealed the destinies of the princes of kingdoms on high with great power, and with which are sealed the lots of the Angel of Death, and the destinies of every nation and language.

Metatron, the angel, the Prince of the Presence; the angel, the Prince of the Wisdom; the angel, the Prince of the Understanding; the angel, the Prince of the Kings; the angel, the Prince of the Rulers; the angel, the Prince of the Splendor; the angel, the Prince of the high ones, and of the princes, the exalted, great and honored ones, in heaven and on earth, said, "Yahweh, the God of Israel, is my witness in this thing, that when I revealed this secret to Moses, all the hosts in every heaven on high raged against me and said to me, 'Why did you reveal this secret to the human, born of woman, tainted and unclean, a human produced by semen, the secret by which were created heaven and earth, the sea and the dry land, the mountains and hills, the rivers and springs, Gehenna of fire and hail, the Garden of Eden and the Tree of Life; and by which were formed Adam and Eve, and the cattle, and the wild animals, and the birds of the air, and the fish of the sea, and Behemoth and Leviathan, and the creeping things, the worms, the dragons of the sea, and the creeping things of the deserts; and the Torah and Wisdom and Knowledge and Thought and the Knowledge of things above and the fear of heaven. Why did you reveal this to flesh and blood?'"

Commentary

Behemoth was described by Job 40:15-24. It eats grass and is very strong, and has been furnished with a sword, which may refer to a horn or tusk/s. It lies under the lotus trees in the swamps and marshes.

Job 41 describes Leviathan as huge, fierce, with scales on its back, states that it breathes fire and smoke, and that arrows and clubs have no effect on it, and that it stirs up the sea when it moves. Job 31 also states that there is no other creature like it on earth. Psalm 71:14 says, "You crushed the heads of Leviathan." The Ugaritic texts have the dragon with 7 heads defeated by the god Baal and by the goddess Anat. *KTU*^{2} 1.3 3 38-39 and

KTU[2] 1.5 I 1-3. Psalm 71:13 says, "You broke the heads of the dragon in the water." The dragon is called "Rahab" (proud one) in Isaiah 51:9 and Job 26:12. Isaiah 27:1 and Job 26:13 describe the dragon as "squirming." Job 41:19-21 states that the dragon breathed fire and smoke.

Behemoth and Leviathan in 1 Enoch 60:1-24

In the five hundredth year, and in the seventh month, on the fourteenth day of the month, in the life of Enoch. In that vision, I saw that the heaven of heavens was shaken fiercely, and that the host of the Most High, and the angels, thousands and thousands, and ten thousand times ten thousand, were agitated and greatly disturbed. And when I looked, the Ancient of Days was sitting on his splendid throne, while the angels and the honest were standing around him. A great trembling seized me, and terror took hold of me. My loins buckled and gave way, my strength dissolved, and I fell on my face.

Then sacred Michael sent another sacred angel, one of the sacred ones, and he raised me up, and when he raised me, my spirit returned, for I had been unable to endure the sight of the host, the disturbance, and the shaking of heaven.

Then sacred Michael said to me, "Why are you disturbed by this vision? The time of compassion

lasted until now, and he has been compassionate and patient toward all the inhabitants of the earth. But the day will come when the power, the punishment, and the judgment will take place, which the Lord of spirits has prepared for those who do not worship the just judgment, those who deny that judgment, and for those who take his name in vain. That day has been prepared for the chosen as a day of covenant, and for wrongdoers as a day of inquisition."

On that day two monsters will be separated from one another, a female monster named Leviathan, to live in the depths of the sea, above the springs of waters, and a male monster named Behemoth, which moves on its chest, and occupies a large desert named Dendayen in the east of the garden, where the chosen and the just live, where my grandfather was received. My grandfather was human, the seventh from Adam, the first human whom the Lord of spirits made. Then I asked the other angel to show me the power of those monsters, how they became separated on the same day, one being thrown into the depths of the sea, and one onto the dry desert. He answered, "You, human, are here wishing to understand secret things."

And the angel of peace, who was with me, said, "These two monsters are prepared by God's power so that God's punishment won't be in vain.

Then children will be slain with their mothers, and sons with their fathers. When the punishment of the Lord of spirits comes on them, it will continue, so that the punishment of the Lord of spirits won't take place in vain. After that, judgment will be with compassion and patience."

I answered them, "Because the Sacred One - may he be blessed! - gave me the authority to do so. Furthermore, I have obtained permission from the high exalted Throne, from which all the explicit Names go out with fiery lightnings and flaming Chashmals."

But they were not placated, until the Sacred One – may he be blessed! - rebuked them and drove them away with a rebuke from his presence. He said to them, "I am delighted with, and have set my love on, and have entrusted and committed them to Metatron, my Servant, alone, for he is unique among all the inhabitants of heaven."

Metatron brought them out of his house of treasuries and committed them to Moses, and Moses to Joshua, and Joshua to the elders, and the elders to the prophets and the prophets to the humans of the Great Synagogue, and the humans of the Great Synagogue to Ezra, and Ezra the Scribe to Hillel the elder, and Hillel the elder to R. Abbahu and R. Abbahu to R. Zera, and R. Zera to the faithful people, and the faithful people committed them to give warning and by them to heal all diseases that rage in the world, as it is written (Exodus

15:26), “If you listen carefully to the voice of Yahweh Elohim and do what is right in his sight, if you pay attention to his statutes and keep all his decrees, I will not bring on you any of the diseases I brought on the Egyptians, for I am Yahweh who heals you.”

Ended and finished! May the Earth’s Creator be praised!

CHAPTER 8: APPENDIX

LIST OF BIBLICAL REFERENCES TO ENOCH

(The other two references in Genesis (4:17 and 4:18) are to a different Enoch.)

Genesis 5:18 When Jared was 162 years old he fathered Enoch.

Genesis 5:19 Jared lived for 800 years after he fathered Enoch and had other sons and daughters.

Genesis 5:21 When Enoch was 65 years old, he fathered Methuselah.

Genesis 5:22 Enoch walked with God after he fathered Methuselah for 300 years and had other sons and daughters.

Genesis 5:23 Thus Enoch lived for 365 years.

Genesis 5:24 Enoch walked with God, and then he was not there, for God took him.

1 Chronicles 1:3 Enoch, Methuselah, Lamech,

Luke 3:37 (...the son of Noah, the son of Lamech,) 37 the son of Methuselah, the son of Enoch, the son of Jared, the son of Mahalalel, the son of Kenan,

Hebrews 11:5 By faith Enoch was transferred from one place to another so that he didn't experience death, and could not be found, because God had taken him away – since before he was transferred from one place to another he had the reputation that he had pleased God.

Jude 1:14-15 Now Enoch, the seventh from Adam, prophesied to these people too. He said, "The Lord comes with tens of thousands of his devoted people, to carry out judgments on everyone, to cross-examine every soul among them who has committed sacrilege, about their sacrilegious acts, and about all the harsh things that sacrilegious sinners have said about him."

ABOUT DR. A. NYLAND

Dr. A. Nyland spent her time on Faculty at the University of New England, Australia, teaching ancient grammar, conducting a lengthy replication of a Bronze Age horse training text, and drinking espresso.

She is the best selling translator of such books as *The Complete Books of Enoch* and author of *What Were the Watchers?* as well as *Nephilim and Giants*.

The information based on her books is not based on her own opinions, but is presented with a view to getting actual facts out there. This is harder and harder in this day and age with misinformation spreading like wildfire on the net, driven by all the books by authors who know no ancient languages, and get their information from English translations rather than the original texts. It is futile to research ancient texts in English translation.

Made in the USA
Las Vegas, NV
10 February 2022